Do-It-Yourself Guide to
CUSTOM PAINTING

BY TOM BROWNELL

D1604782

OVERSEAS DISTRIBUTION BY:

BROOKLANDS BOOKS LTD.
P.O. BOX 146, Cobham, Surrey, KT11 1LG, England
Telephone 01932 865051 • FAX 01932 868803

BROOKLANDS BOOKS LTD.
1/81 Darley Street, P.O. Box 199, Mona Vale, NSW 2103, Australia
Telephone 2 999 78428 • FAX 2 997 95799

PRODUCTION BY
TAMARA BAECHTEL

COPY EDITED BY
MONICA DWYER ABRESS

ISBN 1-884089-49-6
PART No. SA10

CARTECH®, INC., 11605 KOST DAM RD., NORTH BRANCH, MN 55056

ABOUT THE AUTHOR

Tom Brownell's first experience with automotive refinishing came at age 16 when his school bus driver helped him paint his Model A Ford roadster. Today, Brownell is a professor of technical writing at Ferris State University in Michigan. Besides teaching, he writes on automotive topics for a range of hobbyist and enthusiast publications. His syndicated column can be seen in newspapers across the United States.

Tom and his wife Joyce, also a professor of writing, live in a Victorian-era house in their rural Michigan college town.

ACKNOWLEDGEMENTS

A project this extensive isn't possible without the help of others. I wish to publicly thank those who have made this book possible:

Jim Bigelow and Vic Fowler, instructors in Ferris State University's Auto Body program, for answering my questions and allowing me to photograph sequences of their students' work;

Rich Jensen for putting aside his shop's production work to "play" with powder coating;

Jeff Main for sharing his rich expertise in custom painting;

Phil Noder for inviting me to photograph painting steps as he was building his '39 street rod;

John Sloane, Marketing Manager for the Eastwood Company, for help with photographs and for introducing me to Eastwood's marvelous HotCoat™ powder coating system;

Ralph Starek for letting me watch an artist at work. The fish in the coral reef mural he painted on a minivan came alive before my eyes; and Scott Taylor for filling pages of my notes tablet every time I visited his shop.

BY
TOM BROWNELL

TABLE OF CONTENTS

Do-It-Yourself Guide to CUSTOM PAINTING

Introduction

A car's finish sets our first, often lasting impression.

A car's finish sets our first, and often lasting, impression. Sure, I've seen cars that look sharp and run lousy, but I'm still likely to remember their appearance and not their performance. This isn't to say that the car's mechanical ability or its interior and trim don't matter — it's just that the finish counts more, at least in the eyes of most observers. By the finish I don't just mean the body's paint coating. Raise the hood and what do you see — a glob of cast iron with some functional pieces on it, or a sparkling, multi-colored layout that resembles the "spit and polish" engine room on a millionaire's yacht? Function can, and should, be beautiful. The same goes for the car's chassis and running gear. Take a peek through the wheel wells and see what colors are visible — rust orange and grease gray, or tidy chassis black highlighted with the dull silver of fresh steel brake lines? On a car, beauty goes more than skin deep.

Whether you've got questions about automotive refinishing because you're restoring a collector car, truck, or tractor, because you're building one of those artistic self-creations (commonly called a "hot rod" or "Custom"), or because you want to upgrade the finish on your "daily driver," this book seeks to provide the answers. Automotive refinishing is becoming increasingly complex with specialized products for virtually every step of the refinishing process and painting systems that demand compatible products up and down the steps. Using an incompatible product can devastate the process so thoroughly that the refinishing products applied up to that stage may have to be removed and the build-up started all over again — something no one wants to do, even once.

To complexity add the toxic chemicals in many modern painting products and there's another "recipe for disaster," only this time affecting your physical health. Modern automotive refinishing products are intended to be used by professionals who are fully informed of the dangers as well as the safety measures and equipment required. Hobbyists, almost by definition, are relaxed, not just in their work schedules, but also in their approach to safety.

For the paint products described in this book, where safety measures apply, they'll be clearly stated, and should not be overlooked. If used improperly, some automotive refinishing products can, in fact, be lethal.

Then there's cost. Just for the paint alone the cost can exceed what you would have paid a professional shop not long ago for a complete paint job. From simply a cost standpoint, it's important to do things right. Botch the final coating, and you might be shelling out another several hundred dollars more to repurchase the materials you've just wasted, plus additional time and effort to make things right.

Let's begin our look at the refinishing process with safety, something already mentioned, but needing to be fully understood so that the hobbyist approaches modern refinishing products with the same respect they receive from a professional.

Automotive refinishing is becoming increasingly complex with specialized products and painting "systems."

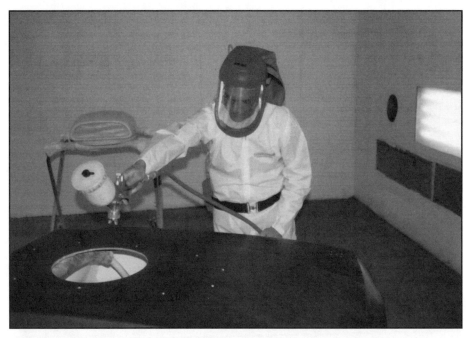

Modern automotive refinishing products are intended to be used by professionals who are fully informed of the dangers as well as the safety measures and equipment required.

Many of today's primer products can be tinted to match the finish coat. Tinting the primer helps build depth in the finish color and assures thorough color coverage.

Most modern paints mix with hardener that limits the paint's usable life. The "pot life" (the spraying time once the hardener has been added) will be listed on the product information sheet.

Do-It-Yourself Guide to
CUSTOM PAINTING
Guidelines to Painting Safely

The modern refinishing shop stands in sharp contrast to its counterpart of 50 years ago. Painters in hooded uniforms work in brightly lit spray booths that prevent any trace of painting chemicals from entering the shop.

Hobby activities are to be enjoyed. None of us would dispute that. So what about a hobby that's potentially dangerous, to the point of being lethal; surely you'd want to take precautions against danger. As an example, those participating in racing vintage cars don't roar around the track blithely ignoring safety, as did the drivers of those same cars 40 or 60 years ago. No, racers today wear high-impact helmets and Nomex driving suits and fit their cars with roll cages. As a result, in a sport where danger is the attraction, no fatalities have occurred that safety equipment could have prevented.

The automotive refinishing process is as potentially dangerous as vintage racing. Yet, the hobbyist is much more likely to ignore safety precautions and approach the painting preparation steps, as well as the actual paint spraying, in the same lax manner that I watched Harvey Bardo paint cars in his body shop in 1955. To be sure,

Harvey's spray area had an exhaust fan, perched on a window ledge in the shop's far wall. I remember looking at the fan shroud and seeing coatings of paint dust a quarter-inch thick in places. Likewise, the paint had encrusted on the fan motor — surely not the safest of all conditions, especially for a wood-constructed shop. I never saw Harvey wear a respirator or a breathing mask of any sort. As for protective clothing, Harvey wore what he'd put on when he got up in the morning.

The modern automotive refinishing shop stands in sharp contrast with its "bump and paint" counterpart of 50 years ago. Though there's plenty of activity, the shop floor around the work area is clean and uncluttered. Painters in hooded uniforms work in brightly lit spray booths that prevent any trace of painting chemicals from entering the shop. Both the cleanliness and the many barriers placed between the workers and the painting chemicals

are evidence of the shop's health and safety priorities.

Which shop is the hobbyist's most likely to resemble, the '50s bump and paint or the modern refinisher? With not a lot of exceptions, the hobbyist has opted for the laid-back, relaxed look of the '50s shop — which probably means it's not a safe place to work.

Each stage in the refinishing process presents health and safety hazards. Stripping off the old finish risks exposure to toxic chemicals, creates fire hazards, and produces irritating dust. Mixing painting products exposes handlers to skin contact, vapor inhalation, and fire hazards from spillage. Spraying greatly increases exposure, while storage and disposal, when done improperly, risk explosion, fire, and contamination. Although some painting chemicals are only mildly irritating, others pose serious health risks — to the point of being lethal. In this setting, there's no margin for laxness in safety.

Respirators need to be worn even while mixing paints. These painters should also be wearing protective gloves as skin contact from two-part catalyzed paints can be toxic.

Shop Safety Rule Number 1, Keep a Clean Shop. Clutter like this packing debris invites accidents.

UPDATING TO PROFESSIONAL STANDARDS

Though they're available to anyone, painting products are manufactured and intended for professional use. Safety begins by adopting a professional's outlook — which means doing everything "by the book."

Rule 1. Keep a clean shop. Mess and clutter invite accidents, whether spilled paint or solvent, tripping over snarled air hose, tangled electrical cords, or other clutter lying about the shop floor. Paint the shop walls and ceiling a light color, preferably white, and install lots of lighting. It's easier to keep things clean and avoid accidents working in a well-lighted shop. Thoroughly clean painting areas after spraying.

Rule 2. Store products in locked, fireproof cabinets. Keeping the cabinets locked prevents the painting chemicals from being reached by children.

Rule 3. Don't smoke inside your shop and don't allow others to smoke. Paint and painting products are flammable. Don't bring matches or a lighter into the work area either. Post no-smoking signs to alert others of shop policy.

Rule 4. Mount fire extinguishers within easy reach. The fire extinguishers need to be foam or dry powder. Do not attempt to extinguish paint product fires with water. Remember to check fire extinguishers annually and get them serviced as necessary.

Rule 5. Keep a first-aid kit in the shop to treat cuts or burns. For medical emergencies resulting from harmful exposure to painting products, draw up and post a list of first-aid procedures. Some of the items your list should include are:

- Irregular or halted breathing: Immediately remove the person to fresh air, call 911, keep him/her warm and at rest, if necessary administer artificial respiration.
- Eye contact with chemicals: Flush eyes with clean water for at least 10 minutes.
- Skin contact with chemicals: Remove contaminated clothing. Wash skin around contact area with soap and water.

It is very helpful if the shop has a sink or other washing facility (a hose). If not, post directions for the quickest route to a washing facility.

Rule 6. Do not bring food or beverage into the painting area. Always wash hands after using painting equipment or handling chemicals.

Rule 7. Wear protective clothing and equipment whenever working with painting products.

Clothing items are available from a painting supplier and should include:

- Lint-free coveralls with elastic

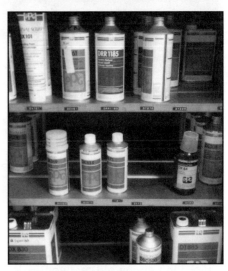

Painting chemicals should be stored inside locked metal cabinets.

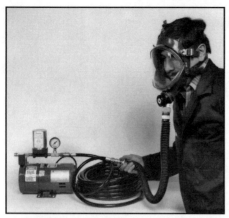

wrists and ankles

Wear protective clothing and equipment whenever working with painting products. This painter's full face mask is equipped with an external air supply. Photo courtesy of the Eastwood Company.

Don't store expired and non-usable painting products. Keep an inventory sheet and properly dispose of all hazardous material.

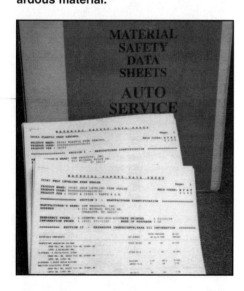

Individuals as well as professional refinishing shops are required by law to have MSDS sheets for all hazardous materials on premises.

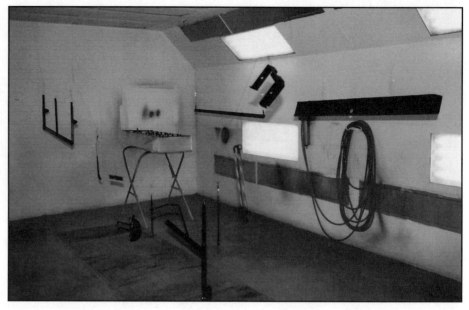

Painting should be confined to a booth or enclosure with a filtered ventilation system.

- Painter's cap with elastic or adjustable band
- Rubber gloves offering chemical resistance to solvents and hardeners

Equipment should include:

- An approved paint spray respirator for use when spraying acrylic enamel. A full face piece respirator is preferred to a respirator alone

-or-

- An air-supplied hood or full face piece, air-supplied respirator and oil-less compressor for use when spraying two-part paints with hardeners.

Rule 8. Confine spraying to booths or enclosures with a filtered ventilation system. Make sure air is exhausted away from buildings and/or people. Remove painting vapors not just from the person doing the spraying, but from others who may be in or near the building where the spraying is occurring.

Rule 9. Properly decontaminate and dispose of all left-over painting products that have been mixed with hardeners, also "empty" paint cans and hardening agents that have reached the end of their relatively short shelf-life. Don't store expired and non-usable products. Never pour coating products or solvents into drains or dump them into the soil.

Rule 10. Remember, safety is a personal and daily decision. Post safety reminders.

REASONS FOR SAFETY PRECAUTIONS

Why all this fuss about safety, you might ask? I'm only using painting products a few hours at a time, not every day as is the case with a professional. Sure the solvents are potentially explosive and it's best not to inhale their vapors. But I'm smart enough to not light a cigarette while mixing paint. So what if I breathe a little of the vapors? It's not like I do this every day! The reason this "so what's the big deal" attitude doesn't work can be stated in one word — isocyanates.

Although they're not found in all automotive refinishing products, two-part coatings where the paint is mixed with hardener are likely to contain reactive isocyanates that pose severe short-term and long-term health risks. The presence of isocyanates will be indicated by the Hazard Ratings of the painting product shown on the Material Safety Data Sheet (MSDS) prepared by the manufacturer. It should be noted, that individuals — as well as professional refinishing shops — using automotive painting products are required by law to have proper MSDS sheets on premises and readily available. When purchasing painting products and supplies, ask for the MSDS package and read the hazard information as well as the spill or leak procedures, first-aid treatment, and protection information.

HEALTH EFFECTS OF ISOCYANATES

Reactions from overexposure to isocyanates can range from acute responses like coughing, dryness of the throat, or a burning sensation of the nose, throat, and lungs, to chronic or long-term respiratory difficulty. Acute symptoms may resemble an asthma attack, possibly resulting in pulmonary edema (fluid on the lungs), or flu-like symptoms of fever and chills. Chronic, long-term breathing difficulty can result in decreased lung function. What's scary is that these reactions do not necessarily result from a single overexposure. It's possible to become "sensitized" to isocyanates by repeated exposures to low levels over a period of time. Becoming sensitized means the body develops an allergy-like response to an amount of chemical that might have no effect on a normal healthy person. It is possible to become sensitized from a single overexposure or from repeated overexposures. Once sensitization has occurred, even a very low exposure (well below the OSHA Permissible Exposure Limit, or PEL) could trigger a reaction. Or the reaction might be triggered by some other completely unrelated irritant — like cold air, pollen, or dust.

Sensitization to isocyanates may be temporary or permanent, and may persist even without continued exposure. Do you see the picture? Casual use of refinishing products containing isocyanates could weaken your respiratory system for the rest of your life. Long after the car has been painted, you could be sitting in your living room and suffer an asthma-like attack for no apparent reason. Or, if the overexposure is really severe or combined with prior sensitization, then ARDS (Acute Respiratory Distress Syndrome), which simulates a heart attack, can occur and cause death.

The harmful effects of isocyanates aren't limited to respiratory conditions. While mild overexposure may cause watery eyes, severe overexposure can cause "clouding" of the eye surface (like cataracts). Skin reactions may range from itching to blisters, severe redness, or swelling. Like respiratory sensitization, the skin can also become sensitized, in which case the reaction may either be immediate (at the moment of contact with isocyanates in liquid form or vapors) or delayed.

The OSHA permissible limit is based on the concentration of chemical and is set for isocyanates at 0.005 ppm (parts per million in air). Workers can be exposed to these permissible limits for 8 hours a day, 40 hours a week, throughout their entire working life without experiencing ill effects to health. The permissible limit for isocyanates is the same concentration as painting a single nickel red and mixing it in with a gigantic mound of nickels totalling 10 million dollars, then setting about to find the red nickel. What the OSHA standards tell us is that exposure to isocyanates is not to occur.

PREVENTING ISOCYANATE EXPOSURE

The simplest way to avoid respiratory or skin contact with isocyanates is to not use products containing the chemical. However, this means spraying primarily single-part refinishing products and avoiding painting products that mix with a catalyst or hardener containing isocyanates. It can be done. A full range of primer products, adhesion primers, primer surfacer, primer sealers, and color coatings can be selected that do not mix with catalysts. Likewise, single-stage color coatings are available that don't require a catalyst or that mix with catalysts not containing harmful isocyanates. For most hobbyists, these isocyanate-free products are the wisest choice from a health and safety standpoint.

In order to take advantage of painting technology and still avoid isocyanate exposure, the hobbyist might apply only the base coatings, leaving the color finish for the professional. This approach makes sense for several reasons. Unless the hobbyist has access to a spray booth, risk of dust, insects, and other contamination in the final finish is good reason to leave the color coating to a professional. The high cost of the paint itself removes much of the financial incentive for the hobbyist attempting a quality finish

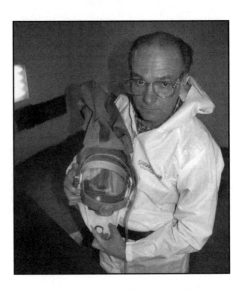

Casual use of refinishing products containing isocyanates could weaken your respiratory system for the rest of your life. This painter preparing to "suit up" with his air-supplied hood isn't taking that chance.

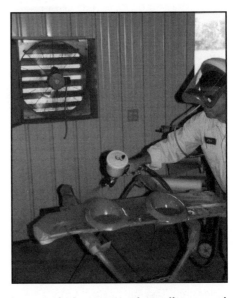

Less toxic lacquer and acrylic enamel paints can be safely sprayed in areas ventilated with an exhaust fan.

coating without the proper equipment. The spray booth functions not only to ensure a dust-free painting environment, but also to help protect the painter from toxic painting chemicals.

Even with non-catalyzed paints, it's still important to wear a proper respirator and other protective clothing. Painting products and solvents can cause respiratory sensitivity and can be caustic to the skin. Approved respirators for acrylic enamel (and lacquer where it is still used) are available through painting product manufacturers and their dealers and distributors.

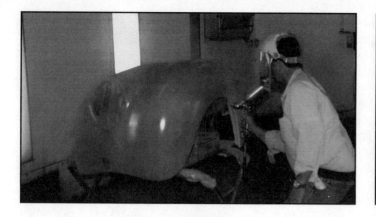

A face shield or full face respirator should be worn to protect eyes from painting mist.

Curtained enclosures can provide a safe spraying environment without losing valuable shop space.

When wearing this type of respirator, it is important to adjust the face piece for a tight seal and to know when the mask is sealing properly. Filters need to be changed at recommended intervals, or when paint vapors are detected through the filters. Lightweight disposable respirators are also available. If the disposable type is used, it's important to have several on hand so that you won't be tempted to spray that "quickie touch-up job" without respirator protection. To protect the eyes from painting mist as well as possible chemical splashes, respirators are available that cover the whole face and provide clear viewing through a replaceable polycarbonate lens.

Use of a respirator doesn't eliminate the need for a ventilated spray area. For the hobbyist, a spray area suitable for isocyanate-free painting products can be created by sectioning off an area of the shop with clear plastic sheeting. The air draft system should be constructed so that air entering the enclosure passes through filters (furnace filters can be used) and exhausted from the spray enclosure and the building as well. The exhaust fan should be placed at the end of the enclosure opposite the filters. The exhaust fan should always be turned on before spraying begins and left running until after the painter has left the enclosure. It's important that the painter avoid spraying "upwind" (against the direction of the air moving through the enclosure) to avoid being engulfed by the painting mist.

A respirator's protection is inadequate for spraying catalyzed painting products containing isocyanates in an enclosed shop without a painting ventilation system. Isocyanates don't have a detectable odor so you're not going to smell anything through the respirator that tips you off to the presence of toxic chemicals. Also, a respirator alone does not provide effective enough filtration. To apply two-part paints with maximum safety, the painter needs to wear a hood or full face piece supplied with air drawn from an external source away from the painting area. The air supply needs to be provided by an oil-less pump or compressor that is located where it can draw fresh air. Although an external air source gives the painter less freedom of movement than a filter-style respirator (the air hose to the hood has to be contended with, along with the spray gun hose), the external air supply system keeps the painter safe from toxic exposure.

Suited up in protective garb of lint-free coveralls, rubber gloves, and an air supplied mask or hood, the painter looks like a decontamination worker at a toxic site — which in a manner of speaking he is. Hobbyists should not consider the modern automotive painter's "uniform" silly or frivolous, but necessary for safe application of highly toxic paints. This safety equipment can also be needed when doing metal work that can burn a catalyzed coating (as in cutting or welding). If you're doing metal repair and wonder if the coating contains isocyanates, you can determine whether it's necessary to wear protective garb, including an air supplied respirator, with a simple test. Soak a corner of a rag with solvent and wipe vigorously across a small area of finish. If some of the color comes off on the rag, the coating does not contain isocyanates but is Thermoplastic, meaning it has not been "set" with a catalyst. Clothing to protect against hot metal and burns will be adequate for these types of coatings.

DANGER TO THE ENVIRONMENT

Beyond health and safety, automotive refinishing products are harmful to the environment. The danger comes from the amount of Volatile Organic Compound (VOC) that is present in virtually all painting products. Without the VOC component, paint would be just a lump of pigment. Volatile (meaning evaporative) compound is needed to give the paint and its catalyst or hardener a liquid consistency. For spraying, additional VOC is added through solvent. To show that we're not talking about insignificant amounts, paint contains 4.5 lbs. of VOC per gallon; reducer has 7 lbs. per gallon, and hardener adds another 4 lbs. per gallon. Of course 1:1:1 is not the mixing ratio, so we wouldn't have 3 gallons of refinishing product containing 15.5 lbs. of VOC. For a gallon of ready-to-spray product, we'll mix 2 quarts of paint with 1 quart of reducer and 1 quart of hardener, having a VOC content of 5 lbs. — a lesser amount, but still not insignificant.

VOCs harm the environment when they evaporate and mix in the atmosphere with other pollutants, creating a greenhouse haze or smog. Concern, both for health and the danger of global warming, has led to air quality regulations limiting VOC in painting products.

These regulations originated in California in response to the severe air pollution in the Los Angeles basin. Rule 1151, passed in the late 1980s, imposed extremely stringent regulations on vehicle refinishing with the intent of drastically reducing the amount of VOC. Subsequently, Northern California, then Washington, Oregon, Texas, and several midwestern and eastern states adopted similar automotive refinishing VOC regulations. In the late 1990s, the Federal government set VOC standards for the entire country.

While the Federal regulations apply to manufacturers of automotive painting products and the regional regulations monitor compliance by professional refinishers, both effect hobbyists 1) in the phase-out of lacquer paints, and 2) through changes in painting technology, both in development of low VOC refinishing products and high-transfer spraying equipment.

Traditional high-pressure spraying wastes a large quantity of painting product through overspray. Reducing product waste is one of the most effective ways of scaling back on VOC. Since both state and federal regulations limit VOC content "as applied" — meaning in paint actually used — more efficient paint transfer technologies like HVLP (high volume low pressure) are necessary to gain compliance with the standards. While hobbyists are not likely to come under the scrutiny of regulators — as is the case in many areas for professional refinishing shops — this does not mean hobbyists should look askance at or ignore regulations on both VOC content and refinishing technology. All of us share responsibility for the quality of the air we breathe. We also need to manage our waste.

CLEANING UP AND DISPOSING OF PAINTS AND SOLVENTS

Cleaning up an accidental spill of painting product instantly becomes serious if that product contains isocyanates. Rubber gloves must be worn to prevent the product from coming in contact with skin and a respirator will need to be worn to avoid exposure to product vapors.

Safety precautions are also required for clean up at the end of a painting session and disposing of leftover painting products and their containers. Spray guns are available that use disposable liners inside the painting cups. With this type of gun, clean up is quick and easy, consisting mainly of removing and disposing of the liner. Clean up needs to be done in a well-ventilated area. With the shop bay open to outside air, clean up can be accomplished with a full face mask and respirator. In a closed shop, an air-supplied hood needs to be worn while cleaning up after spraying catalyzed paints. Full clothing (rubber gloves and coveralls) needs to be worn to make sure none of the activated painting product comes in contact with the skin.

Information on proper disposal of leftover painting product is given on the MSDS sheet, which you'll recall manufacturers prepare for each refinishing product and are available from the retailer. These sheets will state the type of waste storage container required, whether this container should be ventilated or non-ventilated, and recommended storage locations and temperature range. Hobbyists need to read and follow the MSDS guidelines, not just toss leftover painting product into a household waste container. Proper disposal is through OSHA-approved disposal service. Since the hobbyist may consider contacting such a service impractical for the small amount of waste generated by occasional painting activity, a more practical disposal alternative is to bring leftover product to a professional refinishing shop and pay the shop to include your product in its waste. Also, many counties now have designated recycling centers that will accept this type of hazardous waste. Never pour leftover painting product down a wastewater drain or sewer. Product that "cures" in the drainlines or trap can "irreversibly block" the waste lines and add contamination to a leach bed or sewage treatment.

Empty curing agent and paint containers need to be decontaminated before disposal using a solution of 5 percent ammonia and 2-5 percent detergent in water, or alternatively a

Suited up in protective garb of lint-free coveralls, and an air supplied hood, the painter looks like a decontamination worker at a toxic site.

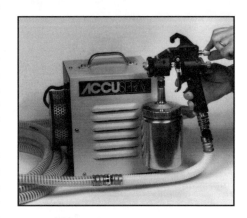

HVLP paint spraying systems lower VOC emissions. Some HVLP guns use a compact, portable turbine compressor to deliver a very high volume of warm, dry air — ideal for spraying automotive paints. Photo courtesy of The Eastwood Company.

20 percent solution of Union Carbide's Tergitol TMN-10 in water. Containers should not be sealed for at least 24 hours after being washed with the decontamination solution due to possible carbon dioxide gas buildup, which could burst the container.

Safe use of modern automotive refinishing products requires hobbyists to:

- familiarize themselves with proper safety procedures
- purchase and use proper safety equipment and clothing
- properly dispose of leftover painting product.

With catalyzed paints especially, the "margin for error" can be fatal.

Do-It-Yourself Guide to CUSTOM PAINTING
Types of Paint

Painting used to be done with lacquer and enamel. Lacquer looked good, but didn't hold up. Enamel had better durability, but lacked gloss. Today's base coat/clear coat systems offer gloss and durability and in many cases can faithfully match the original colors on older vehicles.

Through most of the automobile's first century automotive refinishers talked of two types of paint, lacquer and enamel. Each had its advantages and its disadvantages. Some cars came from the factory with lacquer finishes, some with enamel. Each refinisher had his or her own preference. Today the choice between these (let's call them "original") types of paint is simple. For all practical purposes, lacquer has disappeared from use —swept into history's "dust bin" by the harm to the atmosphere caused by its solvents. But lacquer really wasn't the most practical automotive finish. Its appeal came from lacquer's ability to produce a beautifully deep, mirror gloss and its ease of use. Almost anyone could spray a "decent" lacquer finish. A friend still owns the Model T Ford he painted one summer afternoon in his front yard. "We'd just sprayed the last coat," Ed says, "when a car came ripping

down the dirt road past the house. The dust cloud seemed to engulf the Model T. I was afraid to look. But when we rubbed out the finish, it looked like we'd painted the car in a spray booth." Today, nearly a half-century later, not right up close, but from a bit of a distance, that "T" still looks sharp. Lacquer was really hard to "mess up."

The problem with lacquer arose from its lack of durability. That Model T we've been talking about still looks good from a distance because it sits perpetually in storage. Lacquer finishes are brittle, so they chip easily. Also, with temperature changes lacquer cracks, which makes an old lacquer finish easy to spot.

Enamel's virtues were the opposite of lacquer, and vice versa. Enamel, which is still used today (though reformulated), is a much tougher paint than lacquer. The downsides were that older enamel finishes wouldn't approach lacquer in gloss and the

paint was much harder to spray. The old synthetic enamels dried slow, almost invariably producing runs. The choice came down to this, do you want a paint that lasts, but looks crummy, or a paint that looks like a drill sergeant's spit-shined boot but ages at nearly the same rate as fruit flies?

MODERN FINISHES

Today, appearance and durability aren't the hard choices. Modern acrylic enamel applies with the ease of lacquer and has a much brighter gloss. Further, paint companies rate newer acrylic enamels 50% more durable than their predecessor. With lacquer out of the picture and acrylic enamel closely approaching lacquer's ease of application, the paint choice turns in a new direction. Beginning in the 1970s with DuPont's Imron, polyurethane paints entered the automotive refinishing arena.

Modern painting products are toxic and require respirators and airflow systems to protect the person spraying the paint.

Base coat/clear coat finishes are the choice of manufacturer's and refinishers alike because of their deep, enduring shine.

Technologically, the polyurethane finishes progressed so far from lacquer and the old-style synthetic enamel that the manufacturers don't even call them "paints." These are "coatings" and "refinishing systems." You'll see that "system" word used a lot, not only in this book but also in the paint manufacturer's literature, because it describes an interlocking regimen of primers and finish coatings that's designed into modern automotive paint. The choices today weigh complexity and cost, durability or super durability, gloss or super gloss.

Lowest on the complexity scale is acrylic enamel. An automotive hobbyist with a low-cost paint spraying outfit (portable air compressor and siphon-style spray gun) can achieve satisfactory results — whether a whole car or just touch up work — with this paint. The mixing ratio is 2:1 with reducer, and additives for color blending help simplify spot repair.

Moving up the complexity scale, acrylic enamel can be mixed with hardener to create a urethane-tough, high gloss finish. But whenever a hardener or "catalyzing agent" is added to a painting product, the hobbyist refinisher needs to take notice. Often, catalyzing agents contain isocyanates, chemicals that can be extremely toxic and require special respirators and air flow systems to

protect the person spraying the paint. (See Chapter 1 for a more complete discussion on this topic.) Nor is it advisable or practical to spray the catalyzed refinishing product out-of-doors (where the toxic chemicals are dispersed more quickly). Airborne dust or insects landing in the paint can quickly ruin a substantial investment in painting product and time.

Adding a catalyzing agent changes the paint in yet another way, giving it a "pot life" after which it turns to jelly and can't be used. "Un-catalyzed" paint (meaning older lacquers and acrylic enamel without the hardener) can be stored somewhat indefinitely in an airtight container for later touch-up or some other application. Being able to reuse leftover product naturally helps stretch the paint's cost. Not being able to reuse paint that's been mixed with catalyst means more than just wasted product — the leftover residue has to be disposed of according to hazardous waste procedures, which for the hobbyist are not only cumbersome, but can also be expensive.

Offsetting their drawbacks, catalyzing agents bring several benefits, including ease of repair and the opportunity for clear coating. An innovative feature of modern paints is the two- or three-step finish where the color is applied in a base coat and the gloss and protective layer in a clear

coat. (For creative, very bright, and fluorescent finishes, a third midcoat can be applied between the base and clear.) Although some base coats are not catalyzed (meaning they do not contain toxic isocyanates), most clear coats are, making this more complex finish potentially dangerous for amateur refinishers to apply.

Nonetheless, base coat/clear coat finishes have three major attractions that have made them the "universal" choice for new cars and the "hands down" favorite for show cars. Manufacturers like base coat/clear coat because they save on paint while giving their cars a gleaming, durable finish. (The paint saving comes from the clear coat's ability to protect the underlying color even when only a thin layer is applied.) Car owners like base coat/clear coat because of its deep, enduring shine, which matches and surpasses those legendary "fifteen coats of hand-rubbed lacquer" finishes. Additionally, base coat/clear coat allows dramatic custom finishes with color shifting "harlequin" or "chameleon" paints, bright candy colors, and fluorescent pearls. Finally, the clincher, clear coating protects the finish against airborne pollutants which in low air quality regions can literally "eat" a car's paint.

Paints used in clear coating are most typically urethanes — a funda-

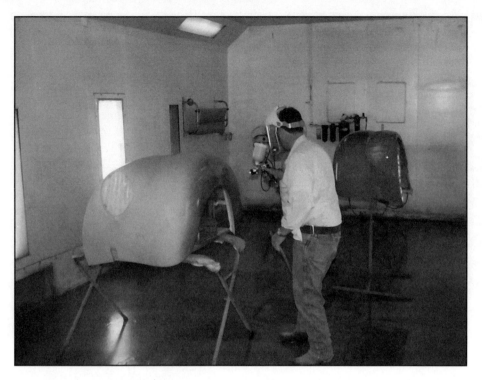

The "systems" approach gives great versatility to the primer coatings.

mentally different kind of coating from a lacquer finish. When the choices were lacquer or enamel, painters had a rule: enamel over lacquer but never lacquer over enamel. The reason was simple — enamel's solvent wouldn't penetrate a lacquer base, but lacquer thinner would cut right through enamel, lifting underlying enamel coatings. Anyone who's had this happen knows the "pit in the stomach" feeling of seeing a bright, new finish suddenly ripple and blister like its been attacked with a heat gun. Once the damage has occurred, the only "fix" is to sand the finish smooth, rebuild the base, and recoat with enamel.

THERMOPLASTIC VS. THERMOSET

The older lacquer and unhardened enamel finishes are called *Thermoplastic* coatings, which means they can be re-flowed by heat or solvent. A favorite "trick" of refinishers back in lacquer's heyday was to "microsand" the final coat, using a very fine sandpaper, then spray a "wet" top coat that was 90% solvent and only 10% paint. The solvent would "melt" the finish, flowing smooth any sanding marks, for a mirror smooth surface. Of course, as just discussed, that "wet"

solvent coat sometimes penetrated and reacted with underlying coatings, undoing all of the painter's painstaking work. Thermoplastic coatings are largely avoided by professional refinishers today because of their susceptibility to damage from airborne pollutants, as well as checking, cracking, and shrinking.

Modern two-part (or catalyzed) paints are called *Thermoset* coatings, meaning they cannot be re-flowed by heat or solvent once cured. As it reacts with the catalyst, the paint undergoes an irreversible chemical reaction that leaves it virtually impermeable to solvents. With the modern "systems" refinishing approach, each primer and finish coating is formulated to interlock chemically with the next. Older thermoplastic coatings relied on mechanical bonding (roughness of underlying surface) to adhere one layer to the other. The thermoset "systems" approach has lots of advantages and a few disadvantages. Among the advantages is very strong bonding between the coatings — with these paints a peeling topcoat is nowhere nearly as common as it was with older enamels or lacquer. The "systems" approach also gives great versatility to the preparation coatings. For example, a catalyzed corrosion-

resistant primer applied can also double as a primer surfacer and be top-coated without need for a separate sealer. The downside of the thermoset "systems" products occurs with the isocyanates used in most of the curing agents. The appropriate warning label on a product containing isocyanates would be a skull and cross bones. These chemicals are that dangerous if used improperly.

So how do you know if an existing finish is thermoplastic or thermoset, in other words whether it is an old-style or modern coating? The test is really simple: just wipe some solvent on a rag and rub the finish. If some of the color shows on the rag, the coating is thermoplastic.

So far we've looked at two thermoset coatings, acrylic enamel with hardener and acrylic urethane (also with hardener) frequently used in base coat/clear coat combinations. Polyurethane coatings offer a third system choice, although in practicality the use of these extremely tough, chemical-resistant coatings is somewhat limited. When DuPont's Imron, one of the first polyurethane products, entered retail markets in the mid-1970s, car restorers and customizers alike quickly became excited by the paint's brilliant shine and toughness. Imron's limitation, or so it seemed, was the coating's very few color choices. Since the paint couldn't be formulated to OEM color matches, it was used primarily for painting chassis and underbody surfaces (black is black, right? Wrong!), or for commercial fleets. Advertised as the paint with the "wet look," an Imron coated chassis looked like it had just been driven through a car wash. In the paint's intended settings, as a coating for trucks and aircraft, for example, the brightness and hardness worked. Underneath a Model T Ford, let's say, no one believed that's how the car looked from the factory. Imron had another, more troublesome, problem. While the paint could hardly be scraped or scratched, it chipped rather easily (as in being hit by a stone chip thrown up from a tire on gravel paving) and was difficult to repair. It's not surprising, then, that whereas ads for collector cars in the early 1980s might boast of an Imron painted chassis, one seldom, if ever, sees this claim today.

POWDER COATINGS

Modern polyurethane finishes have improved chip impact resistance, but their intended use remains the same — airport ground and operation equipment and fleet vehicles like over-the-road trucks. That's not to say a restorer or a customizer wouldn't use a polyurethane coating. However, the most logical application, on chassis parts, can now quite conveniently and inexpensively be powder coated for a finish superior even to polyurethane.

With powder coating the refinishing complexity cycle also comes full circle. This technology is even easier to apply than old-fashioned lacquer, is virtually harmless, and does not endanger the environment. Surely, there's got to be a "hitch," you say. Well, there is. In its raw form, powder coating is just what the name implies, a dust-like coating of finely ground-up plastic. What turns the coating into a finish isn't an iso-cyanate-laden hardener, but baking — and there's the "hitch." The range of powder coating applications is limited to the size of the baking oven, plus an expanding, but still restrictive, range of color choices.

Professional powder coating shops have baking ovens large enough to hold the major components of an automotive chassis, but for the hobbyist doing powder coating in his own shop, a second-hand kitchen oven from an appliance or second-hand store is more likely to be the baking device. What this means is that for smaller pieces, like engine accessories (valve covers, for example), assorted brackets, and chassis parts as large as wheels, powder coating is eminently practical for the hobbyist refinisher. Larger items can either be painted or powder coated by a professional. At this time powder coating isn't used for exterior body panels for reasons beyond the lack of car-sized baking ovens. For one, powder coatings don't exist in the color ranges required for automotive finishes. For another, powder coating looks too much like what it is (melted plastic) to

serve as a body finish. On accessory pieces, however, its resemblance to baked enamel looks "just right."

Unlike the various refinishing systems, powder coating is a "stand-alone" product. No base coating is needed. The part is stripped to bare metal, free of rust, then powder coated. That's it. No micro-sanding, clear coating, rubbing, buffing; just melt the plastic powder, let the part cool, and put it on the car. It's a great one-shot finish, and you'll find two chapters in this book devoted to its application and use: one as a durable coating and another as a custom finish.

HOW COATINGS ARE APPLIED

There used to be a sense that really good automotive refinishers had an "artist's touch," meaning the way a spray gun was held and paint fanned across the surface, or how a refinisher twiddled the spray gun's control knobs or air pressure setting. Some refinishers seemed to have a magical touch. The mystery surrounding good paint jobs ran so deep that a friend insists to this day that the best looking paint he ever saw on a car was applied by an "old-timer" who had concocted a special solvent blend of lacquer thinner and enamel reducer. An apocryphal story to be sure, but so far had automotive refinishing removed itself from "science," that anything seemed possible and plausible.

Today automotive refinishing is all science, Actually technology. Do everything absolutely according to manufacturer's recommendations, and a superior finish will result. This means the paint, solvent, and catalyst have to be mixed in exact proportions, the pressure to the spray gun must be at exactly the right setting, the gun must be held at the exact factory-set distance from the painting surface, the temperature and humidity need to be within manufacturer's standards, and then it works. Like shooting a really good game of golf, the "human factor" has to be gotten out of the way.

How much of the refinishing work you can or want to do yourself depends on how much you want to learn about what products to use, in

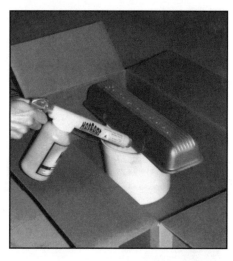

With powder coating the refinishing complexity cycle comes full circle. This technology is even easier to apply than old-fashioned lacquer. Just point the spray gun at the part and pull the trigger. The only preparation is a bare metal surface.

Powder coating's only limitation is the need for a curing oven, something easily solved by an inexpensive second-hand kitchen range.

what sequence and time frame, and how they're mixed. You also need to consider how much you want to invest in proper equipment both to apply the paint and to protect yourself from the physical harm you could suffer by exposing yourself to the paint's toxic chemicals. The equipment can be a substantial investment by itself.

BASE COATINGS

For the hobbyist, starting with the lowest technology products makes the most sense. This means begin-

Really good automotive refinishers used to be thought of as having an artist's touch. The "art" of painting is actually technology — mixing and applying the painting products exactly according to the manufacturer's specifications.

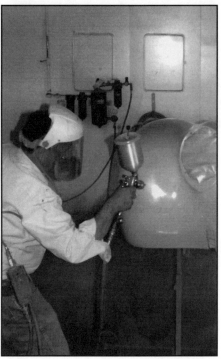

How much of the refinishing process you decide to do yourself will depend on your interest in learning about the products and willingness to invest in the necessary equipment.

ning with non-isocyanate base coatings. Base coatings (primers) are typically applied first and spraying errors such as sags or runs don't present much of a problem since the coating is likely to be sanded. Base coatings have another advantage for the hobbyist. In nearly any setting where you bring in a professional, you can save money by doing as much preparation work as possible yourself. This is especially true where the preparation work is time intensive and low skill. I'm not implying that the base coat for an automotive finish can be put on with a brush and smoothed with household sandpaper, but compared to the skills in color matching, spray gun handling, and product knowledge that are required for a professional quality finish, the base coat is at least feasible.

The hobbyist can do most of his/her own base coating with a moderate investment in equipment, leaving the final color finish to a professional. Or, if the hobbyist plans a final finish in acrylic enamel, by the time the primer and primer surfacer preparation is completed, the hobbyist will likely have acquired the skills to confidently apply the finish. With component parts, powder coating is simple

enough that even a first-timer is almost guaranteed success.

Base coat/clear coat finishes can be challenging for the novice. Since the base coat has a dull, primer-looking, off-color hue and the true color doesn't emerge until the clear coat is applied, color matching can be difficult. Not understanding how the two coatings combine to create the final high-gloss color finish could give the impression that the job has been ruined. Then again, if the base coat color mix is off, the job could well be ruined. Unlike non-clear coated finishes (what the paint manufacturers call "single stage color") the base coat is kept thin — applied only thick enough to hide the undercoat. The hobbyist, not realizing the difference in coatings, could apply the base coat too thick, causing sand scratch swelling and other problems. Also, base coat/clear coat systems mix with hardeners containing isocyanates — chemicals which require a professional breathing mask. Finally, any dust or airborne impurities are very noticeable in base coat/clear coat finishes not easily removed. Lack of access to a spray booth may be reason alone to leave application of base coat/clear coat finishes to a professional.

Some hobbyists do have access to spray booths and other professional refinishing equipment. A retired college professor now enjoying his life's passion, restoring collector cars, showed me his shop located in the basement of his home, which he converted from a Pennsylvania barn. There, tucked away in one corner of his cavernous shop was a downdraft spray booth which he had purchased from a school district that had closed out its vocational educational auto body program. He bought the spray booth, he confided, for a small fraction of its original price. Another hobbyist related that he has access to professional refinishing equipment, including a spray booth, through his employer. By carefully reading the product instructions, practice, and help from professionals, both of these hobbyists have learned to spray modern high-technology automotive finishes. It can be done, but keep in mind that you don't need to apply every stage of the finish to save money — and if you make an error with the final color coating, given the high cost of the refinishing product, you're likely to lose a lot of money.

Paint spraying is converting to a technology called HVLP (High Volume Low Pressure) that results in very little loss of material and greatly reduced toxic overspray.

Once the new finish has been applied, it needs to be cared for and preserved. Proper finish care is a multi-step process that calls for the use of quality products.

SPRAYING METHODS

Two quite different methods are used to spray modern paint coatings. Traditionally, automotive finishes were applied by high-pressure spraying. Today, high volume low pressure (HVLP) has become almost the universal spraying method. HVLP's popularity draws from its substantially higher transfer efficiency (meaning more paint lands on and adheres to the surface being painted), which says simply there's less wasted paint. Conventional spraying blows the paint against the surface being coated at high pressure (35 to 65 psi at the air cap). Much of the paint rebounds off the surface and diffuses in the air, landing on other surfaces as overspray or being sucked out of the spraying room by an exhaust fan and dispersed into the atmosphere.

Air cap pressure for HVLP ranges from 1 to 10 psi, so there's very little rebound. Where the paint lands is where it adheres. Elimination of overspray means easier cleanup, less atmospheric dispersion, and savings in painting product. Both types of spray painting equipment, conventional and HVLP, are marketed to the hobbyist and are within equivalent

price ranges.

Whichever paint spraying system you choose, it's essential that the air supply to the spray gun be free of moisture and other contaminants. Chapter 5 discusses proper air lines with traps, filters, and dryers to ensure a moisture-free air supply. As has already been mentioned, it's essential to wear a proper respirator or breathe from a fresh air supply when spraying painting products containing toxic isocyanates. Chapter 1 details respirator and fresh air supply equipment that meets safe-use requirements.

PRESERVING THE FINISH

Once the new finish is applied, it has to be cared for and preserved. Although the car owner's first concern may be scrapes, scratches, and parking lot dings, damage also results from airborne contaminants as well as tree sap dripped onto the car, bugs splattered against the paint, and oxidation of the finish caused by ultraviolet light. Clear coats are especially susceptible since they can be easily scratched, particularly when wiped off dry.

Proper finish care is a multi-step process. If the full regimen is followed

in the spring when the car is brought out of storage in preparation for the summer show season and again at storage time in the fall (or some other more frequent schedule if the car is operated year 'round), then maintaining the finish is a fairly simple process. The full regimen covers a series of steps, beginning with washing to clean off dirt and grime, then a deep cleaner to remove stains and oxidation, this followed by a deep polish to restore color, then a rich carnauba wax to bring out the finish's full gloss and give long-lasting protection. Clear coats may require an additional step to remove hairline scratches.

During storage, whether long term or just sitting in the garage, the car should be covered. Protective covers with soft inner liners to prevent scratching not only help against accidental damage — someone scraping against the car with a bike, for example; they also shield the finish from dust, pollutants, and harmful sunshine. For long-term storage, it may be advisable to seal the car in a storage wrapper, locking out not only dust and pollutants, but moisture as well. These finish care and storage procedures are described in more detail in this book's closing chapters.

Do-It-Yourself Guide to CUSTOM PAINTING

Powder Coating: Easy, Safe, and Fun

Eastwood's Hotcoat® system plus a used kitchen oven makes powder coating an inexpensive, do-it-yourself process.

"This paint is really fun to use." That's how Rich Jensen owner of Cruzin' Performance, a shop specializing in GM engine upgrades, described his first experience with The Eastwood Company's HotCoat® powder coating system. Rich had seen the HotCoat system demonstrated at Eastwood's tent at the giant Spring Carlisle (Pennsylvania) swap meet, but questioned whether the powder coating process was really as easy as it looked in the demonstration. "I wondered," Rich said, "if I could really get the same results at home in my shop that they were showing us. I tried out my HotCoat system on a timing cover. This stuff works great and is simple, safe, and best of all it's fun."

A DIFFERENT KIND OF PAINT

Since these three claims — easy, safe, and fun — can't be made about any solvent-based painting product, let's find out what's different about powder coating.

Powder coating isn't a paint — at least not in the traditional sense of a liquid coating or pigment suspended in solvent. The powder is finely ground plastic and that requires heat to melt and flow the plastic.

Powder coating makes a tougher, more chemically impervious finish than paint. Have a wrench slip and strike a powder coated surface and you'll think you've nicked through to bare metal, but you're not even likely to see a scratch. Spill solvent or even a corrosive chemical like DOT 3 brake fluid on powder coating and you may see a temporary "wet look," but no lifting, bubbling, or other permanent damage to the finish.

Powder coating is safer to use than solvent-based paints. Safety equipment during spraying consists of a respirator with a charcoal-activated filter, but for mixing and cleanup, a dust mask suffices.

Powder coating won't work for the car body. Though ideal for many smaller chassis, suspension, and

engine parts, powder coating isn't practical for body panels because, most sheet metal items, and certainly the body structure, are too large to fit into the oven needed to melt the powder. Also, even though the selection of powder colors has increased dramatically, it's not the infinite range available with solvent-based paints.

Now that we have a sense of what powder coating is, and what it does and doesn't do, let's find out how you can enjoy the powder coating experience and use this painting technology for a multitude of household and hobby uses, not all strictly automotive.

When my friend Rich and I took our first serious look at powder coating in 1992, I was having my drum brake truck upgraded to front disk brakes. I'd had a powder coating service apply the tough plastic finish to the dust shields for the new braking system. Admiring the hard, glossy finish, Rich could easily see the application of powder coating to much of his shop's specialty work. A few months later he an-

You can't use the kitchen oven for powder coating. It has to be an oven dedicated to this purpose and located in your shop.

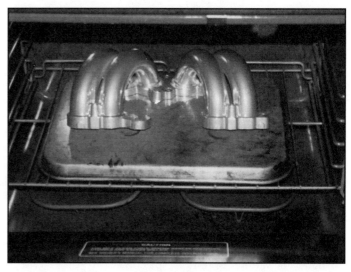

An electric household oven has adequate capacity for baking a variety of engine, chassis, and other bolt-on parts.

nounced that he was planning to add a powder coating system to his shop's equipment. It never happened. "I couldn't justify the cost," he explained. "I'd be doing this as a service, a value-added to my custom work, and there wouldn't be enough volume to pay for the equipment. When I need something powder coated, I can send the part to a shop doing that work."

At that time, powder coating equipment was expensive, about $5,000 for the spraying setup, plus the cost of an industrial baking oven. The breakthrough in do-it-yourself powder coating came in early 1998 when The Eastwood Company released its HotCoat® Powder Coating System. It's an ingenious product. The HotCoat gun has the simplicity of a light bulb, yet it performs comparably to powder spraying units costing more than 10 times its price. Yet, the real genius isn't the gun, it's the solution to baking the plastic. Few hobbyists could be expected to purchase Eastwood's HotCoat powder coating gun if they also had to buy and install an expensive baking oven. John Sloane, Eastwood's marketing manager, says "the light came on" when someone suggested using a regular kitchen oven. "We all knew you couldn't use the same oven for powder coating that you cooked your food in," John explains, "then someone suggested getting a used oven, which can be bought cheap, and putting it in the shop. At first we didn't think big enough parts would fit in the oven to

make the system practical, but a kitchen oven's got a lot more space than you would think." The combination works perfectly.

POWDER COATING IN YOUR SHOP

For low-cost powder coating, you'll need The Eastwood Company's HotCoat® system, which consists of the spray gun, powder cup, and disposable filter, as well as the power supply unit and activation switch. The gun requires both a 110-120 volt AC power source and an air supply. The gun's air requirements are so low, that a portable regulated air tank would suffice for powder coating one or two parts; however for coating a batch of parts you'll need an air compressor capable of being regulated to less than 10 psi. The gun requires less than .5 cfm at 8 psi, so a small hobbyist compressor will easily provide the needed air supply. Along with the gun and air supply, you'll want to order the desired shades of powder. Popular colors include Semi-Gloss Black (for chassis parts), Stamped Steel (for underbody parts that left the factory unpainted), Chevy Orange (for Chevrolet engine parts), Ford Light and Dark Blue (for Ford engine parts), and Satin or Gloss Clear (for protecting and enhancing the appearance of polished items). Some of the translucent specialty colors may also be desirable. Eastwood supplies its HotCoat colors in 8 oz. and 2 lbs.

cans. Since powder coating eliminates virtually all material waste, the powder in an 8 oz. can will coat numerous parts. Before ordering the larger quantity, you'll want to try the system and see how far the material stretches.

Three additional items are highly desirable and should be included on an initial order. The first is the High Performance Deflector, a low-cost tip for the gun that improves transfer efficiency. The second is a roll of high temperature masking tape which is used when you don't want to coat the complete part and you need to cover areas. The third is a set of extra gun cups with lids. Although most cleanup after powder coating can be done with compressed air, having a supply of extra gun cups eliminates the need to clean the cup — either at the end of the powder coating session or when changing powder colors. You can label the cups with a marker and use them to store material until needed.

Depending on the condition of the parts being powder coated, you may decide to purchase a high temperature filler to use in smoothing pits or other flaws in the metal. While powder coating is intended as a one-step finish over bare metal, the coating can also be used over primer and filler if these products can withstand the baking temperatures of up to 500 degrees F. For filler, Eastwood recommends Metal-2-Metal, an Evercoat product. The recommended primer is Corroless Rust Stabilizer.

With the equipment and supplies in

The coating needs to be applied to bare steel. For demonstration, we selected a variety of engine pieces from our scrap pile.

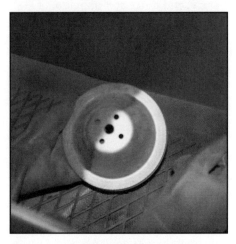

Abrasive blasting quickly removes all traces of paint and rust.

Before powder coating, the metal is wiped clean with wax and grease remover.

place, you'll also need a baking oven. For small items, a toaster oven that plugs into 110v AC household current can be used. For larger pieces, you'll need an electric kitchen oven. Eastwood cautions against using gas

ovens to bake its powder coating. The recommendation is to locate a used electric stove with a working oven and set up the appliance (which will require 220v AC service) in your shop.

Warning: An oven used to prepare food and located inside the household should never be used to bake powder-coated parts.

Rich Jensen at Cruzin' Performance obtained his baking oven by contacting a friend who manages an appliance store. After explaining how the appliance would be used, and emphasizing that only the oven needed to be functional, Rich asked to be notified when a suitable used appliance came into the store. The call came in a few days, saying that two used kitchen stoves had been turned in on new purchases, both with inoperable features, but both with good ovens. Rich selected the cleanest of the two (actually spotlessly clean) and brought it to his shop at no charge. A vacant space along his shop wall directly below the electrical panel made an ideal location, requiring only the 220v outlet.

The HotCoat system has given Rich's shop the same capability as the professional powder coating setup he investigated a few years ago at a small fraction of the cost. As added benefits, powder coating eliminates complicated mixing formulas with solvents, catalysts, and hardeners, exposure to toxic chemicals, and the need for a ventilated painting area, or even a high level of skill. And, for a specialty shop like Cruzin' Performance, the HotCoat system offers "value added" to customers by including powder coating in the service.

HOW THE PROCESS WORKS

Powder coating with Eastwood's HotCoat® system is actually simpler than painting from an aerosol can. The HotCoat system is easier to use because there's no danger of runs from too much powder (if the coating seems a little thick, you blow or wipe it off) and because the item being sprayed is electrostatically charged, the powder gravitates directly to the part, even wrapping around curved edges. The risk of failure is just about zero — even for someone who has

never powder coated before.

As in normal painting, the first step is preparing the parts. The metal needs to be clean and rust free; however, it's possible to powder coat over chrome or a painted finish, providing the paint can withstand the 400 degrees F. baking temperature. For his first trial with the HotCoat system, Rich Jensen selected a timing cover for a GM 350 engine. This aftermarket "dress up" item had a shiny chrome finish which Rich thought would be a good test of powder coat's adhering properties. "I couldn't believe the results," Rich said enthusiastically. "The coating is on to stay." Keep Rich Jensen's comment in mind when you're powder coating items that have surfaces that should remain uncoated. Remember, just because you don't point the gun at a surface you want to keep free of powder doesn't mean it won't be coated. Unlike paint that's blown onto a surface, powder coating is drawn to the surface through an electrical charge, so you'll need to mask any surfaces you don't want coated with a special high temperature tape.

For his second sample, Rich pulled a set of engine pulleys from his scrap metal pile. Both had a thick coating of surface rust, so they were abrasive blasted to bare steel. After blowing off any sand residue, the pulleys were wiped with metal prep. Rich wore vinyl gloves while handling and washing the parts, both to protect his skin from the mild acid solution and to avoid contaminating the metal with skin oil. The most time-consuming and trickiest part of the process was rigging up a hanger to suspend the pulleys during powder coating and also to hold them in the baking oven. Rich used a portable shop light as the support fixture for the coating process and a rack in the broiler position with the oven. To catch any stray powder (which can be reused), Rich placed a box lid under the powder coating fixture.

The actual coating process has to be experienced to be appreciated. The ground lead from the gun is clamped to the part in some location where its mark won't be seen in the finished coating, or to the wire suspending the part. After adding powder to the gun cup and checking the air supply — 8 psi being optimal pressure at the gun — you're ready to begin. It's also important that the air supply be moisture free. Since Rich's air compressor had been working hard for the abrasive blasting and the day was humid, he decided to bleed the air tank before powder coating. Eastwood supplies a disposable moisture separator with the HotCoat gun, but a water extractor or dryer in the air line are also desirable. If the powder gets wet, it turns to unsprayable goo.

The fun of powder coating comes when you trigger the gun. The first time I used Eastwood's HotCoat system, I expected the powder to spray out under fire hydrant pressure, coating everything in the room. The HotCoat gun doesn't eject the powder with anything near the pressure of conventional spraying or even HVLP. Instead, the powder wafts toward the part like HVLP in slow motion, or if you're a little more imaginative, like when you were a child puffing the seed tassels of a dandelion into the air. Incredibly, the powder blows in only one direction, toward the part. That's because the ground clip from the gun has given the part an attracting electrostatic charge. In my first powder coating experience, I held the gun steady, sweeping it across the part as I do when spraying solvent based paints. My instructor told me to loosen my wrist, shake the gun slightly as though I'd just finished a cup of strong coffee. A slight shaking motion agitates the powder and helps assure a constant feed. The powder coating process is so simple, it's just about impossible to goof.

Important: When you've finished coating the part, touch the emitter (metal rod protruding from the tip of the gun) to the grounding clip attached to the part. You'll hear a "snap" and see a spark. This discharges the gun. Failure to do this, can give you a sharp electrical jolt. After setting down the gun, unplug the power unit.

When you're satisfied that you've coated the part evenly and completely, it's time to move the part from the painting rack to the oven. Eastwood's instructions call for preheating the oven to 400 degrees F. and checking the temperature with an oven ther-

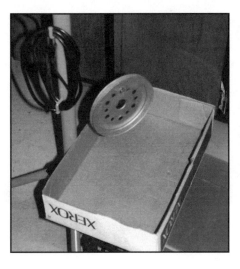

So little powder is wasted from overspray that a box lid can serve as a container for the residue, which can be poured through a paint filter and reused.

To attract the powder to the part, a ground lead is attached to some location where its mark won't be seen in the finished coating

mometer, or an infra red thermometer which they sell. However, if you've checked the accuracy of the oven's temperature settings, you can just turn the dial to 400 and wait for the preheat light to go off. The problem with these instructions is that you're placing parts in a hot oven—and it is very easy to burn yourself, likely causing you to drop the part and probably saying something not to be repeated in polite company. If you're going to follow this procedure, make sure you have worked out the logistics of placing or suspending the part in the oven — with the suspending wire already in

Most powder coating residue can be recycled and reused.

Applying the powder coating is the fun part of the process. The powder just puffs out of the gun and is attracted to the item being coated by an electrical charge that is applied through the wire that can be seen clipped to the front of the pulley. Shaking the gun slightly while spraying helps agitate the powder.

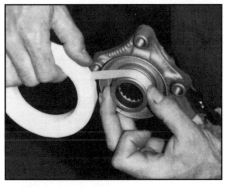

Surfaces you don't want coated can be masked with special heat resistant tape.

place — before reaching your hands into a very hot oven.

Rich Jensen said he singed a finger on a hot oven rack and figured there must be a better way. Why does the oven have to be preheated before the part goes in? After all, the part also has to come up to the powder's melting temperature. Now if Rich is suspending a part in the oven (as opposed to simply sliding in a part on a tray) he heats the oven after he's

A kitchen oven works great for baking powder coating on small parts. You'll need to wear heat-resistant gloves when placing the parts in the hot oven.

Once the powder reaches its curing temperature, you'll see the coating begin to melt and a glossy finish emerge.

Powder coating has the gloss of paint, but gives a much tougher finish that isn't easily chipped.

Powder coating can be used on a variety of shop and household items, as well as car parts — including toys and tools. Photo courtesy of the Eastwood Company.

placed the part. The results appear to be the same.

As the powder nears its curing temperature (about 400 degrees F; 204 degrees C) you'll see the coating begin to melt. If you watch the process through the oven window, you'll see the dull, flat powder transform to a smooth glossy finish. When all the surfaces have turned glossy, the coating needs to cure for another 10 minutes, at which point you can turn off the heat, open the oven door slightly, and let the part gradually cool. Cooling the part too quickly, as in taking it out of the oven immediately after curing, can dull the finish.

While you'll nearly always be pleased with the quality of the gloss and the smoothness of the finish, if the gloss isn't quite as sharp as you want, or the finish has a little too much orange peel texture, the cured powder coating can be smoothed by wet sanding with 400 grit wet/dry sandpaper and then compounded to a higher luster with a paint polishing compound or buffed using white rouge on a loose section buffing wheel.

CLEAN UP

What could be simpler than cleaning the spray gun and powder cup with a few quick shots of compressed air? Although the powder isn't toxic, you'll save cleanup time for yourself by wearing disposable nitrile or vinyl gloves. Throughout the powder coating process you need to wear a dust mask to keep from inhaling the powder. Though not toxic, the powder could be a respiratory irritant and should not be inhaled. Any powder that gets on your skin or clothing should first be blown off with compressed air and can be washed off with soap and water.

Very little powder is likely to be lost in the coating process. Still, if a box, flat sheet of cardboard, or a tarp is placed under the spraying area, any stray powder can be collected and reused. To make sure any powder collected in this way is free of contaminants, the residue should be filtered though a paint strainer as it is poured back into the container.

Caution: Heavy concentrations of powder dust can be flammable. Although it's unlikely that your HotCoat activity would generate a large volume of dust, to avoid the dust's flammable potential, do not use a shop vacuum or other electrical appliance for cleanup.

POWDER COATING DIE-CAST PARTS

Die-cast, also called "pot metal," parts often used as trim pieces on cars and light trucks of the 1930s through 1950s are porous and can present problems both for chrome plating and powder coating. In the plating process, the metal is immersed in vats of chemical which can seep into the metal's pores. Since most die cast that would be powder coated has previously been plated, some of the chemical absorbed during the plating process may still be inside the die cast. When the part is heated to cure the powder coat, contaminants may "boil out" of the metal and show up as bubbles or pits in the finish. To prevent this from happening, die-cast and other porous parts such as cast aluminum or magnesium should be preheated to between 200 and 400 degrees F for the duration needed to bring the metal to the temperature of the oven. Allow the parts to cool and wipe thoroughly with metal prep solution before powder coating.

One of the reasons for powder coating die-cast trim pieces is to avoid having these items replated. The plating process not only traps contaminants, but can release contaminants that were absorbed earlier, presumably during the original plating. When this happens bubbles or pits will show underneath the plating, just as they might with powder coating. However, in plating, there's no way to boil out contaminants ahead of time, so in replating die cast the outcome is always uncertain. Having to replate a part to get rid of the bubbles generally makes things worse. For this reason, if plating isn't needed for authenticity of a "show restoration," powder coating die-cast trim makes a desirable alternative.

While you wouldn't normally powder coat a die-cast trim piece in a standard color, unless you were trying to match the trim to the paint finish, painting trim a special effects color, such as one of Eastwood's translucents, can be very eye-catching. Another popular alternative is coating plated die cast with Eastwood's simulated chrome powder — the closest thing to real chrome plating that you'll ever see from a spray gun. Creative and original color effects can also be created by laying a chrome powder coating over a translucent base, or even a standard color. Powder coating offers nearly as many options for dramatic and special effects as solvent-based paints. These options are explored in Chapter 16: Custom Effects with Powder Coating.

SAFETY AND ENVIRONMENTAL CONCERNS

The biggest safety risk with powder coating is the potential flammability of powder dust suspended in air, if ignited. Adequate ventilation in the spraying area, a clean shop, and being careful to eliminate all possible sources of ignition are the necessary actions to counter this risk. Never smoke or allow someone who is smoking to enter the powder coating area. Make sure the electric oven is in good repair with no dangling wires and that all shop wiring, including the oven connector, conforms with local code. As mentioned earlier, because

of possible sparks from the motor, do not use a shop vacuum to clean up powder coating residue. Also, because of the powder's potential flammability, do not use a gas oven to cure powder coated parts.

A dust mask provides sufficient respiratory protection from the powder when spraying the powder coating. However, Eastwood recommends wearing an activated charcoal respirator when curing the powder. As the powder cures it gives off mildly toxic fumes. You may also smell a slight odor.

One of powder coating's biggest advantages is that any unusable residue can be disposed of as household waste. Since the powder consists primarily of pulverized plastic, spillage does not create an environmental hazard and cleanup requires only the precautions mentioned above.

POWDER COATING OVERSIZED PARTS

While really quite ingenious, using a kitchen oven to melt and cure the powder does have limitations. Valve covers, even wheels will fit inside most ovens, as will suspension "A" arms, and a myriad of smaller parts. But if you want to powder coat a motorcycle frame using your HotCoat system, you're not going to be able to fit the frame in a kitchen oven. Of course one option is to have the oversized part commercially powder coated. But Eastwood now has another alternative — curing the oversized part with a baking lamp. Eastwood offers a heat lamp, like those used in body shops to cure or bake paint, as a means of melting and curing powder on those items that won't fit into a kitchen oven. The lamp severely stretches the curing process since it has to melt and bake coating in segments. Still, the heat lamp gives the HotCoat system virtually unlimited application at low cost.

COLOR SELECTION

Eastwood continuously adds new colors to its HotCoat powder listing, yet the color selection remains limited in comparison to solvent-based paints. Although powder coating has

Clean up is much easier than with solvent based paints—just blast the spray gun and paint canister with a shot compressed air.

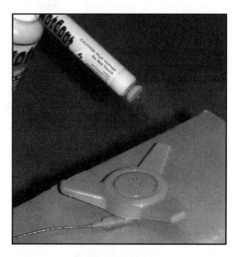

Powder coating makes an attractive alternative to plating for die cast trim parts. The Corvair wheel spinner shown here is being coated with a translucent powder that will let the plating's gleam show through.

replaced liquid paints in many industrial applications, it is likely to remain a supplemental finish in automotive applications for the near future. Still, for many chassis items, wheels, engine accessories, and trim pieces, powder coating can't be beat. The finish is superior to liquid paints in nearly all respects.

A major advantage, and the primary reason powder coating is being used increasingly in industrial applications, is its essential safety and ease of application. But for the hobbyist, the attraction of powder coating is how much fun you'll have doing it. Once you've experienced the HotCoat process I think you'll agree, and you will likely find yourself like Rich Jensen, asking his Dad and other car enthusiasts for items to powder coat.

Do-It-Yourself Guide to CUSTOM PAINTING

Painting Systems

What makes the systems concept so important is the designed-in compatibility between products. The racks of painting products shown here are tinting bases for a color mixing system.

Years ago if an automotive painter ran out of thinner for a lacquer paint job he was spraying, he'd head for the nearest painting supply store to pick up the needed product. Likely the only questions from the counter clerk would be price (solvents used with primer coatings cost less) and evaporation speed. The brand would be whatever the store carried — and it would work with whatever product the painter was using. Almost nothing about this scenario fits today.

Modern paints are "systems" products, meaning all paints, solvents, hardeners, additives used in the entire refinishing process should come from the same manufacturer. Mixing different manufacturer's products not only invites a lousy paint job — solvent from one manufacturer may not be compatible with the paint from another — but you'll find you've voided any warranty the product carries. Said another way: It's your mess, you fix it. But the "system" concept also applies

within a manufacturer's products where it refers to compatibility within the entire refinishing range from primer to finish coating.

WHERE THE PAINTING "SYSTEM" BEGINS

To use a painting "system" successfully, two crucial decisions have to be made at the very start of a refinishing project. The first is what painting manufacturer's products to use. While DuPont, PPG, Sherwin Williams, and Sikkens, to name a few of the "players," all produce high quality automotive painting products, each manufacturer promotes product "extras" the others don't offer. Some of these extras, like being ahead of legislative mandates in VOC content, may not have a lot of significance to hobbyists. However, once you've picked a paint manufacturer you're going to be pretty well locked into its products, so the choice of paint line is important.

Factors to consider include service and technical assistance available from the stores selling the different brands, color availability, specialty finishes, and depth of the product line.

The next decision is the type of final finish: single coat enamel, enamel with hardener, base coat/clear coat, tricoat or multi-stage finish, or a specialty coating. From the final finish you'll work backward to select compatible undercoat products. To help with this decision, Sikkens uses what it calls the "Sikkens Simple System" to select the final finish. Truly simple, the Sikkens approach looks at why the refinisher is painting the car: Will it be "high build" over an existing finish; a spot repair that retains most of the original finish; a fresh finish over new parts; or a repair coating or new finish over plastic parts? Once the purpose is identified, the undercoat and color finish systems can be chosen for maximum compatibility. Even fillers should be selected for their compatibility with the

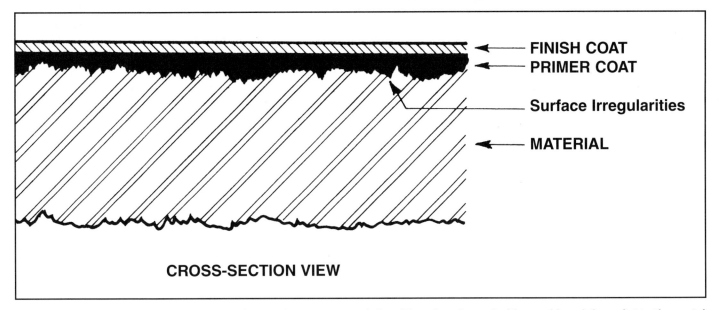

FINISH COAT
PRIMER COAT
Surface Irregularities
MATERIAL

CROSS-SECTION VIEW

A glossy finish rests on primer coatings (the undercoat system) that fill surface irregularities and bond the paint to the metal or plastic substrate.

painting systems being used.

Talk to professional refinishers and you will quickly hear their system preference in their product jargon. In fact you'll hear the system, Deltron, for example, in the PPG product line, or Colorbuild from Sikkens — often without reference to the manufacturer, that detail being assumed.

What makes the systems concept so important is a designed-in compatibility between products. The Sikkens Colorbuild system, for example, uses tinted primers to build an undercoat that's color-compatible with the final finish. Scratch the topcoat of a Sikkens Colorbuild system, and you won't see a telltale primer color of black, gray, or yellow. The scratch may cut away the gloss, but it won't change the color. (Though Sikkens emphasizes color compatibility in its marketing, other paint manufacturers also offer tintable sealers to accomplish the same effect.) While color compatibility has its advantages, more important is the chemical compatibility between painting products. PPG's Deltron Acrylic Urethane System, for example, links an entire set of PPG undercoats, reducers, hardeners, clear coats, and additives. To stray from this systems path is to invite problems.

Since "systems talk" frequently uses technical terminology, a list of terms and their definitions appears at the end of this chapter. A more compre-

hensive list of refinishing terms and their definitions can be found in the Glossary in the back of this book.

TOPCOAT SYSTEMS

Within a manufacturer's system, refinishing products divide into a variety of subsystems that reflect the type of finish coating that's desired and suited to the job. Keeping in mind that the second step in the system decision — after selecting the paint manufacturer — is choice of the color finish or topcoat, let's look at the topcoat options. All the products used to achieve one of these finishes make up a topcoat system. Topcoat options include:

- single-stage color which can be non-catalyzed (acrylic enamel) or catalyzed (urethane enamel)
- base coat/clear coat where a thin color layer (the base coat) is covered by a protective coating (the clear coat) that "enlivens" the color and adds gloss
- tricoat or multi-stage where three finish layers combine for a dramatic effect
- glamour finishes (sometimes base coat/clear coat, sometimes tricoat) of translucent "pearls," high-strength "candy colors," or color-shifting "chameleons."

A single-stage color system can be a relatively simple non-catalyzed coating, or a more complex catalyzed

coating with or without a clear coat. It can be used to spot repair an older finish and is available in metallics as well as solid colors.

The base coat/clear coat system differs from single-stage color in two basic ways: first, both the base coat (color layer) and the clear coat are catalyzed paints; and second, the color coat is sprayed very thin — 1 mil, the thickness of a cellophane food wrapper, being considered an optimal build.

With the tricoat/multistage system, a highly pigmented "ground" or base coat color such as white is often applied over a similarly-tinted undercoat. This gives reflective depth for a midcoat paint containing mica flakes or metallics, which creates playful color effects with a high-solid clear coat sealer resulting in a rich, magnifying gloss.

A glamour system adds mystery and intensity through prismatic color shifts and deep, "live-appearing" colors.

UNDERCOAT SYSTEMS

Each of the topcoat systems links to a corresponding set of undercoat products. The typical undercoat consists of three product types:

- primer which serves as a bonding coating with the substrate, which may be plastic, metal, or an existing finish
- primer surfacer which adds build,

Catalyzed system products require a hardener (the catalyst) in addition to solvent.

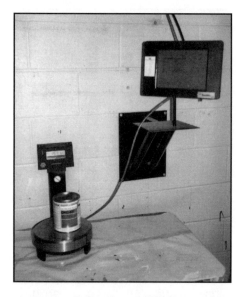

Electronic scales assure the mixing accuracy required by modern refinishing products.

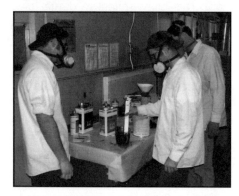

Proper respirators need to be worn even when mixing modern two-part (catalyzed) painting products.

or thickness, to the primer coating and can be sanded to give a smooth base for the finish coating
• sealer which "locks" the underlying coatings (possibly including an old finish) and creates a bonding layer for the new finish.

Within a system, these products interlock to provide a smooth, stable painting base. Because undercoat conditions vary widely — both with the nature of the job (spot repair, recoat, or fresh finish) and the type and condition of the substrate — the products can be called upon to perform a range of functions.

Primer can be formulated for bonding with bare metal, galvanized metal, a plastic surface such as bumper facia, fiberglass, or an existing finish. With bare metal, the initial primer coating will likely contain a corrosion-resistant agent.

Primer surfacer, which some manufacturers are now calling primer filler, can be formulated to spray on thick for fast build-up. Before modern primer filler products, painters sprayed and sanded as many as a dozen "filler" layers. Today's high-build primer surfacers have cut this process to as few as two or three coatings.

Sealer can be tinted to match the color of topcoat so that eventual stone chips in the finish won't create a "salt and pepper" effect, and to help light-color topcoats hide the primer base.

Some undercoat products cross categories. By altering the mixing ratio, some primers can be turned into primer surfacers to create a thick bonding coat that can be sanded. Some products can even do triple-duty as a sealer. Eliminating the need for separate products not only saves money, but also time in the form of fewer spraying steps and shorter drying intervals.

BENEFITS OF THE SYSTEMS APPROACH

For the hobbyist this systems approach can seem mind-bogglingly complex, but actually it's quite simple. Compatible products up and down the system are listed on the product labels and information sheets. As you're making your system selection, ask your supplier for technical literature on the various products and for advice on how to gain the maximum versatility from the products you purchase.

By interlocking the various coatings, the systems approach has leveled the quality standards. Yesterday's general purpose primers were often mixed with reducers or thinners of lower quality than those used with the color coating. Today the same reducers are used across the system, undercoat to topcoat. It makes sense that quality be standardized throughout a manufacturer's refinishing products; otherwise the final finish could fail due to an inferior product at any point in the painting sequence.

SYSTEM VARIABLES

Within a system various products will have different drying times and working or "pot" life — and in some cases different "windows" within which the product can be recoated. It's important to know the properties of the products you are using which can vary widely, both from one product to the next and also with changes in temperature and humidity. The drying and pot life times that are listed on the product label and on information sheets are for temperatures between 70 and 75 F (21-24 C) at 50 percent humidity. For every 15 degree temperature increase, the drying time and pot life are halved. Conversely, a 15 degree drop in temperature doubles these values. Temperature and humidity conditions outside the norm are more likely to be a problem for hobbyists than professionals where shops are often climate-controlled.

For painters working in warmer or cooler climates, drying time can be speeded up or slowed down by reducers that are formulated for different temperatures. Likewise, hardeners (the catalyst used with thermosetting paints) can be selected for cool to warm temperatures. But concerns with shop temperature must not distract from the systems principle. It's not just the paint that makes the system; reducers, hardeners, enhancers, and additives must all share compatibility.

SYSTEM PERIPHERALS

Just as a computer system includes peripheral devices for functions like printing, digitizing images, and storing

Once catalyzed system products are mixed, they have a relatively short "pot life," after which the paint "sets-up" and can no longer be used.

It's important to know the properties of the painting products you are using, which can vary, not just among different products, but also with changes in spraying conditions.

data that increase the computer's capability, so too painting systems use peripheral products like enhancers and additives to improve the paint's versatility. Categories of peripheral products include:

- Accelerators to speed drying or curing time without shorting pot life
- Elastomers to create a flexible coating over rubber or soft plastic parts
- Chip resistant coatings to protect against paint damage from road debris
- Fisheye Preventer to counter the effects of silicones in paint
- Flattener to produce semi-gloss, egg shell, or dull appearing finishes

Within a peripheral category a manufacturer may list several products, each tailored to a different system. It's essential to select a product that's compatible with the painting system you're using.

SYSTEM TERMINOLOGY

To understand the systems concept, it helps to become familiar with the terminology likely to be used with the different systems products. An introduction to that terminology follows.

Additives — chemicals added to paint in small amounts to give certain qualities. For example, flex additives allow coatings to adhere to bendable substrates like bumper facia.

Base coat — the color layer in a base coat/clear coat finish.

Bleeding — color from an underlying coating showing in a fresh finish.

Build — the thickness of a paint coating (measured in mils).

Compatibility — ability of different products to be used together without adverse reactions.

Conversion coating — a coating of zinc phosphate or chromate applied to galvanized metals, steel, or aluminum to improve paint bonding.

Curing — the chemical reaction that occurs in the drying process of catalyzed paints.

Enamel — a durable paint having a high gloss finish.

Epoxy — paints containing resins that are chemically resistant.

OEM — the abbreviation for Original Equipment Manufacturer, referring to the paint originally on the car from the factory, or the factory color.

Pearls — tiny particles of mica embedded in the paint that act like prisms, creating a "rainbow" color effect.

Polyurethane — very high gloss paint with strong chemically-resistant properties.

Pot life — the paint's useful life after mixing with a curing agent or catalyst. The pot life period may range from minutes to hours, depending on the product.

Primer — a type of paint that pre-

pares the surface for the topcoat.

Pretreatment or precoat primers — adhesion coatings that may contain acid for cleaning a bare metal substrate.

Primer surfacer — a high-solids primer that helps fill surface imperfections while providing a bonding layer for the topcoat.

Primer sealer — the coating directly beneath the topcoat, applied both to improve adhesion and to prevent topcoat solvents from penetrating underlying coatings.

Retarder — an additive to slow evaporation of the paint's solvents.

Substrate — the item or material that is being painted. Substrates can be glass or any metal (steel and aluminum being most common), or plastic, wood, paper, or other paintable surface.

Tack — stickiness of a paint coating.

Thermoplastic — a coating that becomes soft when heated and hardens when cooled. A thermoplastic can be softened with solvent.

Thermosetting — a coating that cures permanently hard.

Undercoats — a collective term referring to any or all primer coatings.

Urethanes — types of paint noted for their toughness and abrasion resistance.

For a more comprehensive listing of painting terms, turn to the Glossary in the Appendix.

Do-It-Yourself Guide to
CUSTOM PAINTING
Tools and Techniques

Traditionally, automotive finishes have been applied with high pressure spray guns. Although high pressure paint spraying produces a fine quality finish, only 25-30 percent of the paint actually ends up on the vehicle.

Today's automotive refinishing products are high precision, costly, and toxic — a combination that's not very forgiving of errors. We've looked at the precision aspect of modern paints in their systems design. You'll experience the costly aspect each time you purchase the products. The toxic aspect — which applies most specifically to the two-part paints and primers that require a hardener (or catalyst) for curing — really means that you shouldn't use these paints unless you are willing to familiarize yourself with and follow the safety and environmental precautions that modern refinishing products require. Complying with these precautions means buying and using appropriate safety equipment (as described in Chapter 1). You'll also need to set up a spray area in your shop that filters incoming air to prevent dust and other airborne contaminants from spoiling the paint and exhausts painting fumes from the shop. Finally, in order to be

able to paint, you'll have to purchase the proper spray painting equipment.

Add up the cost for all four elements
• painting product
• safety equipment
• shop set up
• spray painting equipment
and you may decide that it's cheaper to hire a professional to do the painting for you. Of course, the cost ratio changes dramatically if instead of painting just one vehicle, you plan to paint several either as part of an ongoing hobby or working with friends on their projects.

SETTING UP SHOP

With the disappearance of lacquer paints and increasingly stringent environmental controls on VOC emissions, a garage or workshop is rapidly becoming obsolete or unfit as a location for spraying automotive finishes. If you do spray paint in a garage, the paint you would most safely be able to

apply would be acrylic enamel. This isn't to say that an acrylic enamel base coat, or even topcoat, is an undesirable coating, but it has neither the toughness nor the gloss of urethane paints. Also, recall from Chapter 2 that acrylic enamel is a *thermoplastic coating*, which means it is more susceptible to peeling and flaking than *thermoset* paints. To spray acrylic enamel you'll need a supply of compressed air, a spray gun, and a respirator — and the location where you're spraying should also have an exhaust fan. To spray acrylic urethane and other two-part catalyzed paints, you're going to need a compressed air source, spray gun, and full face respirator — ideally a painting hood with an external air supply and some sort of painting booth.

SELECTING THE
AIR COMPRESSOR

A spray gun needs a source of compressed air. For hobbyists this source is often a portable air compressor available from building or tool supply stores. Compressors of this type range from very limited capacity units, designed for little more than pumping up tires or inflating toys, to units with nearly the capacity of a stationary compressor of the type likely to be found in a professional shop. In selecting an air compressor, three items are important:

- the engine's horsepower rating
- the air tank capacity, and
- the SCFM (Standard Cubic Feet per Minute).

Professionals use the rule: A "good" compressor should produce between 3.2 and 3.6 SCFM per horsepower — meaning a 5 hp compressor should have a capacity of 16-18 SCFM. Here's the problem, you won't find an SCFM <u>near</u> these numbers in a hobby-sized 20 to 30 gallon portable air compressor regardless of the motor's rating. To get the professional's performance standard you'll need a stationary compression with an industrial/commercial rating.

You'll see spray painting outfits, spray guns, and accessories advertised with the lower capacity, hobbyist-type air compressors, so you may wonder why a commercial unit is needed. The first reason is logical: The more limited is the air compressor's capacity, the more limited is its use. You may also want to use the compressor to power air tools, perhaps an abrasive blaster as well. By operating continuously, a hobbyist compressor may be able to keep up with the demands of a high speed sander, but doing so puts a great strain on both the compressor and motor. Second, the more the compressor runs, the hotter the air and the more moisture the air contains. Run a compressor continuously and you'll see water droplets streaming out of the air tool, a sure sign that the air tank, piping, and regulator are all moisture laden and contaminated as a painting air supply.

The third reason for purchasing an adequate air compressor is to be able to use HVLP (high volume low pressure) paint spraying technology. While some HVLP spray guns require their own turbine-style compressor, others

The alternative paint spraying method, called HVLP (for High Volume Low Pressure) virtually eliminates overspray, which in turn reduces product waste, lowers VOC dispersal, diminishes toxic fumes, and minimizes cleanup. HVLP spray guns can be used in conjunction with a regular air compressor, or a high output turbine compressor shown here. Photo courtesy of the Eastwood Company.

are designed for conventional air compressors. Although HVLP spray guns are designed to produce 10 psi (pounds per square inch) of pressure at the air cap, their incoming requirement may range from 18 to 80 psi. Further, the SCFM may range from 7.5 to 24. At the low end, 7.5 SCFM at 18 psi can be delivered by a fairly capable portable compressor, but the high end, 24 SCFM at 80 psi is going to require a very strong commercial unit.

Bottom line: Pay a little extra and buy an air compressor that will provide the air flow needed for a quality spray gun and the air tools you expect to use.

PLUMBING THE AIR SUPPLY

The compressor needs to sit where it can draw fresh air. Assuming the compressor has the storage and recovery capacity to power air tools as well as a paint spray gun, it's advisable to pipe the air from the compressor to several drop locations around the shop. Piping results in less pressure loss than air hose, helps condense moisture, and adds convenience and safety. Shorter lengths of air hose can then be used from the drop to the work location.

Although galvanized or black pipe can be used, copper pipe is preferred. A shop air line should not be constructed from PVC because pipe from this material is not rigid and could

burst under pressure. Copper has advantages over metal because copper won't rust and it assembles easily by soldering. Galvanized or black pipe requires threaded connections. Black pipe will corrode and rust on internal surfaces if water gets into the air supply. The size of the pipe (I.D.) varies with the length and capacity of the compressor.

The air will cool as it travels through the metal piping, precipitating water droplets. To remove this water, drains need to be installed at low points in the piping. Hose connections will need to have a filter/dryer with a regulator at each location. While a filter will remove liquid water, oil, and dirt in the air supply, it won't remove vaporized moisture. A dryer containing desiccant is needed to absorb the moisture, delivering dry air to the spray gun.

Air-driven tools need lubrication to prevent internal damage. To improve the performance of grinders, sanders, and other air-driven shop tools, an inline oiler or lubricator should be placed in the line connections for these tools. However, since oil in the air will ruin a paint job, any lubricators for air tools would be "downstream" or in a "loop" piping system at the bottom of special drops to be used only for air tools.

Air hoses should be 3/8 in. I.D., as should fittings and couplers. The air pressure drop is much less with a 3/8

Air line pipe diameters (minimum)

Compressor	Horsepower	Air line piping	
"hobby" compressor	1 ½-2 hp	¾ in.	over 50 ft.
small portable compressor	3-5 hp	¾ in.	up to 200 ft.
		1 in.	over 200 ft.
stationary compressor	5-10 hp	¾ in.	up to 100 ft.
		1 in.	over 100 ft.
		1 ¼ in.	over 200 ft.
professional compressor	10-15 hp	1 in.	up to 100 ft.
		1 ¼ in.	over 100 ft.
		1 ½ in.	over 200 ft.

in. I.D. air hose than a 1/4 in. hose. Using quarter-inch I.D. couplers with a 3/8 in. hose voids the larger I.D. hose's advantage.

Sometimes you'll see spray painting packages with a 2-4 hp compressor, spray gun, air hose, and regulator all sold together at one relatively low $300 to $400 price. While the equipment supplied in these spray painting "packages" may be adequate for primer coatings, it won't be suitable for finish painting and is likely to be under capacity for air tools, both because of the compressor's slow recovery rate and the restrictive 1/4 in. diameter air hose often supplied with such outfits. Another caution, inexpensive (under $100) spray guns that appear identical to the higher cost professional models, do not give the same performance despite what the ads may say.

CHOOSING THE SPRAY GUN

Traditionally, automotive finishes have been applied with high pressure (35 to 65 psi) spray guns. Although high pressure paint spraying produces a fine quality finish, only 25 to 30 percent of the paint actually ends up on the vehicle. The other two-thirds paint and solvent volume is blasted off the vehicle's surface as overspray and either disperses into the atmosphere or settles on nearby surfaces, including the painter. If the painter is not properly clothed by wearing coveralls, gloves, and cap, as well as a full face mask and respirator, a large quantity of paint overspray can be absorbed into the skin as well as inhaled.

The hobbyist painting only one vehicle may not consider the quantity of paint and solvent lost in overspray to be a significant waste, but to the professional painter, losing two-thirds of the painting product has become financially unacceptable. As anyone who has recently purchased automotive refinishing products knows, just the paint alone can cost more than the expense of a complete paint job a few years back. Along with wasted product, high pressure spraying also produces more Volatile Organic Compound (VOC), which is found in painting solvents and constitute a damaging form of environmental pollution. Clean air legislation by federal and state governments is targeting VOC dispersal from automotive painting by placing increasingly stringent restrictions on the production of VOC emissions from automotive painting.

In response to both the waste of high pressure paint spraying and the health and environmental hazards this older technology invites, the automotive refinishing industry has developed a radically different paint spraying technology called High Volume Low Pressure or HVLP. Low pressure spraying virtually eliminates overspray, which in turn reduces product waste, lowers VOC dispersal, diminishes toxic fumes, and minimizes cleanup.

Since HVLP uses a very low pressure of 8 to 10 psi to apply the paint, transfer efficiency of this paint spraying technology reaches 65 percent or higher — meaning that over 2/3 of the product adheres to the painting surface. Early, first generation HVLP spray guns followed the design principles of high pressure guns, so a very large quantity of air (up to 85 cubic feet per minute for HVLP as opposed to 6-8 cfm for traditional paint spraying) had to be provided by the compressor. To provide the air supply, these first generation HVLP spraying systems coupled the spray gun with a high output turbine compressor. Paint spraying equipment of this design offered advantages beyond the HVLP technology. Since a turbine compressor doesn't use a storage tank, risk of moisture contamination in the air line is eliminated. Also, since air becomes heated as it compresses, the turbine supplies air that is both warm and dry, ideal conditions for spraying paint. The major disadvantage of the turbine-supplied HVLP gun is the expense (nearly $1,000) for equipment that is single-purpose.

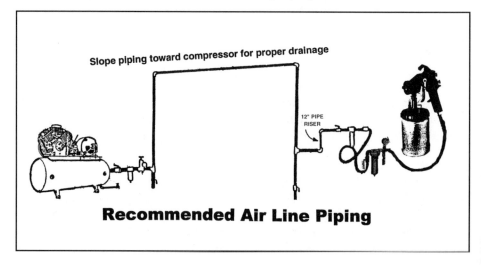

Slope piping toward compressor for proper drainage

12" PIPE RISER

Recommended Air Line Piping

Traditionally, paint spray guns have been mainly the siphon type shown here with the paint canister below the spray nozzle.

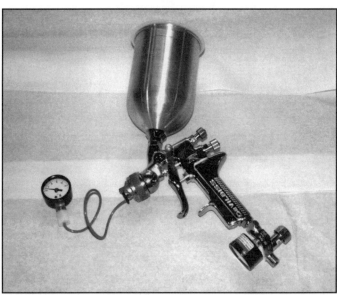

More common today are the gravity style spray guns which place the paint container above the spray nozzle. The gravity flow design helps assure a more precise fluid mix and has the added advantage that most gravity guns use disposable plastic liners that simplify clean-up. Notice the pressure gauge attached to the gun nozzle, which is the only place to accurately measure actual spraying air pressure.

Redesigned HVLP spray guns are now available that can be coupled with standard shop air compressors. The "non-bleeder" design of these guns converts the shop's high pressure air supply to a low pressure spraying force within the spray gun itself. Depending on the gun, compressors as small as 2 to 3 hp capable of delivering 8 cfm at 40 psi can be used for HVLP painting. These small shop compressors are not only very common, they're also inexpensive. From a tool standpoint, HVLP technology is as economical as conventional high pressure paint spraying. Since HVLP offers substantial savings in material waste and toxic as well as environmentally harmful overspray, it has almost entirely replaced high pressure equipment in professional shops and should be the first choice for hobbyists as well.

OPERATING THE SPRAY GUN

When high pressure paint spraying was "the only game in town," selecting a spray gun came down to price and brand. Today the choices are more complex. Price is still a factor. An inexpensive, off-brand spray gun typically sold through a discount tool company or a mass merchandiser may be suit-

able for spraying undercoatings. This is especially the case when variations in pattern and other blemishes can be sanded out. However, an inexpensive, off-brand spray gun is unlikely to perform with the consistency needed for top coatings.

This is why gun design has become the important second consideration. High-pressure (also called conventional) spray guns were typically of one type: siphon design, where the air blast passing through the gun sucked paint and solvent from the painting cup and atomized the mixture as it left the gun nozzle. HVLP spray guns are of three types: siphon, gravity, and pressurized.

A siphon-type HVLP gun will look identical to a conventional spray gun. The difference is internal in the way the gun atomizes the paint. A gravity gun looks and feels very different from the more familiar siphon type. With a gravity gun, the paint cup sits on top, allowing the paint to flow down to the air stream. This gravity flow helps assure a more precise fluid mix. Another advantage, most gravity guns use disposable plastic bladders (or liners) to hold the paint. This bladder keeps paint from spilling, even when the gun is turned upside down, and makes for easy clean-up since the

liner is simply removed from the cup and placed in a suitable storage container for disposal. Conventional high pressure spray guns are also offered with the gravity cup design. Pressurized spray guns have long been used for industrial painting where they were needed to apply heavier-bodied paints. In automotive painting, they're more likely to be used by professionals than hobbyists because their advantage is in a volume and production setting.

Recommended is an HVLP gravity gun from a "name" manufacturer like DeVilbiss, AccuSpray, GEO, Iwatta, Mattson, SATA, or Sharpe. Expect to pay between $200 and $400 for a spray gun that delivers professional performance. You won't be disappointed by the investment because once you learn how to use the gun, providing you keep it clean, you can depend on it functioning the same every time you use it.

SPRAYING TECHNIQUE

Although conventional high pressure and HVLP guns are not completely identical in their painting characteristics, they share the same basics of proper technique: spray gun

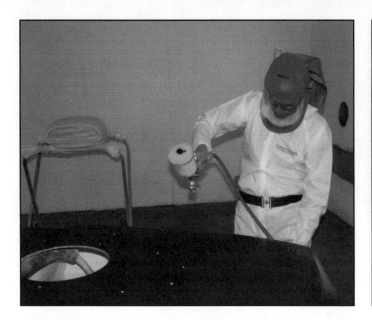

The spray gun should sweep horizontal to the surface being painted.

The "rule of thumb" is to hold the gun 6 to 8 in. from the surface for fast drying paints and 8 to 10 in. for slow drying paints.

The painter needs to see the surface he is painting. When painting lower sections of the car, you'll need to bend or squat down to see the painting surface and keep the gun in a horizontal plane.

angle, distance from surface, and gun travel speed.

Spray gun angle. The gun should sweep horizontal to the surface being painted. Novice and inexperienced painters often sweep the gun across the painting surface in an arc, like cleaning a floor with a broom. Sweeping the spray gun in an arc pattern means the paint will be thicker in the center of the arc than at the ends. What's desired is consistent paint coverage across the sweep.

Distance from the surface. Hold the gun 6 to 8 in. from the surface for fast drying paints (lacquers, when and if they are used) and 8 to 10 inches for slower drying paints (enamels, base coat/clear coat catalyzed products). A closer position interferes with atomization of the painting product and lays down a coating that may be excessively wet. Farther away allows too much atomization and a dry paint film.

It's recommended that you get familiar with your gun's optimal distance by spraying against a sheet of cardboard or scrap metal. Start first with the greater distance and decrease if needed for an even pattern. Keep in mind that the closer you hold the gun to the painting surface, the faster you should move the gun.

Gun travel speed. The gun should move fast enough to provide a uniform build with 50 percent overlap on each sweep. Slowing the rate of travel will lay on more paint. Increasing the speed will decrease the amount of paint. To get the speed right, watch the area you are spraying very closely to make sure you are "wetting" the surface and that about half of your sweep overlaps the previous pass.

Since there's a lot less overspray blowing around the painting path with HVLP, you've got more control with this technology. Don't be afraid to "wet" the panel. If you move too quickly or apply the paint too dry, the finish will either lack gloss or have lots of "orange peel."

Getting the paint too wet could cause a run, but in undercoats these can be sanded out. Small runs can even be micro-sanded out of a clear coating. Never pass directly over the same spot twice. Wait for the paint to "flash" (begins to set) before returning.

ATOMIZING THE PAINTING PRODUCT

Though technique is important, more essential to smooth, even paint application is proper atomization at the gun nozzle. A spray gun does more than blow paint onto a surface; it atomizes, or breaks paint into tiny droplets that fog the surface in a mist. Controlling this atomization is the nozzle set, consisting of the air cap, fluid tip, and paint needle. Spray gun manufacturers offer a multitude of nozzle set combinations or gun setups, each designed for different of refinishing products such as undercoats, single-stage color, or base coat/clear coat. Changing the gun setup (the air cap, fluid tip, and paint needle combination) alters the fluid to air ratio, meaning the amount of paint coming through the fluid tip compared to the amount of air flowing through the air cap.

The fluid-to-air ratio can go out of balance on the side of either fluid or air. With too much fluid, the paint will lay on wet, causing runs and sags. The build (or thickness) may be more than desired, and the paint will dry more slowly. With too much air, the paint will be dry, have very little flow and likely produce an orange peel texture. The build will be thinner than desired and a fast flash dry on the surface may not allow solvents trapped underneath to escape. While either condition could probably be corrected in a base coat by sanding, with a finish coat heavy runs or severe orange peel could result in sanding down the finish and starting over again. This is an expensive, time-consuming process that's better avoided by understanding how to select the gun setup best suited to the painting product you're spraying and how to adjust the spray gun for a balanced fluid-to-air ratio.

Step 1 in setting a proper fluid-to-air ratio is to request the setup chart for your make and model spray gun from your paint supplier. Product manufacturers print these charts showing fluid tip and air cap combinations recommended for various paints and primers, both for spot repair and complete refinishing. You can request the chart for your spray gun from the maunfacturer.

Step 2 is to adjust the spray gun for proper atomization. The adjustment process goes like this:

Set up a test panel to check the spray pattern.

- Adjust the air regulator (at the air line drop) to the appropriate psi range. Use the lowest pressure required to achieve full atomization and a good spray pattern. (Set the regulator near the bottom end of the range and adjust up if needed.)
- Hold the gun stationary at a 90 degree angle, horizontal to the surface and the appropriate distance for the drying speed of the paint (6 to 8 inches for fast drying, 8 to 10 for slow drying) and type of gun (closer for HVLP).
- Squeeze the trigger on the gun to full open.
- Gradually adjust the air/fan control on the gun.
- Repeat the triggering/adjusting operation until you have a smooth elliptical spray pattern 8 to 12 inches in width.

One of the trickier surfaces to spray is the top, which should be painted first.

An assistant can be helpful to make sure the air hose doesn't drag across a freshly painted surface.

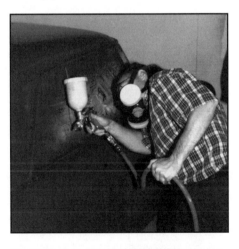

Keeping the spray gun pointed directly at the painting surface sometimes requires careful maneuvering.

RECOGNIZING PROBLEM SPRAY PATTERNS

What you see in the spray pattern is what the finish is going to look like. Where the desired pattern is elliptical and smooth, problem patterns may be sickle or half-moon shaped, split or divided, teardrop shaped, or spotted

The spray gun should not sweep in an arc as this painter is doing; instead, the spray gun nozzle should point directly at the painting surface.

Having an assistant in the spray booth can help assure no spots are missed.

The spray gun should move fast enough to provide a uniform build with 50 percent overlap on each sweep.

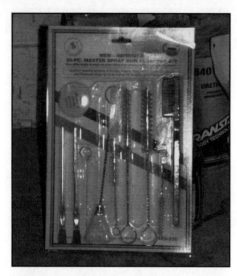

Should the spray gun clog up and need cleaning, use a proper cleaning kit, not a piece of wire or a paper clip. Cleaning kits consist of brush sets designed to open up air passages without damaging the gun.

(looking as though they've been spit upon). The causes of these problem patterns are as follows:

Sickle or quarter-moon pattern — caused by dried paint in one of the side holes of the air nozzle.

Split pattern — caused by too much air pressure, remedy by increasing fluid flow.

Teardrop pattern — caused by dried material on the outside of the fluid tip.

Spitting (paint coming out in spurts) — caused by atomized air entering the fluid supply typically due to a loose fluid tip or air cap. Spitting can also be caused by too little paint in the cup, which leads to an advantage of gravity feed guns. When a gravity feed cup is empty, it's empty; it won't give a little spit of paint as is likely to happen with a siphon feed gun.

CLEANING THE GUN

The best assurance of a proper spray pattern, and cure for problem patterns, is to clean the spray gun properly and thoroughly after each use. Following is the proper spray gun cleaning sequence, recommended by Sharpe's Dr. Gun.

1 As soon as you finish painting, "back pressure" the gun. You'll see professional painters do this by placing a cloth over the nozzle and triggering the gun for a blast or two.

What you may not have noticed is the nozzle is loosened before covering. With a tight cloth seal, pulling the trigger forces painting material back into the cup.

2 Remove the cup, pour out the paint, and pour in about a quarter-cup of solvent. Be sure to use a solvent that's compatible with the paint product.

3 Tighten the air nozzle and trigger the gun as if painting. Do this until the gun sprays clear solvent.

4 Loosen the air nozzle, cover with a cloth, and repeat the back pressure step. If the spray gun is a siphon type, hold the gun vertical and shake it up and down while triggering against the cloth. This motion jiggles solvent out the pressure hole in the cup lid, helping keep the hole clean and open.

5 First, tighten the air nozzle and then remove the cup. Dip the cloth in the remaining solvent and wipe both the outside of the gun and the cup until completely clean.

6 Replace the cup and return the gun to storage.

Following this procedure after each use will keep the gun clean and working properly. Should the air cap passages clog and need cleaning, use a proper cleaning kit not a piece of wire or a paper clip. The air cap is made of aluminum alloy and is easily damaged. Cleaning kits consist of brush sets designed to clean out air passages without damaging the spray gun.

CREATING A SAFE, CLEAN PAINTING ENVIRONMENT

Painting in either an open or enclosed shop presents problems. If the shop is open, dust and insects can settle on the finish. When lacquer was the hobbyist's paint of choice, dust in the finish could be removed by compounding — using a fine grit paste to micro-sand the finish. Acrylic enamel finishes are often micro-sanded for the same purpose. You can also micro-sand base coat/clear coat finishes, but not necessarily with the same success. If dust is trapped in the base coat you can't reach it and if its in the clear coat, you risk sanding through the finish trying to remove the

dust. Sealing up the shop doesn't work because dust inside can be blown onto the finish. Sealing the shop also exposes the painter and others in the vicinity to toxic fumes. If catalyzed paints containing isocyanates are being used, a sealed shop is not a safe painting environment. In either setting, with the shop open or sealed, painting overspray is both a nuisance and a hazard, not only time-consuming to clean up, but potentially toxic as well. The answer is a spray enclosure that filters incoming air and exhausts the fumes.

So your shop doesn't have a spray booth and you want to do "high tech" spraying (meaning the use of catalyzed paints). What to do? The options are very limited, but here are two. Perhaps you'll think of or discover others. The common sense, least expensive possibility is to arrange access to someone else's booth. A retired, former colleague of mine works with a friend who operates a body shop. Newell does all the prep work on the car he's having painted (sanding, masking, etc.). Scott, the body man, does the painting. Scott lets Newell work in his shop right alongside his other employees (the difference, Newell is working for himself, not Scott). In this setting, Newell is able to oversee all the painting phases, but doesn't do the actual painting. A variation on this approach would be to sign up for an auto body course at a technical high school or college where painting is part of the curriculum. If you're allowed to use your car as a project, you can probably paint it in the school's spray booth. The other option is to buy a spray booth. Did I hear someone say, "Oh, yeah, I'm going to spend $100,000 to save $2,000 on a paint job? Maybe when I win the lottery!"

Some shops as well as hobbyists have constructed their own spray enclosures, usually by erecting a partition and placing an exhaust fan at one end. However, such an enclosure can be both dangerous and in violation of fire code. A major risk of a home-built painting enclosure is fire. If the exhaust fan has steel blades and is mounted in a steel housing (as is likely to be the case), a chance spark

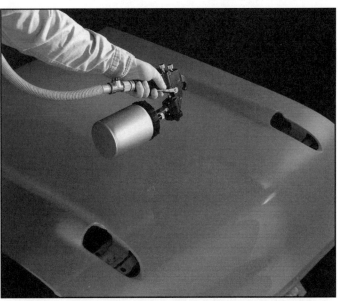

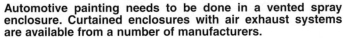
Automotive painting needs to be done in a vented spray enclosure. Curtained enclosures with air exhaust systems are available from a number of manufacturers.

If you're serious about automotive painting, you should consider a professional spray booth. The investment is not as serious as you might think. Photo courtesy of the Eastwood Co.

from the motor or the fan mechanism itself could ignite volatile solvent in painting fumes, potentially creating a conflagration that would be difficult to escape. The second risk is to the painter. An exhaust fan at one end of an enclosure pulls air past the car or other object being painted as well as the painter. What's needed is an airflow pattern that pulls air away from both the work area and the painter.

If you're serious about automotive painting, you should consider a professional spray booth. The investment is not as expensive as you might think. Spray Enclosure Technologies (Spray-Tech) of Ontario, Calif., sells a professional-grade, front-flow spray booth for under $5,000. Shipping and installation are likely to double the price, but here's a booth in which you, your club, and friends can do all your automotive painting for a cost a group could probably reasonably afford. Obviously, you won't set up a Spray-Tech enclosure in your garage, but it or a comparable unit would install nicely in the types of shop buildings many hobbyists are erecting. A complete address listing for Spray-Tech is listed in the Resource Appendix.

For painting small parts, like wheels and suspension pieces, Spray-Tech offers a Table Top Spray Booth. It is constructed much like an abrasive blasting cabinet, except that it uses

charcoal filters to eliminate the need for outside ducting; the cube-shaped 42 in. enclosure allows safe spraying of isocyanate paints inside the shop.

Curtained painting enclosures made of heavy plastic suspended from an overhead track and equipped with proper exhaust fans and air filtration are also available from a number of suppliers. Professional shops used these enclosures to prepare and paint "hang on" items like mirrors and bumpers. These enclosures have the advantage that the plastic curtains can be folded back when not needed for painting, making their space available for storage or other uses.

RECAPPING PAINT SPRAYING TOOLS AND TECHNIQUE

Professional auto refinishers have switched preponderantly to HVLP, partially because of savings in painting material, but also because less overspray means a cleaner spray area and reduced health risk. Further, environmental rulings in some areas, including Southern California and San Francisco, stipulate that only HVLP equipment be used in spraying automotive refinishing products. The hobbyist is well advised to follow the professional's lead. The major change in spraying technique is holding the gun closer to the surface and using a little

faster painting stroke.

Unlike conventional paint spraying which requires high pressure, HVLP requires a high rate of air delivery. Some HVLP spray outfits combine the spray gun with a specially designed high-output turbine compressor. This combination has advantages: The units are compact and self-contained, there's no guessing about the air supply, and the air is delivered dry to the gun. Other HVLP guns are designed for use with conventional air compressors. The primary advantage of this combination is the compressor's multi-purpose uses. However, the air piping for a conventional pressure has to be laid out so that moisture can be drained from the system and includes moisture filters and dryers at the spray gun drops.

The often-mentioned health hazard of two-part catalyzed paints containing isocyanates requires a painting enclosure that filters incoming air and pulls spraying fumes away from the painter. Since the design of such an enclosure is complex and requires adherence to applicable fire and electrical codes, professional spray enclosures are strongly recommended to anyone planning to finish paint using catalyzed products.

With the tools and equipment in place, the next step in the painting process is preparing the vehicle.

When the base metal is sound, showing no signs of rust, paint can be removed to straighten the metal or smooth surface irregularities with a sanding disk.

Paint coatings serve two functions: To protect bare metal from corrosion, and to give metal (or other base materials which are called "substrates" in painter's jargon) an attractive finish. Corrosion is a naturally occurring process by which metal returns to its oxide state. The process occurs through electro-chemical reactions which require moisture and oxygen. In order to stop corrosion, the metal has to be sealed against moisture and oxygen, and fundamentally that's what paint coatings do.

As long as a finish is intact, with no blisters, chips, cracking, or peeling, it may be fulfilling its sealing function well enough to be scuffed up and recoated. But if the paint has failed, allowing "germs" of corrosion that may be visible through blisters or actual rust, or if the paint is chipped, cracked, or peeling, then the old finish needs to be stripped off, all rust removed, and the metal prepared for repainting.

Every break in the paint seal is a potential "corrosion battery" (a spot where moisture and oxygen can begin to react with

the metal). With a small break like a stone chip or a scratch, the corrosion battery may occupy just a tiny spot on the car's finish. Yet once the battery is activated, it becomes conductive — especially where road salt is also present. As the tiny seed of corrosion grows, it first blisters the paint around its battery. With the paint seal broken, the corrosion spreads, lifting more of the paint and eating into the metal.

Stopping corrosion requires more than grinding off damaged paint, cleaning and recoating the metal. The corrosion batteries have to be neutralized or eliminated. Just cutting out and replacing rusted metal often does not eliminate all seeds of corrosion. If the metal shows any signs of rust, the old finish will have to be removed. Sometimes it may be necessary only to strip the finish from one panel or a portion of a panel. But to assure that the new finish makes a proper bond, to eliminate any problems with the old finish, and to make sure the substrate is rust free, it's going to be necessary to remove the old finish. Several processes can be used.

STRIPPING PAINT CHEMICALLY

Two chemical processes can be used to strip off old automotive finishes: You can attack the paint yourself using a stripper product, or you can have the car – or parts of the car – chemically dipped. The chemical dip is a commercial process available in various locations around the country. Naturally, the commercial process is more expensive, but far less time-consuming, safer, and 100 percent effective.

Chemically stripping a car's finish yourself is a slow, tedious, somewhat dangerous process that can leave inaccessible surfaces untouched. You can buy strippers for automotive finishes from the same source where you buy your refinishing products. You'll also need a scraper (plastic only, no steel tools are used to prevent gouging the metal), a D/A (dual action) sander, Scotchbrite scouring pads, thick rubber gloves, a face shield, and respirator.

In preparation for stripping, all decorative trim should be removed. Bright metal trim like decorative side-spears seen prominently on cars of the '40s and '50s is held in place with clips, which can be carefully pried out of holes in the body panels. Hood ornaments and deck medallions are likely to be secured with clips or nuts. Be sure to find out how these pieces are fastened before trying to pry them off. Later, (in Chapter 17) when we reattach these ornaments and medallions, we'll learn a trick that will make them easier to remove, should that be called for again in the future.

Chemical strippers are of two types: liquid and paste. The paste type seems to be favored and thought to be more effective. To remove the paint, you apply the stripper (spread or squirt), wait about the time period recommended on the product label (about five minutes), and attack the bubbled-up "goo" with a scraper. Older baked-enamel finishes can be very stubborn, requiring several stripper applications and sanding off the remaining residue. Be prepared to use lots of chemical and, depending on the type of finish, spend lots of time.

As you're peeling off the paint, it's a good idea to save a sample. If the original finish proves difficult to match, you can have the color sample electronically scanned for an identical color match.

CAUTIONS WHEN USING CHEMICAL STRIPPERS

1 Always read product labels, paying attention to the product's chemical composition and hazard warnings. Some labels will tell you point-blank this chemical causes cancer!

2 Be sure to wear chemical-resistant gloves, available at home improvement and building supply stores, not lightweight latex kitchen gloves.

3 Work in a well-ventilated area with shop doors open or outside.

4 Be careful with sparks or flame; some chemicals are flammable.

5 Follow instructions on the label to dispose of residue.

6 Avoid contact with eyes or skin. This means that in addition to a face mask or goggles, full clothing also needs to be worn when using these chemicals.

CHEMICALS IN PAINT STRIPPING PRODUCTS AND THEIR DANGERS*

Methylene chloride — causes cancer in laboratory animals, considered a potential cancer causing agent in humans. Evaporates quickly so is easily inhaled. High concentrations can cause irritation to eyes, skin, nose, and lungs. Use only in well-ventilated areas. High exposures over extended periods can cause liver and kidney damage. May be combined with other flammable materials, or nonflammable.

Acetone, toluene, methanol — all highly flammable. Do not use near sparks or flame. Inhaling high concentrations can be harmful to unborn children. Very high levels for prolonged periods can cause brain damage. Use in well-ventilated areas.

N-methylpyrrolidone (MNP) — can cause skin swelling, blisters, and burns. Absorbed through the skin, can cause health problems, including harm to unborn children. Very important to wear chemical-resistant gloves. Even when wearing gloves, wash hands immediately after use. Use only in well-ventilated areas.

Dibastic esters (DBE) — repeated inhalation causes cell and respiratory damage in laboratory animals. Wear respirator; use only in well-ventilated area. Wear protective clothing.

*Health warning information is from the U.S. Environmental Protection Agency, http://www.epa. gov/iaq/pubs/paintstr.html

CAUSTIC STRIPPING

Paint can be removed from small parts by immersing in solutions of lye or Drano. Depending on the concentration and temperature of the mix, cleaning — which removes grease and grime as well as paint — may take from a few minutes to a few hours. When using the caustic solution to clean heavily grease-encrusted parts, a grease film will sit on top of the liquid. This grease film should be skimmed off before removing parts; otherwise they will pick up a light grease coating as they are pulled through the film. Rinse the parts thoroughly after removing and if necessary to remove grease, spray with GUNK degreaser and wash. A strong detergent solution using Trisodium Phosphate (TSP), available in hardware

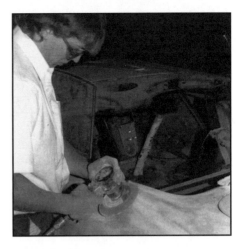

Where a chemical paint remover is used, sanding is still often required to remove the residue.

Paint and light surface rust can be removed from smaller items with caustic solutions of lye or Drano. Depending on the temperature of the solution and the concentration of the mix, the process may take from a few minutes to several hours, so it is important to carefully monitor the solution's progress.

aisles of discount marts and building supply stores, will also remove paint. You can also use a solution of molasses and water, though it will not work as rapidly nor as thoroughly as a caustic chemical solution.

When you've gotten off all the old paint (or at least all the paint you can reach), be sure to wash off all the chemical. Any residue will interfere with the paint bond. Be especially alert to chemical that may have seeped into seams and crevices.

DERUSTING

With the paint removed, you may find yourself looking at rust. Most paint strippers won't touch even light surface rust. Chemically, rust can be removed either with acids or organic anti-oxidants. Though the process is similar, the chemicals differ greatly, as do precautions associated with their use and their ultimate disposal.

Caustic solutions won't work if the parts are coated with grease. Trisodium Phosphate works well both as a grease remover and for stripping light paint coatings. Gunk works well for heavy grease coatings but usually will not strip paint, while GreaseMaster, shown on the left, is a fully biodegradable degreasing agent that is gentle to paint coatings.

Rust can be removed with mild acids available from both refinishing and restoration suppliers. If the part can be dipped in the acid solution, as with this antique wheel rim, even thick rust coatings can be scoured off in a short time. The acid can also be wiped onto surface rust, but the trick becomes keeping the acid from drying before it eats the rust.

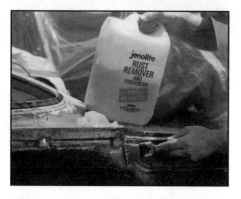

Mild acids are also available as a jell, which is less likely to dry before dissolving the rust.

Acid Derusting

Because they attack metal, acids are effective in removing rust. Harsh acids (such as hydrochloric) should be avoided, both because of their potential danger to the user and possible destruction of the metal. For light surface rust, phosphoric acid, which is readily available from refinishing and restoration suppliers under product names such as Metal Cleaner (PPG) or Rust Remover (OxiSolv), is a convenient, easy-to-use derusting chemical. At the recommended working strength this acid solution is relatively harmless, but even so, full clothing, rubber gloves, and a face shield should be worn to protect skin and eyes. If any acid does splash onto exposed skin, it should be washed off immediately with water.

The acid is sprayed, brushed, or dabbed onto the metal with a cloth. The surface needs to be kept moist while the acid works. Light rust dissolves relatively quickly, leaving a yellowish-gray zinc phosphate coating on steel and galvanized surfaces. This residue will retard rerusting, but the metal should be prepped and primed for lasting protection.

Since the acid will react with the metal, it's unlikely that any residue will be left for disposing. However, if an acid bath is used to derust small parts, then the depleted acid and sludge should be transferred to a plastic container that can be sealed and disposed of in a safe manner.

Organic Derusting

A new process called organic derusting chemically deoxidizes rust, leaving a black, powdery coating, which is easily removed by wiping, brushing, or pressure washing. Currently, the organic derusting product is available only from the specialty supplier listed in the Resource Appendix.

What makes organic derusting unique is that the active ingredients are manufactured primarily from plants and are not harmful, either to the user or the environment. Rusteco, currently the only product in this category, is available either as a liquid or gel enabling it to be used on vertical as well as horizontal surfaces. This

product works with any metal, removing oxidation from aluminum or copper as well as steel. Parts cleaned with this product can be prepared for temporary storage by brushing or wiping on another light coating. Rusteco's supplier maintains that product residue need not be treated as hazardous waste and requires no special disposal.

STRIPPING PAINT AND RUST COMMERCIALLY

An alternative to tediously stripping off paint by hand and then having to deal with rust, is to have major panels like the doors, trunk, and hood, or even the entire car chemically stripped by a commercial "metal laundry." The leading franchiser in this process is the Redi Strip Company, whose operations are located in major cities, primarily in the East and Upper Midwest. Numerous independents also offer metal cleaning services. These are best located through the telephone yellow pages or the World Wide Web. Check out the listings in the Resource Appendix at the back of this book.

Having a commercial stripper tackle the dirty work of cleaning off caked-on grease and mud, layers of paint, and gobs of body filler saves time, but metal laundering isn't a drive-through process. Parts that are candidates for the stripper's bath have to be disassembled as completely

An alternative to tediously stripping off paint and rust by hand is to have parts or the whole car chemically stripped in a commercial facility. Here a batch of small parts is being lowered into one of the stripping tanks.

When the parts are removed, they're as clean as the day they were made.

Entire car bodies can be chemically stripped with the same effectiveness—all grease, rust, and paint coatings, including caulking and body filler, being removed.

as possible. Immersion in the stripper's vats will remove rust proofing, seam caulking, bondo — virtually all applied fillings — but it won't clean covered surfaces. In preparation for stripping, not only would the interior be gutted (seats, upholstery, and carpeting), but also dash instruments, glass, weather seal, all exterior trim, doors, hood and deck lid, everything down to the metal.

When the parts emerge from the stripper's tanks all surfaces, including hidden interior areas, are thoroughly stripped of all coatings except rust. A second, reverse-electrolysis process typically follows which removes all rust without harming the metal. Since the bare metal will quickly surface-corrode, most services will apply a temporary water-soluble rust inhibitor. For long-term rust prevention, both the interior and exterior surfaces need to be thoroughly coated with a self-etching primer. On hoods, doors, and trunk lids, an effective way to coat inside surfaces is to pour the rust-inhibiting primer through holes in the stiffening panels, then rock the part back and forth, swishing the paint around until all inside surfaces are coated. Interior surfaces of fully enclosed panels like door pillars can be rust-proofed using wax-based coatings available from commercial services like Ziebart.

The downside to commercial chemical stripping is cost, both for the service and transportation. Rates are based on time-in-the-tanks plus labor, which means that batches of small parts can often be stripped for the same price as individual items.

STRIPPING PAINT AND RUST WITH ABRASIVE MEDIA

What used to be generically called sandblasting is now termed abrasive blasting. The process hasn't changed; rather a wider variety of media than just sand is used to prevent damage to the items being cleaned. For softer metals like aluminum or brass, engine blocks where sand dust could block vital internal passages, and for some plastics, glass beads are the ideal blast media. Walnut shells, too, are used when a softer abrasive material is needed. Sodium bicarbonate, another mild blasting media, offers the advantage that any residue can simply be washed off, the soda quickly dissolving. Using sand as the blasting media can be risky to large, flat sheet-metal panels as the blast's force and heat can stretch or distort the metal.

Abrasive blasting works best on parts that have been completely disassembled, either in preparation for metal repair or rebuilding. The blasting process has to be done outdoors or inside a blasting cabinet. The dust from most abrasive blasting media is not easily contained. It will penetrate a sealed differential or transmission, gas tank, even dash gauges if these parts aren't removed before blasting. If you're looking for a quick and easy way to strip rust and paint from metal, and the body hasn't been completely gutted and removed from the frame and the chassis disassembled, then use a chemical paint removing process described above.

Doing abrasive blasting is noisy, and when sand is used as the abrasive media, the dust that's produced acts like a desert sand storm. At the end of a blasting session, you'll find your clothes have been saturated by the fine dust. Besides full clothing, protective garb includes a protective hood with full face shield, respirator, and leather gloves such as those worn by welders. The air compressor used to power the blasting unit must be located outside the blast area, since dust particles could clog the compressor's filters and ruin the motor's bearings.

Great care needs to be taken when abrading sheet metal. Even mild blast media like glass beads can quickly deform thin metal, especially on flat surfaces. Panels with curves or creases, like

A spot sandblaster is the ideal tool for spot removing paint or cleaning small areas of surface rust. Photo courtesy of the Eastwood Company.

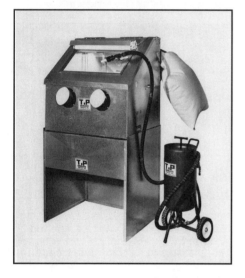

A media blasting cabinet contains the dust when stripping smaller parts. Photo courtesy of TiP Tools and Equipment.

When media blasting inside a cabinet, the worker's hands and arms are protected by heavy rubber gloves. Photo courtesy of TiP Tools and Equipment.

Abrasive blasting is noisy and dusty. It's important to wear proper protective clothing including a respirator.

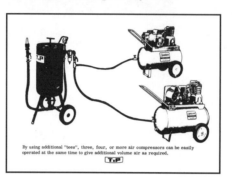

By using additional "tees", three, four, or more air compressors can be easily operated at the same time to give additional volume air as required.

Larger areas will require a pressurized blasting device, which calls for a large volume of air. If an industrial-capacity air compressor is not available, "hobby" sized compressors can be coupled to provide the needed air supply. Illustration courtesy of TiP Tools and Equipment.

a trunk lid or fender crown, are more resistant to distortion. To prevent heat buildup that can cause the metal to expand, it's better to make several light passes, rather than attempting to strip to bare metal in one "heavy" pass.

While aggressive media (sand, aluminum oxide, or aluma glass) will remove both paint and rust, milder media (plastic or glass beads) will only remove paint, leaving rust to be cleaned by some other method. Milder media will not remove body filler, but the filler will be visible and can be ground off if desired. Milder media also requires the metal to be etched before painting, or use of a self-etching primer.

Where the metal has been stripped of all coatings including rust, a wash-coating of dilute phosphoric acid should be applied soon after blasting to protect against surface corrosion, which can occur in just a few hours in high humidity conditions. Any necessary straightening,

Smaller jobs can be accomplished with an inexpensive siphon blasting gun.

welding, or filling should be done on bare metal. If no body work is needed, the metal should be given a protective primer coating right away.

CONVERTING AND STABILIZING RUST

Sometimes rust can't be conveniently removed either because the vehicle isn't being disassembled to the extent needed for chemical dipping or abrasive blasting, or the corrosion is inaccessible. In these situations, the best response, usually, is to stabilize the rust with a product that converts active rust into an inert coating. While not a total solution to the corrosion problem, these products are effective at arresting rust and preventing the rust from spreading for the period of time you are likely to use and enjoy the car. The permanent solution to rust is always to remove and replace the rusted metal.

Popular rust stabilizer/converter products include POR-15 (the product name literally means Paint Over Rust), Corroless, Rust Ender, and ChemSafe

When blasting an entire car body mild media should be used and great care needs to be taken to avoid overheating and warping panels. Expect to find the media dust in every crevice and cranny of the body.

Fiberglass can also be stripped of paint using mild media.

CSM 66. Since the rust stabilizers are liquid, they can be brushed, rolled, or sprayed onto the metal. POR-15 and Corroless are similar in that both react chemically with rust, converting the active corrosion to a more stable magnetite. POR-15 and Corroless also act like a paint, sealing the metal against moisture. A difference in the two products, besides color (POR-15 is available in either black or aluminum colors; Corroless has the color of red oxide primer), Corroless does not need to be recoated — either with primer or a finish paint. However, it is compatible with most automotive enamel and urethane paints and can be topcoated if desired. POR-15 can deteriorate when exposed to ultraviolet light and needs to be topcoated.

The Destroyer and ChemSafe CSM 66 also convert metallic oxides into a more stable and inert compound; however, their application is different than POR-15 and Corroless (which simply apply like paint) and both need to be topcoated with primer or paint soon after application. Following application, both The Destroyer and CSM 66 are washed down with water. As the metal dries, a rust inhibiting coating forms that helps with paint adhesion. Both products are recommended for sheet metal that has light surface rust, as well as deep corrosion.

Cleaning off any wax or grease, scraping off loose rust and scale, and scouring the metal with a wire brush are recommended preparation steps for all rust converter products. Although none of the converter/stabilizers contains isocyanates, application should be done in a well-ventilated area, wearing gloves and eye protection. The Destroyer and CSM 66 have added application as etching products to prepare aluminum, brass, copper, or

chrome for paint. Applying a wash coating of these products improves conductivity for welding, making their use a helpful preparation step to metal repair.

COATING THE METAL

Whatever stripping process has been used, the metal should be cleaned and conditioned (using cleaning and conditioning products available from the refinishing products supplier), then coated with an appropriate self-etching or direct-to-metal primer. Sandblasted metal will likely need one or more coatings of high build primer to fill pocks and fissures.

WRAPPING UP

Removing the old paint provides the best starting point for a new finish. Advantages include:
- a uniform surface
- no hidden surprises, undetected rust, or poorly applied filler to undermine the new finish
- no risk of checking, or bleed-through from the underlying finish
- no danger of finish incompatibility
- superior bonding, especially where the old finish is factory-baked enamel
- avoids excessive paint build which is especially important when applying multistage finishes.

Unless a car is being completely disassembled for restoration or converting into a street rod where the body can be conveniently dipped or abrasive blasted, some combination of the paint stripping and derusting methods described above are likely to be used. In fact, you may want to test different products and approaches on various parts to see which works best. Be sure to observe all health and safety

By whichever process, a bare surface makes the best preparation for new paint.

Rust converter/stabilizer products are popular with restoration refinishers who use these specialty paints to seal the metal against future corrosion. These rear fenders from a street rod have been coated with POR-15 rust stabilizer on the underside, a purely preventative measure since the metal has been stripped of paint and rust through abrasive blasting.

warnings — those on the product label as well as listed in this chapter. About halfway through the process, you'll probably wonder why you didn't take the easy way and paint over the old finish. Sometimes the old finish is an adequate base, but building the finish on bare metal, fiberglass, or composite can't be beat.

If the car hasn't been repainted and the original finish is sound (the paint isn't checked and shows no signs of flaking or peeling), then the finish can be sanded, primed, and prepped for a new finish coating. Often you'll find that some areas of the finish are in better condition than others. For example, unless the car has been exposed to ocean salt spray or intense sunshine, upper body paint is likely to be in relatively good condition — lacking gloss, perhaps, and maybe even "chalky," but intact enough to make a good platform for the new finish. (Sometimes it's possible to rejuvenate a deteriorated finish to save the expense of repainting. The rejuvenating process is described at the end of this chapter.)

Other areas may not be as sound: Door panels, for example, may show "Wisconsin daisies," a euphemism for rust blisters. Along lower door edges and around wheel wells rust's ugly presence may be even more visible. Quite commonly, repainting requires some of the old finish to be

stripped off, both in preparation for metal repair and to provide a proper substrate for refinishing, and some of the finish left intact to be prepped for repainting.

Trouble signs to look for as you inspect the finish include:

• Rust blisters — circular spots where festering rust is lifting the paint. Usually found on lower body panels where a stone chip or parking lot ding has broken the painting bond, sparking a "corrosion battery."

• Peeling — paint that's broken with the substrate. Possibly only the finish paint is peeling and the primer intact. However, any loose paint will have to be removed, back to a firm bonding layer.

• Cracking or checking — lines running through the paint that resemble fissures in an ice cube. Brittle finishes, notably lacquer, are prone to cracking and checking when exposed to severe temperature changes. Some mid-'80s factory finishes failed through severe cracking.

• Chip marks and pocking — damage caused by highway debris that has broken the finish, often leaving the primer intact. Damage of this sort is usually most visible at the front of the vehicle, often on the hood and bumper. The chipping may not be severe enough to warrant stripping down to bare substrate, but will require sanding and feathering to ensure a smooth base for the new finish.

The extent to which these conditions exist and their severity will guide whether or not the existing finish can serve as a base for the new. But even where the finish looks sound, it may not be suitable for recoating. Two settings where you have to say "no" to using the old finish as a base are: 1) where the old paint is lacquer, and 2) where the substrate (metal, fiberglass, or composite) is unsound.

Scott Taylor, a highly skilled refinisher, pointed out the lacquer problem on a street rod that came to his shop for body work and painting after a tree fell on the car's top. "Here's the problem," Scott said, inviting me to sight across the car's rear deck. The paint had the pocked look that painters call an "orange peel" texture — not Scott's usual standards. "Are you going to block sand the finish?" I asked, thinking Scott was showing me a painting flaw. I was assuming Scott had used a single-coat finish and applied enough paint to sand the finish smooth using extremely fine sandpaper so as not to destroy the gloss. "Wouldn't help," Scott answered. "That paint was perfectly smooth. The rippling you see is caused by the lacquer shrinking underneath the new paint. The lacquer will continue to shrink and the pocks will continue to grow. I told the owner he should have the old lacquer stripped off. He didn't want to pay the extra cost."

Lacquer is not a stable finish. It swells and shrinks with temperature changes, a condition that continues even under a new finish. The orange peel texture I saw resulted from pin prick indentations eaten into the old lacquer finish by acid rain, that magnified as the paint shrank. "The hood is the worst spot for lacquer," Scott Taylor explained. "As it absorbs heat from the engine, the paint swells, then when the engine's shut off, the hood cools and the paint shrinks. This goes on constantly. Eventually, you see a checkerboard of cracks, like an ice cube that's been rapped by a hammer, across the finish."

How do you tell if the finish is lacquer? The easiest way — assuming you can find some lacquer thinner (which no longer is universally available) — is to dip a cloth in thinner and wipe it across the finish. You won't have to rub hard; if color shows on the rag, it's lacquer. Another test, lacquer is softer than enamel. Pressing only mildly, you should be able to make in indentation in the paint with your fingernail. Follow Scott Taylor's advice. If the finish is lacquer, strip it off.

Unsound substrate could be anything from rust to flux leaching out of metal repair, to something as fundamentally unsound as holes plugged with body filler. Filler is porous and if used as a body material, it will absorb moisture and blister (or bubble up) paint. Where the substrate is fiberglass or composite, problems include splitting, cracking, or microchecking. Splits, tears, or cracks in bumper facia and other composite panels are easy to recognize on a fairly close inspection. Where such damage exists, it should be repaired before starting refinishing. To do the repair properly, paint in the localized area will have to be removed, usually by sanding. Micro-checking in the form of stress cracks is common on fiberglass-bodied cars of the 1950s and '60s, Corvettes from that era being a prime example. It's easy to see these cracks and think, "the old finish is a little checkered, but the marks will fill easily with high build primer." Yes, the cracks will fill, but they won't go away — like checking in an old lacquer finish discussed above. Getting a smooth substrate for the new finish will require stripping off the paint and filling the maze of tiny cracks with glazing putty.

If the substrate is sound and you're not working with a lacquer finish, preparation steps for refinishing consist of removing trim, decals, and sometimes weather stripping, then thoroughly cleaning the old finish to remove all contaminants and then sanding the paint to "scuff up" the surface for a good primer bond.

REMOVING TRIM, DECALS, AND WEATHER STRIPPING

Although its possible to mask and paint around trim, you'll have a more professional looking finish if you remove trim items. On modern cars, much of the trim glues on and is pried off carefully with a putty knife. On older cars, the trim is held in place with clips and threaded studs. You'll often need to do some "Sherlocking" to figure out what holds the trim in place. Clips can be popped loose with gentle prying. A putty knife works well here, too. Threaded connectors have nuts on the underside. Sometimes these are reached through holes in the body

Removing bumpers and trim items results in a more professional looking finish. The paint on this Corvette is being scuff sanded in preparation for priming and sealing before repainting.

Body moldings should also be removed. These trim pieces are usually held in place by press-in clips.

If the rubber weatherseal on the doors and trunk has lost its resiliency, these items too would be removed for refinishing. Weatherseal removes easiest if it can be heated from the back side. Otherwise, you'll scrape off rubber fragments with a putty knife and loosen the glue with solvent. New weatherseal can be purchased and glued in place after the car has been painted.

Making sure the old finish is thoroughly clean of contaminants requires several steps. Not only is it important to remove any grease or wax, but all traces of silicone that can produce a "fisheye" effect in the new finish.

The old paint is scuff sanded to remove oxidation and improve bonding with the new finish.

panel's stiffening structure. Don't attempt to twist the nuts with force. If they don't turn loose relatively easily, spray on WD40 and wait for the penetrating fluid to work. Twisting off the threaded fasteners makes the trim items difficult to reattach.

Decals come off relatively easily with heat, either from a hair dryer or paint stripping gun. As the decal softens, you may be able to pull it loose. If not, you can scrape it off with a single-edge razor blade. Be careful with the heat — you don't want to blister or burn the paint.

Weather stripping used to seal doors and the trunk lid would only be removed if the rubber has lost its resiliency and is allowing water seepage. Pools of water on the trunk floor after washing or rain are a sign the trunk weather seal needs replacing.

Rather than tear off the rubber and have to clean the residue, you'll find rubber peels off easily with little cleanup if you heat the back side of the weather seal channel with a propane torch or heat gun. This "trick" works best on trunk rubber where the underside of the weather seal channel is easy to reach. Otherwise, you'll scrape off rubber fragments with a putty knife or razor blade, whatever will fit in the channel, and loosen the glue with paint

solvent. The process can be time-consuming and tedious.

If the weather seal has been leaking, you'll often find rust, which needs to be removed following steps described in the previous chapter. When all traces of weather stripping, glue, and rust are gone, you can clean the channel for painting.

CLEANING THE OLD FINISH

Making sure the finish is thoroughly clean of all contaminants requires a few steps.

Step 1. Wash all painted surfaces thoroughly with soap and water. The soap solution will clean off dirt and grime, but it won't remove nonwater soluble finish coatings like wax. Stubborn grease coatings may require a stronger cleaning solution of TSP (trisodium phosphate) or other heavy-duty cleaning product available on "housewares" shelves of home supply marts.

Step 2. Highly recommended: Wash again, this time with a solution of baking soda and water. The baking soda will neutralize acid residue on the finish, or acid that may have begun to penetrate the finish as a result of acid rain. Few, if any, areas of the country are free of airborne pollution that settles on any stationary object and releases acids when

moistened by rainfall or heavy dew.

Step 3. Wipe the finish with a wax and grease remover. A refinishing supplier may stock several wax and grease remover products. Ask for a cleaning product capable of removing silicone, an ingredient in many discount mart variety car waxes and also likely to have accumulated on some areas of the finish as overspray from spraying rubber protectorant on tires. Silicone residue on the old finish may induce a "fisheye" effect in the new paint. Since even traces of silicone can ruin a finish, refinishing shops ban the use of any product containing this chemical.

Note: Original formula Windex (without ammonia) also works well as a cleaning product for removing traces of silicone.

This cleaning process needs to be thorough. Overlooked spots of dirt or grime could be abraded deeply into the finish by the sanding step that follows. Wax residue will quickly clog sandpaper, and airborne pollutants could interfere with the refinishing paint bond. Silicone's fisheye effect was presented in Step 3 above.

A clean surface is easier to inspect for flaws. Be especially alert to paint blisters, which are indications of rust festering underneath the paint. The blisters can be scraped off with a putty knife, sanded, or removed with a grinder. If the rust is flaky, you should probe with a pick or sharp pointed phillips screwdriver to test the soundness of the metal. If the pick pokes through, you've got serious rust damage that needs to be repaired. Sound metal will repel the pick, even when jabbed with force. If the metal is sound, additional steps are still needed to remove the rust.

ELIMINATING RUST

If surface rust is detected, the surrounding finish needs to be removed until only shiny metal is exposed. The finish around a rust blister can be scoured off with a wire brush mounted in the chuck of an electric drill, a grinder, hand-held rough grit sandpaper, or a D/A (dual action) sander with 220 grit sandpaper. The more abrasive the tool, the more clean up work will be required to smooth the abraded spot into the surrounding paint.

Scouring or sanding won't remove the rust; even wire brushing will leave tiny "seeds" of rust that will germinate under the new finish. To eliminate the corrosion battery (which is what you have actually exposed), you'll need to treat the metal under the blister with a rust-removing chemical (discussed in the previous chapter) or use an abrasive blaster to clean the spot to bare metal.

It's overkill to point a sandblast nozzle at a tiny dime- or quarter-sized rust blister. The tool to use is a spot blaster, available from restoration suppliers like The Eastwood Company. A spot blaster is the ideal tool to remove rust blisters or other small blemishes. A soft rubber shield surrounding the nozzle makes it possible to blast close to window glass or trim. With the rubber shield pressed tight against the panel, the spot blaster quickly cuts through paint and rust, leaving a small circle, about the size of a quarter, of bare metal. Provided that the shield is pressed tightly against the surface, almost no media or dust escapes so there's no concern about blasting grit seeping into the car body and

Paint as well as any loose rust and scale can be soured off with a wire brush or abrasive wheel as shown here. Photo courtesy The Eastwood Company.

soiling upholstery or contaminating mechanical assemblies. For blisters larger than a quarter, just move the blaster so that the shield covers more of the blister and squeeze the trigger again. The version of this tool offered by The Eastwood Company can be fitted with different shaped rubber shields (oblong, square, round) for blasting in various tight locations. A spot blaster cleans off paint and rust so efficiently, it's not necessary to scrape or sand the blemish.

SANDING THE OLD FINISH

Where a rust blister or other finish flaw has been cleaned to bare metal, the surrounding paint needs to be sanded so that instead of a sharp edge, the finish tapers smoothly into the bare spot. This process of sanding a smooth tapered seam is called "feathering" or "feather edge" sanding and is necessary to prevent the sharp paint edge from showing in the new finish.

To remove oxidation that may have developed on the surface of the old paint, and to scuff the surface for improved bonding, the areas that are going to be repainted should be sanded with 600 grit wet/dry (or finer) sandpaper or a gray Scotchbrite pad. Professionals typically use a D/A sander for this step,

since the tool both speeds the process and prevents ridges in the finish which might result from hand sanding. To help assure a uniform surface, hand sanding should be done with a soft hand or sponge pad using sandpaper one grade finer than with machine sanding.

Tips when using a D/A sander:
- turn down the speed when sanding next to body creases
- sand perpendicular to the surface, not at an angle
- sand lengthwise with the vehicle, not up and down

Make sure that all areas of the finish that will be repainted are sanded. After wiping off the sanding residue and cleaning with wax and grease remover, spots that may have been missed will stand out clearly, still having their glossy or chalky finish, as opposed to a dull sanded look.

PREPARING FOR PRIMING

When all areas of the finish slated for repainting have been scuff-sanded, sanding dust needs to be blown out of crevices such as weatherstrip edges and panel seams using an air gun nozzle at the end of the air hose. Then the entire finish needs to be wiped down to remove sanding dust and other residue with a painting preparation product. All paint

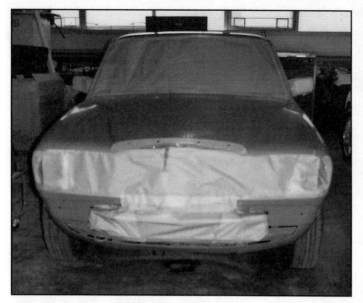

All areas of the car that aren't going to be painted need to be masked. With the bumper and grille removed from this Mercedes, even the radiator and headlight areas are covered by masking paper.

When masking, tape is first used to outline the masking area, then the paper is applied and taped around the edges and along seams.

manufacturers have their version of this product: PPG calls its Multi-Prep. After a thorough wipe down with soft shop towels, sticky tack cloths are used to pick up any remaining dust.

Following this cleaning process, the surface should be mist sprayed with a preparation product capable of neutralizing static electricity which builds up in the wipe-down steps and holds dust particles and other residue to the surface. This anti-static step is especially important when painting over plastic. With the finish clean and ready for primer, all surfaces not being painted need to be masked.

MASKING SURFACES NOT BEING PAINTED

As mentioned earlier, trim — which can include bumpers, door and trunk handles, mirrors, and medallions, in addition to bright metal side spears and other decorative pieces — is typically removed as one of the preparation steps for refinishing. To the extent that any of these items have been left on the car, they need to be masked, also all glass. Since we're preparing for the primer coating, not the color finish, no special masking for two-toning or special effects like flames needs to

be done at this time. At the moment, we're only concerned with surfaces of the vehicle that might pick up unwanted overspray.

Tape used for masking should be purchased where you buy your refinishing supplies, not at a discount mart or hardware store. Masking tape used with refinishing is of higher quality and available in a variety of widths from 1/8 in. to 2 in. The narrowest widths are used for masking designs — a process that is described in detail in Chapters 15 and 16. To mask the vehicle for repainting, you'll use mainly 3/4 inch tape, 1 to 2 rolls. You'll need a roll of wider 2 in. tape for masking headlights, parking lights, and some trim items. You'll also need to purchase masking paper. Although hobbyists often use newspaper as their masking material, masking paper should be used. Paint can seep through newspaper if the paper becomes saturated and the ink can transfer to the surface being covered. Masking paper comes in 60 yard 12 inch rolls; if you're covering more than just the window glass you'll probably need a couple of rolls.

Proper masking is a little more complicated than the job looks. Sealing the edges is most important, so you'll mask these first, running an outline of tape around the wind-

shield trim and other areas being covered. Smaller surfaces like headlights and parking lights are often just covered with tape (here's where the 2-inch tape is used). Rather than tear the tape to run a new strip, cut the edge clean with a single-edge razor blade or x-acto knife. The clean edge will make a better seal and you won't stretch the tape. On surfaces being covered with tape, overlap each strip by at least half. This prevents the seams from opening and overspray from penetrating the cracks.

On larger areas that will be covered with paper, go around the edging tape with a thumb or index finger to make sure the edge is tightly sealed. Then tear off a sheet of paper long enough for the area you're covering. Tape the paper to the outline you've previously taped. Each strip of masking paper should also overlap, also by about half, and the seams taped to prevent overspray. It's a lot easier to unroll needed lengths of masking paper if the paper rolls are mounted on a stand. If you're painting more than one car you may want to consider purchasing a masking stand, which allows the paper to be easily unrolled and the sheets torn off to the right lengths by pulling the tape against a cutter.

Besides window areas and trim, it's important to mask the door jambs and underhood. The reason for applying a tape seal to the door jambs and covering the engine compartment with a sheet of visquine (lightweight plastic) is to prevent overspray from blowing into the car's interior and soiling or possibly coating some of the upholstery and the same with the engine compartment. If you're planning on painting the door jambs, then the door openings have to be masked, along with the trim side of the doors, and the weatherstripping. Likewise, painting the underhood requires careful masking of all mechanical assemblies and accessories.

On the exterior, overspray will land most noticeably on tires and wheels. While tires and wheels can be draped with plastic garbage bags, they can be masked more efficiently and conveniently with a water soluble product called Micro Mask. Available from refinishing suppliers, Micro Mask sprays on and creates a film that looks like a thin layer of visquine (the plastic material used by dry cleaners to protect garments). One of the advantages of Micro Mask is the masking material doesn't have to be removed to roll

In order to repaint matching surfaces on the hood and front fenders, the engine compartment also needs to be masked.

the car around the shop, as would be the case with garbage bags or other coverings. At the end of the refinishing process, the wheels and tires can be rinsed with a hose, washing off the Micro Mask. This product is especially important with alloy wheels where trying to remove overspray can erode the wheel's protective coating.

SAVING MONEY

All the painting preparation steps described in this and the previous chapter are work the typical hobbyist can do him/herself. Although a few special tools have been called for, most notably a sandblaster or spot blaster and a D/A sander (both requiring an air compressor), the

Masking door openings so the door jambs can be painted gives more professional looking results and is necessary when changing exterior colors.

The early stage of masking where the tape outline has been applied can be clearly seen on this Camaro.

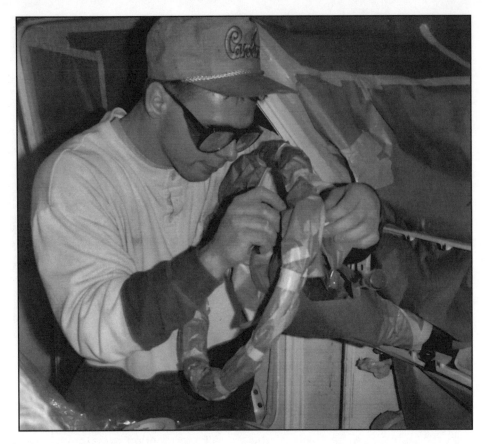

Where interior metal is being painted, masking is extensive.

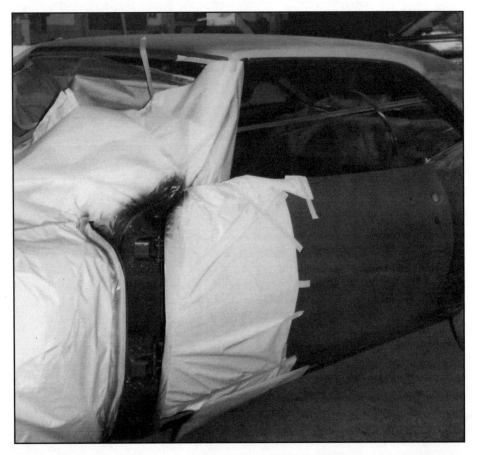

When the car is partially disassembled for repair, it's important to mask and paint areas such as this front cowl support that are now accessible before assembling is complete.

work is mostly time-consuming and painstaking. But this is exactly when contributing your labor and attention to detail not only spares the refinishing shop from work they don't want to do in the first place — because it distracts from their production pace and you're going to wince (or worse) when you see the bill — but also makes you a part of the project. A friend who constructed houses during summers to supplement his teaching income said one client insisted on installing the siding. "I want to tell my friends, 'Everything you see I did,'" was the client's reasoning. By doing the preparation work, you can tell your friends, "Everything you don't see, I did." However, this is one place where what you don't see is as important as what you do see.

MOVING TOWARD REFINISHING

In the next chapter we'll look at the preparation steps for refinishing plastic parts, including fiberglass. Besides bumper facia, plastic is found in nose or grille pieces and sometimes, as with the Pontiac Fiero, the car's entire exterior. Fiberglass has many applications besides Corvettes, including kit cars and in some cases repair panels used on an otherwise steel-bodied car.

Once the preparation processes are completed, the surfaces need to be primed. Chapter 4 described the Systems principle of modern paint. Primer coatings need to be from the same refinishing system as the finish coatings. This means the decision as to the type of finish, single-stage color, catalyzed color, base coat/clear coat, needs to be made prior to priming. Specifying the type of paint also means selecting the color. Otherwise, when the time comes to mix the color, if the color match can't be made in the painting choice you could have an undercoat system different from the finish system. So if making final painting decisions before beginning the first refinishing step seems odd, just blame it on the "system."

REJUVENATING AN OLD FINISH

Sometimes a finish can be renewed or improved sufficiently to avoid repainting. However, rejuvenation only works for conditions on the paint's surface, such as a dull chalky film having replaced the original gloss, extensive "orange peel," small scratches and abrasions, and sometimes minor dents. Blistering, cracking, flaking, and other signs of paint failure can only be remedied by repainting.

My sons and I were able to renew the gloss on a Dodge Omni they drove through high school using the rejuvenation process. A friend smoothed and drastically improved the paint on a vintage Thunderbird that he described as "awful looking" and "pocked with orange peel." The renewal-rejuvenation process is "low tech," requiring more patience than skill. It starts by thoroughly cleaning the old finish following the steps described earlier in this chapter, assessing the condition of the paint, and attempting to estimate the paint thickness or "build." Our Omni had its factory non-clear coat finish — typically 4-5 mils, all coatings. Newell said his Thunderbird had been amateurishly repainted, leading him to assume (correctly) an extra thick color coating.

The Omni's finish felt rough — the result of severe oxidation from several years of curbside parking in a sunny climate. We removed the oxidation, smoothed the paint, and restored the gloss with a combination of finish restoration/ cleaning/wax products from One Grand. The polish phase took the most work, carefully and painstakingly hand rubbing the mild scouring abrasive in the polishing compound against the oxidized paint.

Newell used what he (and others) call the "Meguiars Treatment." Included in Meguiars' line of car care products are microfine 1500 and 2000 grit sandpaper. Newell block wet-sanded his Thunderbird's finish with 1500 then 2000 sandpaper, followed by the polishing steps described in Chapter 17. To prevent

The polishing steps described in Chapter 17 can sometimes be used to rejuvenate a mildly oxidized or orange peel finish.

sanding through the finish on panel edges and creases, Newell covered these areas more likely to be thinly coated with masking tape. After sanding and polishing, he removed the masking tape and very carefully hand rubbed these more delicate spots. Newell's result is a car that looks almost freshly painted. Our Omni looked like a car a few years old that had enjoyed fairly good care — a substantial upgrade from its former appearance as a car several years old with poor care.

If only the surface shows deterioration and your goal isn't a completely new finish, you might try these rejuvenation techniques. The "Meguiars Treatment" boosted the value of Newell's Thunderbird several thousand dollars and saved an equal or greater amount in the cost of a complete repaint.

PAINTLESS DENT REMOVAL

One drawback of a glossy finish is that it shows parking lot dings and dents ("lot rash" a friend calls this minor damage) a lot more visibly than dull paint. Dents and dings are one reason to repaint, but they can sometimes be removed and made almost invisible without repainting. You'll probably want to have the dents removed by a professional trained in this technique. Paintless dent removal specialists often are listed in the telephone yellow pages or can be contacted on the World Wide Web.

If you want to try paintless dent removal yourself, the technique requires accessing the dent from the back side and gently massaging it with various shaped "spoons" (pry bars with flat or slightly curved ends). On doors you may be able to reach the dent by removing inner door coverings, on front fenders by loosening the inner shield, and on rear panels by pulling back the trunk liner. The trick is not to stretch the metal. With the dent as smooth as possible, the finish is microsanded and polished as described above.

Do-It-Yourself Guide to CUSTOM PAINTING
Painting Over Plastic

Corvette pioneered the development of plastics and composites for entire bodies, beginning in 1953. Both the 1962 and 1970s vintage Corvette shown here used fiberglass body construction which won't rust, but is prone to hairline cracks.

Starting with the first Corvette in 1953, manufacturers have made increasing use of plastics and composites in car bodies and trim parts. Today, bumper coverings are exclusively made from some form of plastic, as are rear spoilers, lower body cladding, and ground effects panels. Besides the Corvette, where composites replaced fiberglass in 1993, General Motors has used plastic on body panels for the Pontiac Fiero mid-engined sports car, some models of which are now considered collectible, its Lumina MPV vans, and Saturn cars. Preparing plastic panels and coverings for refinishing employs some of the steps and processes described in the preceding two chapters, but adds a few new elements, including identifying the type of plastic — which is necessary for selecting the proper primer and finish coatings — and making any needed repair.

Thankfully, plastic doesn't rust. However, it is subject to other dam-age, most notably cracks and tears. To repair the damage, you've got to know the type of plastic. Once that's determined, you'll be able to select the proper repair materials and right procedure for making the repair.

Although hundreds of kinds of plastic materials are found on modern vehicles, plastics used in the automotive industry can be categorized into two basic types: thermoplastic and thermoset. (You've seen these terms before used to describe the basic differences in paint. They're used again here because the characteristics they describe apply to plastics as well.) Thermoplastics have the advantage that they can be melted and reused, which is a benefit to the manufacturer in the reuse of production scrap and to society generally through recyclable waste. A commonly used thermoplastic is ABS used both in grillework and dashboards. Another example is TPO, used for impact resistance in under-grille rock shields, among other appli-cations. Besides heat, thermoplastics can be softened with solvent, which in some cases makes plastics of this type difficult to refinish.

Thermoset plastics cannot be melt-ed with heat or solvent and therefore cannot be reused. Plastics of this type have a much more complex molecular structure, the result of extensive chemical cross-linking during the curing process, which makes the plastic both heat and solvent resistant. Refinishing procedures for this type of plastics are relatively straight-forward. Examples of thermoset plastics include SMC (Sheet Molded Composite Compounds) used with exterior panels on General Motors MPVs, RIM (injection molded polyurethane material which can be formulated to various degrees of stiff-ness), R-RIM (reinforced RIM, a very hard material), and fiberglass. These plastics are found in bumper covers and fascia as well as exterior body panels.

The fiberglass-constructed bodies on older Corvettes use thermoset plastic which repairs easily with resin and filler.

Preparation for repainting an older Corvette usually entails stripping of the existing finish using a chemical stripper or a mild blasting media like a poly abrasive, then filling cracks and repairing any damage, followed by priming to assure a smooth surface for the new finish.

DETERMINING THE TYPE OF PLASTIC

In recent years, interest in recycling has led manufacturers to code plastic parts with marking designations that tell the type of plastic. The marking symbols typically appear on a surface that's visible only when the part is removed or disassembled and refer to the type of resin or compound used in forming the part. SAE (Society of Automotive Engineers) standards call for the plastic symbol to appear in 3 mm. tall letters inside an oval. Where this symbol appears, the information it gives will be helpful in directing the repair method and selecting refinishing products. However, many plastic parts will lack the symbol (either because they were manufactured before recycling interest led to the symbol standard or because the symbol can't be located). In these settings, another method will be used to determine the type of plastic used in manufacturing the parts.

Since plastics in the two basic categories respond differently to heat, a test can be made with a heat gun to determine the basic characteristics of the plastic from which the part has been formed. To make the heat test, you'll want to select a spot that won't be seen, likely on the back side of the part, and warm it moderately with a heat gun.

Thermoplastic parts will turn shiny, producing a "wet look." If the plastic is heated to the point of softening, it will harden again when cooled. Repairing this type of plastic is done by "plastic welding."

Thermoset parts will turn dull looking, lacking a "wet look." If heated to the point of softening, the plastic will remain sticky or gooey. Repairing is done with adhesives.

It's important to realize that when talking about plastic, we're not concerned just with the vehicle's exterior. Plastic has likely been used extensively inside the vehicle. Examples of interior plastic parts include padded dashboard coverings, instrument panels and dash facia, seat coverings, and door panels. Here, too, damage may have occurred where plastic parts need to be repaired and refinished, or replaced with new or better condition pieces.

REPAIRING PLASTIC PARTS

Most thermoplastics can be repaired by "welding," which in this context means to heat the material and fuse it with a stick of like-composition plastic. A plastic welding kit designed for the hobbyist is available from The Eastwood Company. This versatile kit consists of a heat gun with nozzles of different shapes to work inside corners, fill V-

grooves, make edge welds, or repair outside corners and filler rods for the most common types of thermoplastic material: ABS, PVC, Polypropylene, Polyurethane, and Polyethylene. As in a metal weld, you'll smooth the filler by grinding and sanding. The heat gun can also be used to strip paint and undercoating.

Thermoset plastics are repaired with epoxy or adhesive. When the plastic is cracked or punctured, the procedure is to bond a reinforcing patch of similar

Plastic doesn't need to be soft and pliable to be considered flexible. If it bends so as to absorb impact, as with a grille or bumper fascia, it's considered flexible. For topcoats, a flex additive isn't required when the flexible part is painted on the vehicle. If the color finish is basecoat/clear coat, flex additive is mixed with the clear, not the basecoat.

If the plastic isn't broken or badly cracked, grille assemblies, like this nose piece from a Dodge Viper are repaired similar to steel with filler and glazing putty.

Repairing plastic and vinyl interior coverings is complicated by the different types of material: rigid door panels, soft seat coverings, and flexible dash coverings.

material to the backside of the damaged area. The patch needs to overlap the crack or puncture by at least 1.5 in. in each direction. If epoxy is used as the bonding material, some clamping device (such as pop rivets) will be needed to hold the patch in place while the epoxy dries. Adhesives are much faster drying and may require only minimal clamping.

With the patch firmly bonded in place, you'll grind the repair smooth using 36 grit paper, making an even taper 2 to 4 inches outside the damaged area onto the patch. The rough grinding will be followed by feather-edging with 80 and then 180 grit using a D/A sander and then filling the repair area with a quality filler. The filler should be block sanded

Interior plastic and vinyl coverings can be cleaned with soap and water and scrubbed with a soft bristle brush.

with 80 grit to check for low spots and other flaws in the surface. If additional filler material is needed, it is applied, followed by block sanding with 180 grit.

Although most thermoset plastics are not sensitive to solvent, as a precaution (in case the type of thermoset you're working with is solvent sensitive), you should avoid wiping down the repair area with a solvent-based cleaner. Instead, blow off the area with compressed air and wipe clean with a tack cloth. The surrounding painted surfaces will need to be cleaned with wax and grease remover, but check the label before using them. Products that are solvent-based must not be applied to any areas where the plastic substrate is exposed. The cleaner to use there is Windex. Following cleaning, the repair area and surrounding panel can be primed with an epoxy sealer.

Damage to fiberglass is repaired similarly to thermoset plastics, except that — depending on the severity of the damage — fiberglass cloth and resin (or fiberglass strands, often referred to as "angel hair") may be used in place of, or in addition to, a reinforcing patch. Much the same approach is used to attach patch panels.

One of the most common kinds of damage to older fiberglass car body panels is hairline cracking, sometimes covering virtually all body surfaces. Attempting to fill these cracks with high solids primer during the refinishing process will not be effective. The correct

procedure is to strip off all existing paint coatings using a chemical stripper or a mild blasting media like a poly abrasive, then fill the cracks with glazing putty. Once the hairline cracks are repaired, the fiberglass can be primed and refinished.

Repairing plastic or vinyl interior coverings is complicated by the different types of material — rigid (door panels, for example), flexible (like dash coverings), and soft (like seat coverings) — and the need to match the grain typically stamped into the plastic or vinyl surface. Vinyl, plastic, and leather repair kits, available from The Eastwood Company and Fitzgerald's Restoration Products, use flexible adhesives and graining compounds to seal the crack, tear, or puncture and match the repair to the surrounding material. While repairs made with these kits may not be completely invisible when examined close-up, they can be nearly invisible, at least from a distance.

Although interior plastics and vinyl coverings can be cleaned with soap and water, Fitzgerald's makes a non-flammable, water-based cleaner specially formulated to remove all dirt from vinyl and leather upholstery, as well as other interior plastic surfaces. Once repaired and thoroughly cleaned, the vinyl, plastic, or leather covering should also be repainted. This process for repainting interior coverings is described later in this chapter.

Those engaged in refinishing projects

where the car body is extensively plastic or fiberglass and in need of repair may wish to attend a Plastic Repair course offered by I-CAR, the auto body industry's professional training and standards organization. Contact information for I-CAR course listings is provided in the Resource Appendix.

PREPARING PLASTIC FOR PAINTING

Where an old finish needs to be removed, the first question is whether or not it's safe to use a chemical stripper. Thermoplastics can be highly sensitive to solvents and with these materials, chemical strippers should not be used. While most thermoset plastics are not solvent sensitive, some are. Unless you have a scrap piece of panel on which to test the action of the chemical stripper, it's safest to remove paint buildup either by sanding or blasting with a mild abrasive. Fiberglass can be chemically stripped. However, the material is easily gouged if a metal scraper is used to peel off old paint coatings. A better scraping tool is a plastic applicator for spreading filler. When all of the old finish has been removed and the surface sanded smooth, ultimately with 600 grit wet/dry or finer sandpaper, or gray Scotchbrite pads, all refinish areas are thoroughly cleaned by:

- blowing off all sanding dust with compressed air
- wiping down surfaces being refinished with a painting preparation product that releases static electricity
- thoroughly going over all surfaces with a tack rag
- following paint manufacturer's recommendations and spraying a mist coat of the painting prep product as an anti-static treatment before painting.

The sequence for painting over an existing finish adds a few preparation steps. This process begins by:

- thoroughly washing all surfaces with soap and water
- wiping the finish with a wax and grease remover
- lightly scuffing all areas being refinished with gray Scotchbrite pads, to improve paint adhesion

With new plastic parts, such as the reproduction front fender on this 1956 Ford, preparation steps include wiping with an anti-static painting preparation product. If the new part appears to be primed, test to make sure the coating is actually primer by pressing on a piece of masking tape and removing it in a quick, jerking motion. If the tape removes the coating, the part will need to be prepped then primed.

- wiping down with a quality anti-static painting preparation product

Where new plastic parts are being refinished — a repair panel, for example, or a new bumper cover — it is sometimes helpful to warm the panel (using a heat light of the type professional refinishing shops use to cure paint) to make sure the factory primer is fully cured. If you add this step when refinishing a new plastic part, be sure to observe these cautions:

- Make sure the part is rigidly supported. Excessive heat could cause the part to droop or stretch
- Avoid excessive heat by keeping lamps at least three feet from the part.

There's also the possibility that a new plastic replacement panel (either aftermarket or from the manufacturer) may be not be coated with primer, but rather a primer-appearing coating. To test whether or not the coating is actually primer, press masking tape to the coating. Rub the tape firmly in place and then pull the tape off in a quick, jerking motion. If the tape removes any of the coating, the part will need to be cleaned and prepared for priming, beginning with a thorough washing and wipedown to remove the protective coating.

UNDERCOATING PLASTIC PARTS

Exterior plastic surfaces should be primed with a universal plastic primer or an epoxy primer. These coatings can be used for both rigid and flexible plastic, or flexible parts (such as bumper covers and filler panels) can be coated with flexible primer. Rigid interior plastic (door panels, for example) should be

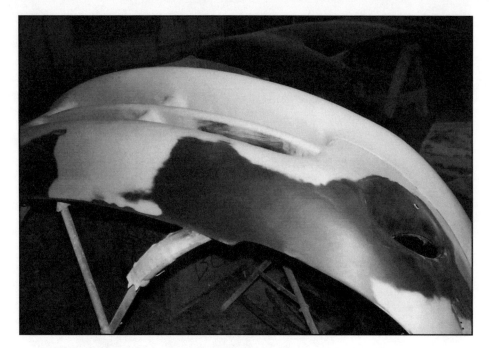

The primer is sanded to fill surface imperfections.

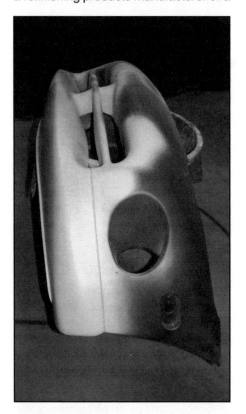

Exterior plastic surfaces, like this Viper grille assembly, should be primed with a universal plastic primer or epoxy primer.

coated with polypropylene primer when bare substrate (the raw plastic surface) has been exposed. Both flexible interior plastic (like dash pads) and soft interior coverings (seat upholstery) are coated with a vinyl color system, available from a refinishing products manufacturer or a specialty restoration products supplier.

For additional undercoats and the topcoat system, determination has to be made as to whether the plastic is rigid or flexible. Often, this difference is obvious, but sometimes you may wonder. Basically, rigid plastic is like the steel part it replaces, it is not easily bendable. Plastic doesn't need to be soft and pliable as a vinyl seat covering to be flexible. If it bends fairly easily so as to absorb impact, it's considered flexible. Bumper fascia is a prime example. If you're not sure (some plastic parts could be considered semi-rigid or semi-flexible, with no clear distinction as to which category they fit), then treat the plastic as if it is flexible. Using a flexible refinishing system on rigid plastic parts will not affect the life or quality of the finish.

Coatings for Rigid Plastic

Additional undercoating with a high build primer surfacer may be needed to fill repair areas or surface irregularities. The primer surfacer and sealer products need to be selected for compatibility with the universal plastic primer or epoxy primer used as the initial undercoat as well as the topcoat finish. No flexible additive is needed. Fiberglass uses the same primer coatings and has the same refinishing options as rigid plastic.

Coatings for Flexible Plastic

A flex additive is required with undercoats after the initial plastic primer. With the topcoat, however, flex additive is required only if the finish painting is done with the flexible part off the vehicle. If the part is mounted on the vehicle, a flex additive does not have to be added. If the color finish is a base coat/clear coat, flex additive is not included in the base coat. Whether or not the part is mounted on the car determines the need for flexible additive in the clear coat.

Painting manufacturers have additional restrictions on the use of certain refinishing products on specific types of plastics. Ask the sales representative where you purchase the refinishing products about potential conflicts. Also, be sure that undercoat and topcoat products are compatible within a system.

RECOLORING VINYL AND LEATHER COVERINGS

Earlier, the discussion of plastic and vinyl interior coverings focused on repair, usually to mend a crack or puncture. Whether or not original interior plastics need repair, they often can benefit from recoloring (another way of saying repainting). This coloring process, which can be applied to leather as well as plastic and vinyl, is straight-forward. First, the material needs to be thoroughly cleaned. The multi-purpose household cleaner Simple Green works well to remove grease as well as ground-in grime. Suppliers of professional refinishing products also supply detergent-based vinyl cleaners. Solvents should not be used for cleaning.

After cleaning, the plastic, vinyl, or leather is "painted" with a product specially formulated for this use. For ease-of-use, The Eastwood Company offers vinyl and plastic coloring products in aerosol spray cans. The color selection, however, is limited. Most manufacturers of automotive refinishing products carry vinyl color systems in their line-up. Since these color systems consist of mixing colors, virtually any color can be reproduced. Additionally, the color systems include clear coatings for non-

REFINISHING TRAINING FROM I-CAR

The automotive enthusiast who wants to learn refinishing tricks and techniques used by professionals can get that training conveniently and inexpensively from I-CAR (Inter-Industry Conference on Auto Collision Repair). An international, not-for-profit (self-financing) organization, I-CAR was founded to provide quality technical programs to the collision repair industry, thereby raising the standards of that industry.

I-CAR training courses exist in three formats: on-site seminars typically offered week nights or Saturdays, CD ROM self-study, and autobody/refinishing courses offered through high school skill centers and technical colleges using I-CAR teaching materials. You may be thinking, I'm a hobbyist, not an auto refinishing professional, would I really want to sit in a training class with people who do this work for a living? Would I understand the information and would the training really be worthwhile to my project? Quite possibly, the answer to each of these questions is "Yes." For example, one of the I-CAR training courses covers Plastic Repair, the topic of this chapter. According to the course description, in this three-unit course (units refer to the course's time requirements which is 4 hours per unit) you'll learn

- Welding and adhesive repair methods
- Re-texturing options for finishing plastics
- Differences between repair methods for sheet-molded compounds (SMC) and fiberglass

- SMC panel replacement, sectioning, and repair
- Refinishing of plastics and composites

With the exception of repair and refinishing interior plastics, the topics covered in this course are those you're likely to encounter if you're working on a vehicle that uses plastics or fiberglass to any extent. The cost of the on-site course is extremely reasonable, about the equivalent of the same number of hours of body shop labor. If the repair/restoration work in your automotive refinishing project is extensive, what you'd learn in the course, translated into work you could do yourself, could make the course fee a savings not an expense. As mentioned, many of the I-CAR courses are on self-study CD-ROM for even greater savings.

Besides training courses, I-CAR offers a bi-monthly Technical Newsletter and Technical Video whose topics include replacing quarter panels on the 1993-94 Camaro/Firebird, glass replacement, and working with aluminum. Information on I-CAR training, including current offerings, is available on the World Wide Web. Check the listing in the Resource Appendix.

---

glare, semi-gloss, or gloss finishes. Fitzgerald's water-based Color Coat products can be used with leather as well as plastic and vinyl.

Even though the coloring system may allow a good match with an interior's existing color scheme, you won't be satisfied recoloring a single covering — one door panel, for example. As a rule, all coverings of similar function have to be refinished together. Seat coverings that are multi-colored or a combination of vinyl or leather and cloth present the added challenge of masking areas where the color treatment won't be applied.

Seat belts can be recolored using the same process, as can vinyl tops (both convertibles and top coverings), top boots, spare tire covers — any vinyl, plastic, or leather application on the car. Keep in mind that recoloring can be used to create a distinctive — even dramatic — color effect.

Soft plastic or vinyl interior coverings, like this convertible top boot, can be renewed with coloring products specially formulated for this use. Most manufacturers of automotive refinishing products carry vinyl color systems in their line-up.

Primer Coatings

Primer coatings are applied in different layers: first the base primer, then the primer surfacer, and finally the sealer. Each coating has a separate purpose. The base primer offers corrosion resistance and adhesion. The primer surfacer fills surface imperfections, while the sealer helps prepare a strong bond with the color finish.

Depending on one's familiarity with the auto refinishing process, the coating that underlies a color finish might be thought of as a "one-size-fits-all" product that does everything needed to prepare an acceptable base. In automotive painting, however, the primer performs a number of functions, typically accomplished through three primer coatings. Collectively, the primer coatings are called "undercoats" and perform five functions.

Function 1: seal metal substrates. Corrosion results from a metal's desire to return to its natural oxide state. To prevent this natural corrosion process from occurring, the metal's surface has to be sealed against moisture. As long as this seal remains intact, the "corrosion batteries" that "spark" the metal's oxidation (rusting) process are not able to develop. Some primers contain zinc which can be "sacrificed" to the corrosion process, instead of the metal.

Function 2: create a bond with the substrate. Some primers chemically roughen the surface for a stronger bond.

Function 3: provide a bonding link with other coatings. Traditional painting products (lacquer and enamel) bond mechanically — meaning that the painting layers physically "interlock." Modern catalyzed painting products bond chemically making the link essentially unbreakable.

Function 4: fill surface blemishes. High build (also called high solids) primers spray at least twice the thickness of normal paint. This thick coating can be sanded to fill minor blemishes.

Function 5: seal old finishes against color bleed and solvent penetration. When painting over an existing finish, it's important to prevent solvents in the fresh coatings from penetrating the old paint — especially if the old coatings are lacquer or enamel which can be softened or "melted" with solvent.

Achieving all of these functions calls for three different primer products: base primers, primer surfacers, and primer sealers.

Base primers provide corrosion resistance and strong adhesion to the underlying surface, whether bare substrate or an old paint coating that's been properly prepared. Usually the base primer is not sanded. When selecting a base primer, the following factors need to be considered: 1) type of substrate, steel, aluminum, plastic or fiberglass; 2) condition of the substrate, bare or old finish; 3) choice of topcoat system — single-stage color, base coat/clear coat, or specialty coating.

Note: The primers discussed in this chapter are not intended for use over rust. For corrosion problems, see rust removal techniques and paint over rust products described in Chapter 6.

While base primers vary with manufacturer, common types and their applications include:

- Self-etching primer — used over bare steel or aluminum substrate

If the old finish or an earlier primer layer has been sanded, wipe off sanding dust before recoating.

An air gun helps blow dust and debris out of body seams.

that has not been sandblasted or treated with metal conditioner. Also recommended over body filler.

- Corrosion resistant primer — used over sanded original finish or cleaned bare metal. Depending on manufacturer's recommendations, galvanized steel may require prior treatment with metal conditioner.
- Urethane primer — used over bare metal and fiberglass, but not over plastic. Works as primer, primer surfacer, and primer sealer, all in one product.
- Epoxy primer — used over virtually all prepared surfaces. Has superior adhesion and corrosion-resistance. Requires a catalyst.
- Plastics primer — used with plastic and rubber.

Primer surfacers help fill surface imperfections and must be sanded. Considerations in selecting a primer surfacer are the product's compatibility with both the base primer and topcoat system, build capacity (thickness of the coating), and tinting capability. Some base primers can also function as primer surfacers, either by building up several coatings or by varying the mixing ratio. Likewise, some products specifically designated primer surfacers can be mixed for normal or high build. The thicker "high build" coating allows heavier sanding to fill surface blemishes. Tinting capability is advantageous for two reasons: 1) tinting improves color coverage and depth when topcoating with base coat/clear coat systems, and 2) tinting allows "color sanding,

" to help spot surface flaws.

Primer sealers improve adhesion of the topcoat, assure a uniform color base, and prevent bleeding from underlying coatings. Sealers and their use are discussed in detail in Chapter 11.

APPLYING PRIMER COATINGS

Before applying any primer product, it's important to read the manufacturer's Product Information sheet. Here you'll find a short statement of the product's characteristics and intended use, necessary preparation steps, mixing ratio and pot life, spraying technique and recommended drying times, recoat time frame, compatible base and topcoatings, product color, any applicable restrictions (such as incompatibility with additives), and basic safety instructions. Detailed safety instructions are found on the can labels and the Material Safety Data sheet. Both Product Information and Material Safety Data sheets are available from the painting products distributor. You'll also find Product Information sheets for many automotive refinishing products on the World Wide Web, either by searching on a topic like Automotive Refinishing or by looking directly at the refinishing manufacturer's website. What makes the Product Information sheets so valuable is that the application details vary for each product.

Let's say you're priming bare metal that has been prepared by chemical stripping and sanding. Your painting products retailer has recommended using a self-

etching primer. Several refinishing manufacturers offer equivalent products, but for this example, we'll use a PPG product, DX 1791. The Product Information sheet describes this product as being fast drying and providing excellent adhesion and corrosion resistance. Further, it is compatible with virtually all topcoats and intended for use over bare metal — ideal in all aspects for the application at hand. So we've got the right product, now we'll look at the Product Information sheet for instructions about the primer's use.

Mixing Ratio

The Product Information sheet reviews preparation steps for priming over bare substrate (as described in Chapter 6) and recommends (though it doesn't require) wiping down the painting surfaces with metal treatment product. This step is not required because of this primer's "self-etching" capability, meaning the formula includes a metal conditioner. Next comes the mixing ratio, which for this product is 1:1 with a corresponding catalyst. Where the mixing combination is paint and solvent, painters are sometimes haphazard, filling the spray gun cup part way with painting product, then pouring in solvent until the mix flows at the right consistency from the stirring stick. Such haphazard practices should not be used when reducing painting products with solvent and definitely do not apply when mixing with a catalyst. The wrong amount of catalyst can cause a number of problems from shrinkage, cracking, to

It's good practice to wipe down the surface with wax and grease remover before applying any coatings.

Tires should be draped with covers or coated with a sprayable masking.

the primer remaining gummy — none of which are easy to correct. It's extremely important that the mixing ratio be exact. At a minimum, the products being mixed should be carefully measured by volume using the gradations on a chemist's measuring bowl (available from photographic supply stores) to make sure the mixing ratio is correct. Mixing scales, available from automotive painting products suppliers, assure a more accurate mix.

Once mixed, catalyzed products have a "pot life" after which they can no longer be used and have to be discarded. For our example, PPG DX 1791 Self-Etching Primer, the pot life is 8 hours at 70 degrees F., meaning that all mixed product has to be sprayed within that time frame. PPG lists pot life and other critical times at a stable temperature of 70 degrees F. Some other manufacturers set pot life at a warmer 77 degrees F. In warmer temperatures, the pot life expires sooner. Colder temperatures extend the pot life, though most automotive refinishing products should not be sprayed at temperatures below 65 degrees F.

Be sure to wear a proper respirator for the product you are spraying.

Spraying Technique and Drying Times

For self-etching primer, PPG recommends air pressure settings between 35 and 40 psi for conventional spraying and 5 to 10 psi at the gun for HVLP. The coating should be light enough to "see through," giving the substrate a slight yellowish tint. Sags or drips are evidence that the primer is being applied too wet, or the spray gun is being held too close, or gun movement is too slow. Since this primer is only intended as a base coating, it must be sealed before the color finish can be applied. A 10 minute drying time at 70 degrees F. is required before self-etching primer can be recoated with a primer surfacer or sealer. If any sags or drips appear in the coating, the primer should be firm enough to sand after one hour.

With traditional painting products, painters concerned themselves with drying times only for recoating and sanding. Today's two-part refinishing products that use a catalyst for drying (curing or hardening), require attention be paid as well to the "recoating window," a period after which the coating has hardened to the point that other topcoats no longer bond. When the "recoat window" closes, options typically are to sand and recoat with the same product — additional steps that are avoided by observing the recoating time window. If a catalyzed coating has hardened over an extended period, let's say 6 months, sanding the coating may feel like you're trying to roughen up granite. It's best not to miss the recoat window, which means planning the priming and topcoating sequence so that all coatings are applied before their respective recoat windows expire. This "long

view" of the painting sequence was unheard of before the advent of catalyzed paints. In the decades of lacquer and enamel paints, a car might sit for years in primer before receiving its color finish — with no ill effects unless moisture had penetrated the primer coating. Today, a lapse of even 6 months could make preparations for topcoating more difficult than readying the old finish for priming. With PPG's Self-Etching primer, the recoat window is 24 hours at 70 degrees F.

You'll also want to check the Product Information sheet for tinting and additive compatibility. Tinting is useful both with primer surfacers to create a color guide for sanding and with sealers to help with topcoat coverage. Color tinting primers as a guide for sanding is described in detail in the next chapter, but briefly stated works like this. A high-build coating of primer surfacer is applied uniformly to all painting surfaces. Then, as soon as the recoating window opens (drying times vary with the primer product), a thin "guide coat" of contrasting color primer (gray over red or vice versa) or tinted primer (dark over light or vice versa) is sprayed on. As this guide coat is sanded, spots where the contrasting color quickly shows through reveal high points that need more vigorous sanding. Spots where the guide color remains show low points that need to be filled. Possibly, two or three high build/guide coatings may be needed — with sanding between applications — to cut down the ridges and fill the cavities for a uniformly smooth surface ready for topcoating. Without the guide coat, you'll find the microscopic surface variations difficult to detect, though they'll show up under the gloss of a professionally applied color finish.

Since PPG's Self-Etching Primer is intended as a base coat, it does not have tinting or additive compatibility.

Additives, where they apply, might include a hardener, accelerator (to speed drying), or a flexibilizer. Product information sheets for the additives will list the primers with which these products are compatible.

Safety Precautions

Detailed guidelines for spraying and handling painting products are found on the container label and Material Safety Data sheets, also available from the supplier. It's important to read and follow the safety instructions — which at a minimum will require a respirator, face mask, and full clothing, and may require an external air supply. Keep in mind that most automotive refinishing products need to be considered hazardous materials if spilled. Instructions on cleaning up spilled paint chemicals are presented in Chapter 2.

APPLYING PRIMER SURFACERS

While most bonding primers do not require sanding, primer surfacers are used so that they can be sanded, their thick coating filling small flaws that would otherwise be noticeable in the final finish. The next chapter discusses the use of fillers and sanding techniques.

Like base primers, refinishing manufacturers offer several primer surfacer products. Both the supplier's recommendation and the Product Information sheets can guide you in selecting the right primer surfacer for your painting application. Types of primer surfacer products and their characteristics include:

- Multi-purpose primer surfacer — offers fast drying and no shrinkage. For use under acrylic lacquer or enamel topcoats.
- Acrylic primer surfacer — offers fast film build and compatibility with most topcoat systems.
- Urethane primer surfacer — combines fast build with strong adhesion, easy sanding, superior color holdout, and no shrinkage. Some urethane primers offer the flexibility of serving as a sealer for the topcoat and can be mixed with flex additives for paint-

ing plastic and rubber parts.
- Epoxy high build primer — offers wide compatibility with urethane and other coatings. Some epoxy primers are isocyanate-free.

Since the base coat primer example above used a self-etching product, we'll follow that coating with a compatible urethane primer surfacer. Again, we'll follow the mixing and spraying guidelines from the Product Information sheet. As mentioned in the painting systems discussion in Chapter 4, to assure compatibility all refinishing products are often selected from one manufacturer. However, the primer surfacer chosen for this example is from a different manufacturer, Matrix System Manufacturing, and selected to illustrate what this company calls Technical Data sheets.

Preparation for Matrix Systems 2KPB urethane primer surfacer assumes that repaired areas have been base coated with an epoxy primer or fresh metal with a self-etching primer. The next step is mixing the product.

Mixing Ratio

As a high build primer surfacer 2KPB mixes 4:1 with activator. For greater flow-out, at the end of the build-up/sanding process, 2KPB primer surfacer can be reduced 10 percent with a compatible reducer. Additional reduction allows the product to serve as a primer sealer. This mixing flexibility also allows some base primer products to serve as high build primer surfacers, and with an epoxy primer such as PPG's DP 40 to function as a sealer. These mixing variations and additional product functions are detailed on the Product Information or Technical Data sheets.

Once mixed, this urethane primer surfacer has a pot life of only 1 to 2 hours at 77 degrees F. Such a short pot life means everything needs to be ready to spray when the paint is mixed.

Spraying Technique and Drying Times

For 2KPB urethane primer surfacer, Matrix Systems recommends air pressure settings between 40 and 50 psi at the gun for conventional spraying and 5 to 10 psi when using HVLP. "Flash time" between coats is 10 to 15 minutes. A dry-

To avoid drips and sags, the spray gun is typically held 8-10 inches from the painting surface.

Often you'll spray a thin guide coat of contrasting color primer to reveal high and low spots when sanding.

When priming body panels such as fenders separate from the car you'll want to use a support that will hold the part from tipping or falling.

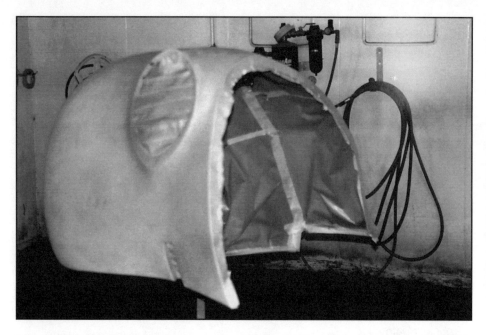

Where different topcoatings are used, surfaces such as the undersides of a fender as shown here may be masked during the priming process — either to avoid expiration of the "recoat window" or to allow for color tinting.

Spot repairs have to be primed to prepare a base for the new finish.

ing time of 4-5 hours at 77 degrees F. is recommended before sanding. If recoating is needed for additional buildup, a 30 minute drying period is recommended. If recoating occurs after 8 hours, the surface must first be sanded. (The recoat window for this product is very short.)

When needed, Matrix Systems' urethane primer surfacer can be mixed with an accelerator (the mixing ratio is up to 1/2 fluid ounces of accelerator per sprayable quart). Adding the accelerator shortens drying time and pot life by half. Accelerator additives are used when the temperature is below the recommended 77 degrees or when it is desirable to shorten curing times in order to speed the sanding process. The purpose of an accelerator is not to make the paint sprayable at any temperature. As a rule, professional painting products should not be sprayed below 60 degrees F. Since warmer temperatures hasten curing and the expiration of a paint's pot life, an accelerator would typically be used only when spraying this product at a temperature between 60 and 77 degrees F.

When spraying sandable primers, it's important to check the Product Information or Technical Data sheets for whether tinting is allowed. The 2KPB urethane primer surfacer tints with a universal black tint base. Since this product has a light buff color, spraying a tinted guide coat will give sharp color contrast for "block sanding," a sanding technique

used across doors and fenders to make sure the surface is perfectly smooth with no ridges or valleys. This block sanding process is described in more detail in the next chapter.

Safety Guidelines

The Tech Data sheets for this primer surfacer, as well as other Matrix System products, specifically call for reading the Material Safety Data Sheets (MSDS) before mixing or using the paint and related products. The user is reminded that the material in these products is designed for "...professionally trained personnel using proper equipment under controlled conditions, and is not intended for sale to the general public." Even professionals can get careless. It's important to read the safety instructions, both from the product label and the MSDS, before using any automotive refinishing product.

DEALING WITH RUNS AND SAGS

Although runs and sags on vertical surfaces are possible with topcoats as well as primer coatings, they're especially likely in the primer process because the painter isn't always being as careful with paint buildup and other factors as when topcoating. Causes of runs and sags include the following:

- spraying coatings too thick
- holding the spray gun too close to

the painting surface
- mixing an incorrect ratio or painting product and catalyst or reducer
- using a hardener or reducer intended for warm temperatures when spraying in a colder temperature or using a drying retarder in colder temperatures
- painting below 65 degrees ambient temperature
- allowing too little flash time between coats

Runs or sags that occur during priming are easy to correct. Simply wait until the coating has dried and sand the run smooth with the surrounding surface. In topcoats, runs are more difficult to repair and may require recoating.

Although runs and sags are avoided by doing the opposite of the list above, specific prevention techniques include:

- hold the spray gun the recommended 8 to 10 in. distance from the painting surface
- make sure the hardener/reducer matches the spraying conditions
- check the flash time on the Product Information sheet and observe this time frame when recoating
- if you're using a mixing method that's giving incorrect results, use a viscosity cup to make sure the paint has the proper ratio or product and catalyst or reducer

Fortunately, primer coatings are very forgiving. Spraying the various under-

SPECIALIZED UNDERCOATINGS

Besides the primers available from your refinishing suppliers, you may find some of the specialized undercoat products helpful — especially where rust has been a problem or the metal has been repaired. These specialty products include:

Corroless rust stabilizer and POR-15 — these "paint over rust" products were described in Chapter 6. These products are used as an alternative to abrasive blasting or chemical derusting in that they convert active surface rust to an inert seal-in chemical and seal the surface against moisture and other agents that could re-start the corrosion cycle.

Cold galvanizing — not a paint, but a compound used when repairing galvanized metal. Since welds can be made through this compound, it is ideal as corrosion prevention around metal repairs. Cold galvanizing is also ideal for treating inside surfaces of replacement panels that will not be painted.

Rubberized undercoating — ideal for coating the undersides of fenders that lack inner wheel wells (the types of fenders used on cars and trucks through the 1950s and on all original-style VW "Beetles"). The rubberized coating deflects small pebbles and other road debris without impacting the metal and damaging the paint.

Gravel Guard — a chip-resistant coating intended to replace the rough texture/impact resistant paint applied by the factory to rocker panels and lower sections of fenders and doors. Sold under various names (PPG calls its product RoadGuard), the coating is applied over a sanded OEM finish or primer and must be topcoated. Texture and thickness vary with the amount of solvent, enabling a single product to match various texture OEM coatings.

Note: POR-15 is available from POR-15, Inc. (See Resource Appendix for address). Gravel Guard, sold under various trade names, is available from your refinishing supplier. Other special undercoatings are available from The Eastwood Company.

Corroless rust stabilizer is compatible with most automotive enamel and urethane paints and can be topcoated if desired. Photo courtesy The Eastwood Co.

coats gives an opportunity not just to correct errors, but more importantly to practice and develop spray painting techniques so that mistakes like runs and sags that could spoil the color finish don't happen in the final coatings.

SPECIALTY PRIMER PRODUCTS

Although most paint manufacturers' primer products cover a range of applications and needs, for special conditions you may want to use a primer product outside the paint system you've selected. Examples are special purpose primers and other refinishing products from Restorer's Choice, whose high quality paints are often used on restoration and custom show cars.

Restorer's Choice primers, which are compatible with other manufacturer's paint systems, include a fast dry, low overspray primer called "Fat Bunny," which is ideal for spot repair. The high build primer "Sumo Usagi" also has self-etching and sealer capabilities making it an all-purpose three-in-one polyester epoxy. Another specialty product, "Body Cavity Etch Primer," is often used in restoration to seal and counteract surface rust inside fender wells, door cavities, and inner quarter panels. The product also works well on mildly rusted or sandblasted frames.

The repair needs to feather into the surrounding finish.

Primer is a "working" coating intended to provide a smooth base for the finish

In addition to selecting from the various primers offered by your painting manufacturer and available from your local retailer, you may also want to investigate what other specialty products are available, especially those suited to your priming and painting. Your best source of information on these specialty products, other than tips given in this book, is to search the world wide web. Some companies are listed in the Resource Appendix.

Do-It-Yourself Guide to CUSTOM PAINTING

Sanding and Filling

This fender was "new-old-stock"(meaning it had sat in a dealer's inventory and had never been on a car). Nonetheless, it had minor damage from handling which would require filling, as would the seam around the plate being welded for a signal light cutout.

Experienced refinishers will tell you: the final finish is only as flawless as the primer coating it covers. In order to arrive at a glossy base for the finish coatings, any imperfections — such as sanding scratches, pits, ridges, or ripples — have to be filled and sanded. Most of the filling and sanding occurs during the primer surfacer stage of the undercoating process.

As discussed in the previous chapter, high build primer surfacers function as fillers by laying a thick, soft coating that is easily sanded. If the base substrate hasn't needed repair and the painting surface is either smooth metal or an intact OEM finish that has been prepared by sanding, then a single high build coating should provide a sufficiently flawless base for the color finish. However, if repair work has left grinding marks and deep sand scratches, or if paint and rust removal processes have roughened the surface, then several coats of high build

primer, multiple sanding steps, and possibly spot applications of glazing putty may be needed to create a surface smooth enough for finish painting.

SANDING MATERIALS AND TECHNIQUES

Just as painting products and how they're applied has changed dramatically in recent years, so too have the materials and techniques used in smoothing the undercoat base. Sanding used to be done almost exclusively with sandpaper. Now, along with sandpaper, refinishers use Scotchbrite pads, sanding pastes, and sanding lubricants. The sandpaper is different too, with manufacturers switching to a European standard for grading the abrasiveness of the sandpaper. The same numbering system for the various grits, or coarseness of the sandpaper, continues to be used, but the new standards provide addi-

tional in-between grits. Sandpaper from a European supplier typically has a P in front of the grade number. If your refinishing supplier stocks the European products, you'll want to select a sandpaper one or two grits finer than the older U.S. type you may be used to for the same sanding effect. For example, a P prefix 1200 grit sandpaper would be comparable to a U.S. 600 grade. The American corporation 3M manufacturers its automotive sandpapers to the European P-grade standard, but adheres to the familiar numbering system. Accordingly, a 3M P-600 sandpaper gives the same finish as a regular 600 grade sandpaper.

The sandpaper used with automotive refinishing differs substantially from sandpaper intended for household use. The more abrasive "dry" sandpaper comes in sheets sized to fit various length sanding blocks and can be purchased with adhesive backing that holds the sandpaper to the block.

The fender now has a light "skim coating" of filler across the entire repair area.

The sanding area can conveniently be kept wet by squirting water from a dish soap container.

The finer grit "wet/dry" sandpaper has a special paper backing that softens, but doesn't tear or crumble when immersed in water and holds its grit.

WET SANDING

Using lubricants (typically water) in the sanding process helps prevent loose grit and pigment from scratching the sanding surface. It also extends the life of the sandpaper by washing away sanding residue. Wet sanding is done like this:

1 Crease a sheet of sandpaper in the middle (across the shorter width), tear along the crease, then fold in thirds. This makes a convenient size to wrap over a sanding block.
2 Fill a bucket with water and place convenient to the sanding surface.
3 Wet the sanding surface with water. (A sponge or shop towel makes a convenient applicator.)
4 Immerse the sandpaper in water.
5 Sand longitudinally (along the car's length) using long strokes on wide surfaces.
6 Immerse the sandpaper frequently in water to wash off loose grit and pigment. Wash the sanding surface as needed to help with lubrication and remove grit and pigment buildup.
7 Wash the surface after sanding. Often the sandpaper can be reused if rinsed in water and unfolded to dry.

Sandpaper should be wrapped around some type of flat surface, rather than held against the palm and fingers of your hand. The reason is obvious when you look at your hand palm side up. The fingers are all curved surfaces and the palm is concave. Using your hand as backing for the sandpaper will cut tiny grooves in the sanding surface. Instead, use a flat object — such as a plastic spreader for filler, a section of a paint stirring stick, or a sanding block made for this purpose and available from the refinishing supplier.

BLOCK SANDING

Different surfaces call for sanding blocks of different sizes and different hardness. Essentially flat surfaces can be sanded using hard blocks. Contoured surfaces require softer, more flexible blocks. Block sanding is done like this:

1 Wrap or clamp the sandpaper to the block. Avoid ragged edges to the sandpaper that can gouge the sanding surface.
2 If wet sanding, immerse the sandpaper and block in water or sanding fluid.
3 Sand longitudinally (along the length of the vehicle) in one direction. **Note:** Sanding in only one direction becomes more important with later sanding steps using finer grit sand-paper.
4 Use increasingly higher number

The filler is block sanded with 220 grit sandpaper.

As much as possible, sanding is done longitudinally — along the length of the part or vehicle.

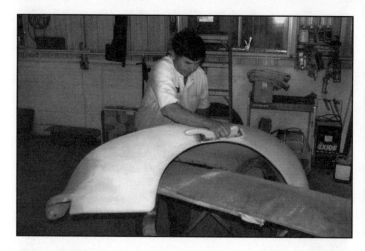

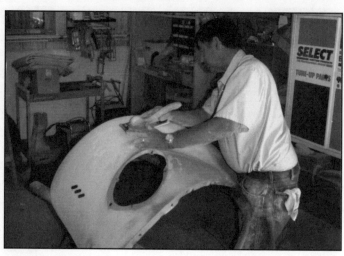

With a flexible body part like a fender, it's important to construct a support platform that will hold the item securely and fairly rigid.

You'll use a sanding block even on curved surfaces.

(milder grit) sandpaper as the surface becomes smoother. The finer sandpaper will remove scratch marks from the coarser grits. Final wet sanding before applying sealer is typically done with 400 or 600 grit sandpaper.

Although sanding is normally done longitudinally across the body surface, sometimes panels need to be sanded up-and-down, as well as across, to assure a smooth surface without bulges or ripples. This is especially the case over repair areas like patch panel seams.

CROSS-BLOCK SANDING

If a panel has had repair work to smooth a dent or replace rusted metal, horizontal sanding may still leave ridges or ripples in the surface. To ensure a smooth surface, the panel should be block sanded both horizontally (lengthwise with the vehicle) and vertically (up-and-down). When cross-block sanding, do the up-and-down strokes first and follow with the horizontal sanding. An additional coating of primer surfacer, sanded longitudinally (lengthwise with the vehicle) may be needed to remove marks from the vertical sanding.

FEATHER-EDGE SANDING

When spot repairs cut into an existing finish, it's necessary to sand the finish so that it tapers gradually into the repair. The taper, or feather-edge, extends in all directions from the spot where the finish has been abraded for the repair. A sanding block or power sander should be used to keep the feather-edge uniformly smooth. When the spot repair is coated with primer surfacer, the filler coating will extend over the area of the finish that has been feather-edge sanded. The spot repair can then be brought to the same level as the surrounding finish by block sanding.

POWER SANDING

Hand sanding one or more primer surfacer coatings can be tedious and time-consuming. A dual action (D/A) sander (when using a soft or tapered pad) can substitute for hand sanding. Be sure the tool selected can be used for wet sanding. Guidelines when machine sanding include:

• decrease the speed next to body

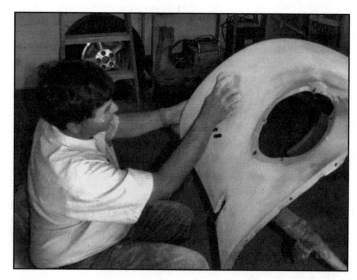

To prevent ridges, a smaller sanding block is now used and the direction is now across the fender instead of lengthwise.

Professional shops use power sanders coupled to a vacuum system that removes hazardous filler and paint dust.

A technique for noticing blemishes in the surface is to dust on a contrasting color primer coating. Blemishes show up as spots of different color as the surface is sanded.

The contrasting color primer has been applied here in areas where slight irregularities have been detected.

lines and in tight spots
- don't use a hard pad that can gouge the soft primer coating
- hold the sander flat with the sanding surface
use light to medium pressure, letting the tool do the work

COLOR SANDING

High build primer coatings serve their filling and smoothing function well; they apply relatively easily and are soft and easily sanded. But the dried coating has a dull finish which makes blemishes hard to see. Often you can feel irregularities like waves in the surface, abrupt edges around a repair spot, grinding gouges, and deeper pits by running your fingers lightly across the coating. Good lighting, preferably sunlight, will help make most blemishes visible. But the easiest way to detect flaws while sanding is to spray a color guide coat.

Color or guide coat sanding follows these steps.

Step 1. After the high build primer surfacer has dried, and within the allowable recoat time, spray a light coating of a contrasting color primer. Where compatible primers are available in light and dark colors, tan and red for example, the light colored product would typically be applied first then guide coated with the darker product. With tintable primer surfacers, the guide coat is easily created using the same product, simply by adding contrasting color tint.

Step 2. When the guide coat has dried, it is wet sanded using a sanding block and 400 or 600 grit sandpaper. As the sanding cuts through the guide coat, high and low spots as well as grinding marks, pits, even scratches from earlier sanding become easily visible.

Step 3. If the blemishes are deep, they should be filled with a thin coating of polyester glazing putty, which — depending on the product — can be either brushed on or applied with a plastic squeegee. When the glazing putty dries, it is sanded using a hard sanding block for flat surfaces, a flexible block for contours.

Step 4. Sand scratches and other minor blemishes can be filled with an additional coating of high build primer surfacer.

Color guide coats tell the truth about the surface preparation. When the color coating sands smoothly and evenly with 600 or finer sandpaper, with no indications of surface irregularities, you will know that the preparation process has been successful and you're ready for the next step: applying the primer sealer.

SANDPAPER SUBSTITUTES

As an alternative for fine 600 or 1000 grit sandpaper, Scotchbrite pads may be used to lightly smooth the surface in preparation for finishing painting. These pads are color coded to the type and coarseness of abrasive. The pads we're talking about are specially

designed for automotive refinishing — not housewares products from a discount mart — and are available from painting products suppliers who can select the correct pad for the sanding operation.

Scotchbrite automotive sanding pads are also used to scuff up a plastic substrate or a color finish in preparation for priming and refinishing. Also, Scotchbrite pads are used to lightly abrade a catalyzed coating that has been allowed to dry beyond the recoat time frame. As catalyzed refinishing products dry, their surface hardens causing possible adhesion problems. Lightly scuffing a hardened coating with a Scotchbrite pad can provide enough surface roughness to good adhesion and chemical bonding.

Sanding paste is also gaining favor as a sandpaper substitute, especially where a very fine abrasive is called for, such as spot repairs and blend areas. The term sanding paste is generic; you'll find this product sold under various names (PPG calls its sanding paste "Final Scuff"). Your refinishing supplier should be able to recommend a product and provide instructions for its use.

While water is used most commonly as a sanding lubricant, wax and grease remover can also be used as a wet sanding lubricant, and may be more effective than water when sanding out defects. Examples of painting defects where you may want to use wax and grease remover as the sanding lubricant include drips or sags and

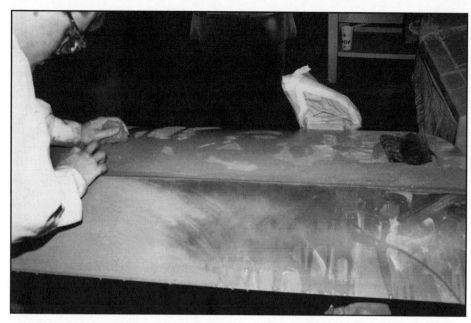

Wet sanding helps prevent loose grit and pigment from scratching the sanding surface. It also extends the life of the sandpaper and reduces sanding dust.

Small, spot imperfections are filled with glazing putty. Like body filler, modern putty products also mix with hardener.

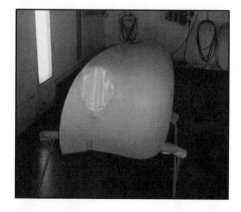

Glazing putty is sanded with milder grit paper and does not require additional priming.

The contrasting color primer is wet sanded using a sanding block and mild 400-600 grit sandpaper.

trapped dirt or insects. Wet sanding to remove these common defects can be done in the sealer, color, or clear stages of the finish application.

SANDING DOS AND DON'TS

- Be sure to clean the surface before sanding. Areas being wet sanded can be rinsed lightly with water. Always prep an old finish with wax and grease remover before sanding.
- When wet sanding, keep the wet sanding bucket filled with clean water. Dump and refill the bucket when the water becomes cloudy with sanding residue.
- When dry sanding, blow off sanding dust frequently using an air gun attachment in the shop's air line. Important: wear a dust mask.
- Don't hand sand without a sanding block.
- Don't use hard, inflexible pads when machine sanding.

FILLING BLEMISHES

While high build primer surfacer will serve as the filler for most surface blemishes, pits in derusted metal, grinding gouges, or other deeper flaws may need a light coating of filler. Refinishers use two types of filler:

- **Body filler** — used over either properly cleaned, bare substrate or epoxy primer and covers slight imperfections remaining after dent or rust repair
- **Glazing putty** — applied over any primer coating, or directly over body filler, and intended for spot imperfections.

Many refinishers will apply a very light skim coating of body filler over sandblast pits or other roughness in the surface that could be filled either with high build primer surfacer or glazing putty because body filler is a more shrink-resistant coating.

In the days of lacquer paints, a red putty, which was actually a non-dilute primer that could be squeezed out of a tube and applied with a rubber squeegee, was commonly used for filling defects in the primer coating. Today, polyester glazing putties have replaced the older lacquer-based red putty, mainly because of better compatibility with modern paints but also due to improvements in shrinkage and less risk of color staining in the finish coating.

Like other catalyzed refinishing products, body filler and most glazing putties mix with hardener, which is squeezed from a toothpaste-type tube. The hardener has a contrasting color (red or blue) and a uniform tint indicates thorough mixing. Proper mixing is important as over-catalyzed filler can bleed its color through the

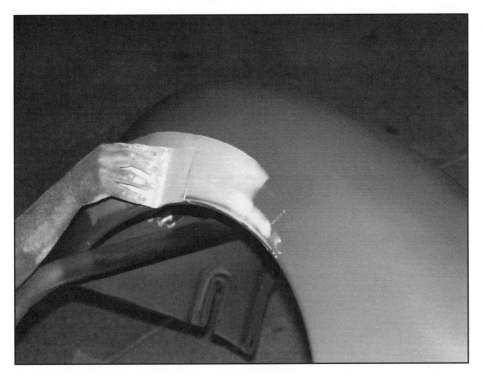

Filler is applied in a light coating (not exceeding 1/8 in.), but over a wider area than just the imperfections. Filler is applied with a flexible plastic spreader.

spread thin, not exceeding 1/8 in. Although filler can be applied directly to bare metal, over time it can have a corrosive effect, so the recommended sequence is to coat the bare substrate with epoxy primer, then apply the filler coating. Body filler should not be applied either to an old finish or other primer coatings.

When set up, body filler is dry sanded with 220 grit sandpaper (using a sanding block) and then coated with self-etching primer. To remove sand scratches from the more abrasive 220 sandpaper, two or three coats of high build primer surfacer are typically applied over the self-etching primer either dry or wet sanded. Glazing putty does not require an additional primer coating. If used at the end of the surface preparation process, glazing putty can be seal coated and finish painted.

PREVENTING COLOR STAINS FROM BODY FILLER

finish. Under-catalyzed filler causes other problems. It's also important to use filler that's fresh. Old filler that's been sitting on your shop shelf should be discarded. When purchasing body filler, buy a quality product from your refinishing supplier — not a no-brand filler from a discount mart — and check the expiration date on the can. If the date is coded, ask the supplier to read it for you.

The filler or putty needs to be

While sealer is effective in "locking" glazing putty so that the product's color doesn't show in the finish coating, body fillers can "stain" the final finish. The problem is not uncommon

Each filler coating is block sanded.

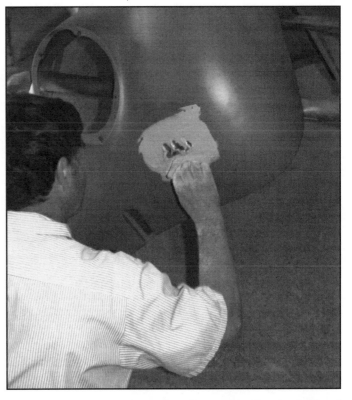

After initial sanding, the surface is reprimed and additional filler applied where needed.

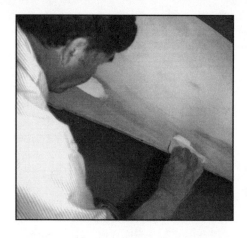

Glazing putty is applied only to small imperfections.

A piece of cardboard serves as the putty palette.

and can be a nightmare if the filler's yellow-brown tint begins to show through a gleaming silver paint job.

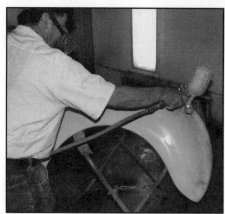

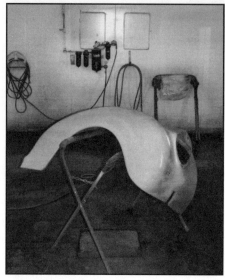

Using lighter colored sealer helps hide the primer for the finish coating.

When staining occurs, it can be traced to one of two causes. The most common is using too much hardener when

mixing the filler; the other is use of a lacquer finish. It's common to think that the amount of hardener only effects the set-up time, but too little hardener can affect the filler's strength and too much can result in color bleeding through to the final finish. With lacquer being phased out as an automotive finish, too much hardener is the more likely cause of this staining process.

PREPARATION MAKES PERFECTION

This is the stage that establishes the quality base for the final finish, so it's important that no steps be skipped. The process can be tedious and time-consuming, with extra high build priming and sanding seeming to improve the preparation base only marginally. However, blemishes that appear small and insignificant in primer can magnify in a glossy finish. Patience and perseverance are the keys to achieving your goal — a primer base so smooth that it could be clear coated and only color would be lacking. To achieve absolute smoothness, the final primer surfacer coating is often micro sanded with 1200 or 1500 grit sandpaper.

Now only one step remains in the preparation process, sealing the primer coating. Sealers and their application are the subject of the next chapter.

Sanding and filling is a time-consuming process intended to produce a surface that is entirely free of defects.

After priming and filling, the surface is ready for sealing—the last step in the priming preparation process.

Plastic Filler Application

Plastic filler is used to fill small dents (not exceeding 1/8-inch), left after you have straightened a large dent. To apply plastic filler, you will need a mixing board, putty knife, spreader, plastic filler, and a tube of hardener. All these items can be purchased at your local auto supply store.

Application of filler involves four steps: (1) mixing, (2) applying the bond coat, (3) applying the fill coat, and (4) applying the finish coat. Mix the filler and hardener on the mixing board (a sheet of heavy cardboard or masonite roughly 12" x 18" works well) by folding and spreading the filler with a putty knife. Do not stir the filler because this causes air bubbles.

When the filler has been mixed to uniform color, a very thin bond coat is applied to the damaged area. Be sure to press down hard on the spreader in order to force the filler into scratches in the metal, assuring a good bond -- hence the name "bond" coat.

By the time you've cleaned your tools, the bond coat will be set and you can apply the fill coat. This time apply slight pressure with the spreader over the damaged area and harder pressure over the good metal adjacent to the dent. More than one fill coat may be necessary.

Now you are ready to apply the finish coat. This is applied much like the bond coat, but can be thicker. After application of this coat, the filler should be above the contour of the undamaged metal. After the filler sets up (about ten minutes) it is ready for smoothing and sanding.

MIKE BARNES

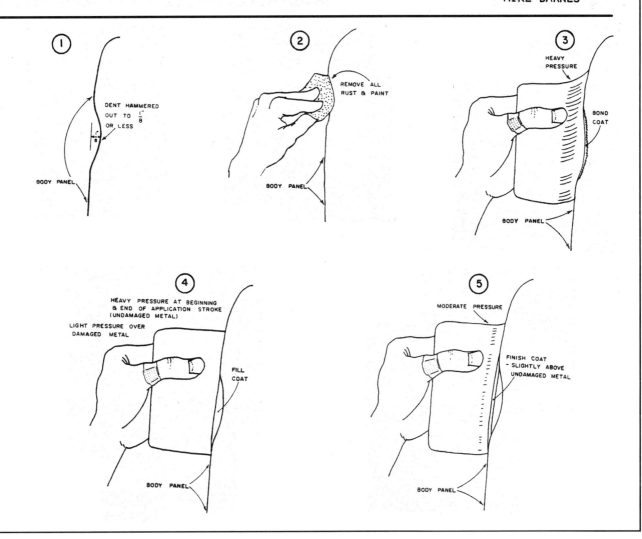

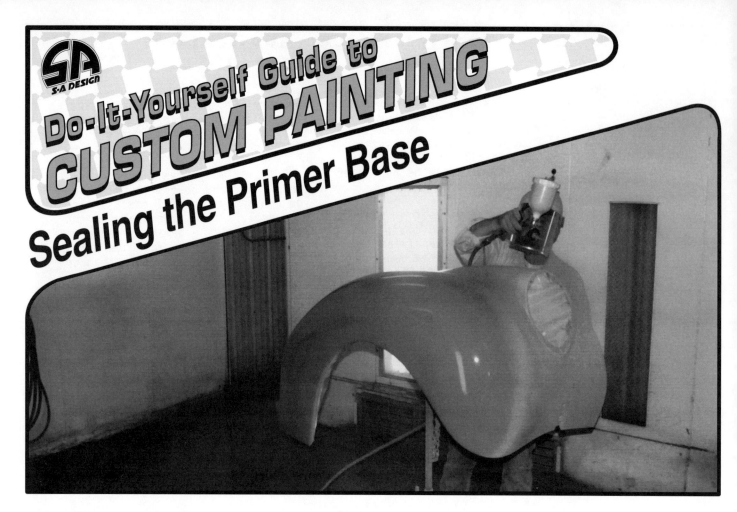

Do-It-Yourself Guide to
CUSTOM PAINTING
Sealing the Primer Base

Although the sealer coating may be optional, skipping the primer sealer step is very short-sighted. Among sealer's benefits, the coating helps improve topcoat adhesion, improves color holdout, and prevents sanding scratches from showing in the finish paint.

Before the primer base receives its color finish, it needs to be sealed. The third primer coating, called the sealer or primer sealer, performs this function as well as several others. While a specific sealer product can be used, multi-purpose primers such as PPG's Deltron Urethane Primer can serve as primer, primer surfacer, and primer sealer just by varying the mixing formula. Using a single product throughout the undercoat process has advantages: You become familiar with the product and may save money by buying in larger quantities. However, it's not essential — and indeed may not be desirable — to use a single product for all three undercoat stages. As described in Chapter 10, painting over metal that has been stripped and cleaned (possibly using abrasive blasting) may call for a corrosion resistant primer that does not have sealer properties. Another example would be using a plastics primer to provide strong adhesion to a plastic or rub-

ber substrate. These special-purpose primers may even be compatible with the topcoat you are using, suggesting that a sealer coating is not needed. Nonetheless, sealer should still be used. Similarly, a multi-purpose primer should be mixed to its sealer formula and applied over the ready-to-paint base coatings. To understand the importance of including the sealer step in the undercoat sequence, consider the functions sealer performs.

BENEFITS OF THE PRIMER SEALER COATING

Although a sealer coating may be optional (in cases where the primer base and topcoat are compatible) skipping the primer sealer step is very short-sighted. Among the benefits:

- Sealers improve topcoat adhesion. You can think of the primer sealer coating as an adhesion enhancer for the color finish.

- Sealers help assure a uniform color base. This is especially beneficial over a multi-colored primer base resulting from guide coat sanding or over spot repair of an original finish.

- Many primer sealers can be tinted to match the topcoat color. Tinting not only benefits light colored topcoats, but also helps camouflage stone chips and other minor damage to the finish that is likely to occur as the car is driven.

- Sealers improve color holdout, which means longer life for the color finish.

- Sealers prevent sand scratches from swelling and showing through in the final finish, and <u>very important</u>, sealers keep finish coat solvents from penetrating underlying layers.

- Sealer coatings also help prevent color bleed through. As mentioned in Chapter 10, body filler is one source of color staining. Pigments

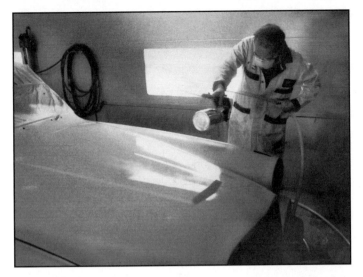

Some sealer products can be color tinted to help with color coverage in a basecoat/clearcoat finish. Color tinting the undercoat also helps hide chips that may occur in the finish paint.

Sealer is the last step in the undercoating process. You'll want to prepare as you would for the finish paint, blowing off all sanding dust and wiping the surface with a tack cloth.

from an earlier, underlying finish can also stain or bleed into a new finish.

While a sealer coating may add marginally to the refinishing expense, its benefits far outweigh the cost, and the step adds minimally to the overall refinishing effort.

APPLYING THE SEALER COATING

Sealer is the last step in the undercoating process, applied only when the primer base is complete and ready for finish painting. If you're doing the undercoat steps yourself and having a professional apply the color finish, you'll want to time the sealer's application with the car's appointment for finish painting to avoid additional sanding (providing the sealer is finish painted within the recoat time window, the sealer coating typically does not require sanding) and other problems likely to occur when the product's recoat window has expired.

Most single-purpose sealers are not intended for use over bare metal, factory finishes, or lacquer refinishes. The Product Information sheet will list these restrictions, along with proper preparation steps. Depending on the sealer product, bare metal may be more or less of a problem. The Product Information sheet may advise priming any bare metal (typically resulting from sanding through the primer surfacer coating) before applying the sealer coating.

Small sand-through spots (less than 4 inches in diameter) may be allowable with larger spots needing priming. Tinting the sealer may affect its ability to cover bare metal, requiring any exposed metal to be primer coated before sealing. Where this is the case, be sure to observe the drying time of the primer coating. Overnight drying may be required before the sealer can be applied.

MIXING FORMULA

If you've used a multi-purpose product for earlier primer coatings, that same product may convert to a sealer simply by modifying the mixing formula. For example, when used as a base primer the mixing ratio may be 1:1 (primer to catalyst), as a sealer the ratio may be 1:1:1/2 (primer to catalyst to thinner). If the sealer coating can be tinted, this will also affect the mixing ratio. When tinting a multi-purpose primer, such as PPG's K36, the formula is likely to have four components (primer-catalyst-thinner-tint color).

Tip: Restorer's Choice has a product called Tigers Claw that allows color paint to be used as an adhesive sealer, or Tigers Claw can be used with the first base coat color to convert it into an adhesive primer sealer.

Even for a single-purpose sealer the mixing formula is likely to include more components, and therefore be more complex, than for a single-purpose

Depending on the sealer product, sand-through spots in the primer and primer surfacer coatings may or may not be a problem. As a general rule, small sand-through spots may be allowable with larger spots needing recoating.

primer or primer surfacer. Besides adhering to the mixing ratio and making sure all mixing components are compatible, it's also important to follow the correct mixing sequence. With tinted sealers, for example, the tint may be added first in a ratio of two parts sealer to one part color. After thorough stirring, the activator may be added at a 1:1 ratio. Skipping the first mixing step and misinterpreting the ratio as a straight 2:1:1 would not produce the correct mix. Similarly, additives such as flex agents for sealing over flexible parts such as bumper fascia need to be included in the mix in the proper sequence as well as the correct amount.

Once mixed, catalyzed products have a relatively short pot life (usually just a few hours) so it's important that all preparation steps be completed before mixing the sealer with its activator.

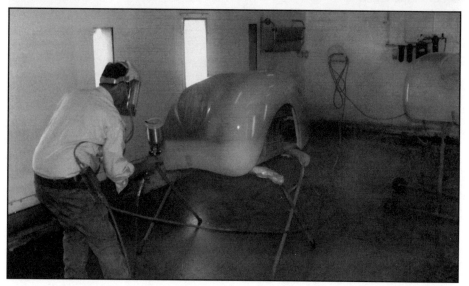

Primer sealers can be applied in two ways: wet-on-wet (meaning the sealer is allowed to set up, but not dry thoroughly before topcoating) or as a barrier coating (in which case the sealer is allowed to dry, then topcoated). Here we see the wet-on-wet sequence with the topcoat color applied as soon as the sealer has become tacky.

For barrier coatings, more sealer is applied and given a longer drying time.

Before applying the sealer coating, use an air gun to blow all sanding dust out of creases and crevices in the masking and tape. Depending on the length of time since wet sanding, water may also be trapped in crevices along the edges of the masking. Run the air gun along the taping seams to blow out any moisture. If the air gun has loosened the masking, you may have to retape some of the seams and overlaps. You'll also want to make sure the tape at the edges of the masking is firmly attached and won't lift or blow loose when you spray on the sealer. This done, you can wipe down the painting surfaces with a pre-

paint cleaner (to remove oil from running your hand across the primer surfacer coating to check for smoothness or from handling). As the last preparation step, you'll chase all dust from surfaces to be painted with a tack cloth.

SPRAYING TECHNIQUES

Many primer sealers can be applied two ways: wet-on-wet (meaning the sealer is allowed to set up, but not dry thoroughly before topcoating) or as a barrier coating (in which case the sealer is allowed to dry, then topcoated).

For wet-on-wet, air pressure at the gun is typically set for 40-45 psi when conventional spraying with a siphon feed gun, 30-35 psi with a gravity feed gun, or 5-10 psi for HVLP. *Be sure to check the Product Information sheets for recommended air pressure settings for the sealer product you are using.* Either one wet coat or two medium coats are applied and given only 15 to 20 minutes tack time before topcoating. The short drying time is sufficient to prevent runs or sags from developing, yet allows the color finish to be applied nearly immediately.

For barrier coatings, the air pressure settings remain the same, but more sealer is applied (2-3 coats for nearly twice the build of wet-on-wet) and given a longer drying time, perhaps until nearly to the expiration of the recoat window.

If any slight blemishes appear in the sealer (such as dust particles), the dry coating can be micro-sanded with 2500 grit sandpaper. If this light sanding removes the blemish without cutting through the sealer, wiping with a tack rag is usually all that's required before finish coating. But if any of the primer surfacer has been exposed, then the part or panel should be given another mist coating of sealer, applied slightly thicker over the fill-in spot.

Sealer coatings typically require sanding only if the recoat window has expired. However, certain finishes may require scuff sanding regardless of the recoat time frame. Be sure to read the Product Information sheet for all instructions relating to the sealer's proper application, as well as requirements (time frame and additional sanding steps) before topcoating.

SAFETY GUIDELINES

Sealers require the same safety precautions as other catalyzed painting products. Remember to be alert to the product's pot life, making sure to clean the spray gun thoroughly before the pot life expires (if the sealer hardens in the gun orifices, cleaning may be difficult at best). Treat any left-over product that has been mixed with hardener as hazardous waste and follow proper disposal procedures. Be especially careful cleaning up any spills. Remember, skin contact can be as toxic as inhalation.

INTERRUPTING THE PAINTING SEQUENCE

It's best not to interrupt the painting process at any stage short of the completed color finish. However, when a car is completely disassembled for restoration, or built from a collection of parts as is often the case with street rods, refinishing often proceeds with batches — the body, doors, fenders — at different times and stages of the project. In this setting, a decision has to be made whether to finish paint the various batches of parts separately or to interrupt the painting sequence at the sealer stage, then wait until all preparation work is completed, and finish paint everything at the same time.

Parts such as fenders, doors, and the hood can be finish painted separately from the body and carefully stored for later assembly. In fact, this batch painting approach is common with show cars because it allows all surfaces to be painted — something not easily done with the parts assembled on the car. The question is whether to finish paint all the various parts individually, or to bring parts such as the fenders and hood through the sealer step in the undercoat process and store them for finish painting later. There are benefits and drawbacks to both approaches.

Finishing painting various sheet metal parts individually at different times risks color shifts in the finish. Noticeable color differences are nearly certain to occur if the finish color is mixed fresh for each batch of parts. If you'll be finish painting parts for the car at different times, be sure to have enough paint color mixed at the start for all the parts. You'll only

add catalyst or hardener to the amount of color mix needed for each batch, so you'll be using a consistent color base throughout. However, there's still the possibility of slight color shifts due to painting in different temperature and humidity conditions. You also have to be very careful to store the parts where they won't be scratched and equally careful to avoid scratches in the finish when assembling the parts on the car.

Holding off finish painting until all parts are ready may mean interrupting the painting sequence on some parts at the sealer stage. With modern paints, storing parts that have been sealer coated does not invite the risk of corrosion that was common with lacquer and older enamel primers. These old-style primers which were applied without a sealer coating were water-porous, allowing the metal to rust right through the primer if exposed to moisture or humidity. Today's catalyzed primer sealers form a barrier against moisture, protecting the underlying metal allowing parts to be stored in somewhat humid conditions without rusting. Still, it's not advisable to store sealer coated parts outside.

If the painting sequence is interrupted at the sealer step, the recoat window is certain to expire before the finish coating is applied. This means that the sealer will need to be scuff sanded and recoated to reactivate the recoat window for the color finish. The problem that can occur is a progressive hardening of the sealer coating. While this may not happen with all sealer products, it's a potential with some. A friend found the sealer coating rock hard on his 1950 Plymouth when he got ready to finish paint the car after storing it at sealer stage for several months. (He'd been waiting to make up his mind on the color he wanted for the final finish. Color selection should really come at the start of the refinishing process, as we'll discuss in the next chapter.) Eventually, he got the sealer sanded and recoated, and was able to finish paint the car — but only after expending a degree of effort he hadn't anticipated.

The bottom line: the painting sequence can be interrupted at the sealer stage, but it's not advised. Modern primer coatings don't allow water to penetrate, so the risk isn't of the metal's

When spraying catalyzed sealers, be alert to the product's pot life, making sure to clean the spray gun thoroughly before the pot life expires.

When a car is completely disassembled for restoration or built from a collection of parts as is often the case with street rods, refinishing often proceeds in batches. Where this is the case, parts such as doors can be primed and finish painted separately from the body and stored for later assembly.

rusting, but of the sealer's hardening. However, if the interruption is short — a few days or a couple of weeks — while the car waits its turn for the spray booth and finish painting, then the delay only results in some additional effort to scuff sand and recoat the sealer. The best approach, proceed directly to the finish coating. If the parts need to be stored before assembly, handle them carefully and store them where the finish won't be damaged.

Holding off finish painting until all parts are ready may mean interrupting the painting sequence on some parts at the sealer stage. On this Corvette, the hood is out of sequence in the painting stages from the surrounding panels. By the time the hood is sealed and ready for finish painting, the recoat window on other sealed surfaces will likely have expired, requiring those areas to be scuff sanded and recoated with sealer.

In preparation for the color finish, masking that has been on the car for priming should be replaced with fresh paper and tape. This re-masking step may seem unnecessary, but sanding and overspray dust could blow out of seams and crevices and spoil the finish.

MASKING AND TAPING FOR THE COLOR FINISH

The masking that has been on the car should be replaced with fresh paper and tape for the final finish. This step may seem unnecessary, but the amount of sanding and overspray dust that has collected on the paper and settled into seams and crevices risks some dust and debris blowing out of the masking during finish painting and settling onto the fresh color coating. If you're applying a two-tone finish, the masking needs to be changed anyway (to cover areas that won't be coated with the initial color), so why not remask and retape the vehicle overall.

The same masking techniques described in Chapter 7 apply. Don't mask with newspaper and don't use hardware store or discount mart masking tape. Use tape and masking paper purchased from your automotive refinishing supplier. What's new is masking for two-toning. The color you'll be applying first depends on the painting sequence, which often starts at the top of the vehicle, then proceeds to the hood and works around the lower surfaces from there. In this sequence, if the top and upper body are painted a contrasting (often lighter) color, then the lower body areas that will be painted a different (often darker) color would be masked first.

Where a multi-color finish is being applied as part of a show restoration, one of the "tricks" is knowing where the factory paint shop put the two-tone color lines. If you're painting over an original finish, hopefully you took photos of the car's original state. You can use these to locate the masking lines for the two-toning. If the car had previously been repainted so that the two-tone lines were obliterated, you may have to do some research, looking at photos of original cars from dealer brochures or books, to figure out the correct masking points. Phil Noder, whose national prize-winning 1955 yellow and black Ford convertible is shown in this book, made the assumption that the color line at the front of the car occurred at the fender seam underneath the headlight. So he masked and painted the car accordingly. In show competition he learned that the factory masked the color break slightly away from the seam, and lost points accordingly. Details of this nature often separate the winners from the runners up in national show competitions.

PREPARING FOR FINISH PAINTING

You can save yourself lots of trouble with the color finish if you follow these final preparation steps:
- remask as described above if sanding has been extensive
- thoroughly blow off all surfaces, taking special care to blow dust out of

While the contrasting color often follows trim lines, for a show car it's important to research the color break points. Phil Noder who painted this prize-winning 1955 Ford convertible, assumed the color line under the headlights followed the fender seam. At the factory, the break point was a taped line under the center of the headlight — a small detail that cost a judging point.

By law, all chemical products that contain a hazardous substance as defined by OSHA (Occupational Safety and Health Administration) must be supplied with an MSDS (Material Safety and Data Sheet) document. Commercial shops are required to maintain copies of the MSDS for the products they use.

Painting supplies received via UPS or other shipping methods will have the MSDS packed with the product. You may have to request the MSDS documents for painting supplies purchased from local suppliers. Don't throw these sheets away! They're for your safety and should be read, then placed in an MSDS folder for reference.

Each MSDS document is divided into 9 sections of information.

Section 1: Hazardous Materials lists components above 1% in mixture that present a physical or health hazard. Possible carcinogens are listed if above 0.1% in the mixture. Exposure limitations are for individual components as established by OSHA.

Section 2: Physical and Chemical Properties describes the product's physical appearance as well as color and smell.

Section 3: Fire and Explosion Hazard Data tells what type of extinguisher to use in the event of fire as well as possible hazardous products resulting from burning.

Section 4: Reactivity Hazard Data explains conditions to avoid to prevent hazardous reactions.

Section 5: Health Hazard Data describes the signs and symptoms of exposure, emergency and first-aid procedures, effects of overexposure, and medical conditions aggravated by overexposure.

Section 6: Control and Protective Measures describes protective equipment that is needed when handling or using the product.

Section 7: Spill or Leak Procedures states precautions that need to be taken when cleaning up and disposing of spilled product. Materials declared hazardous wastes or hazardous substances are identified in this section.

Section 8: Hazardous Material Identification provides a rating system for individual components and emergency response codes.

Section 9: Special Precautions and Comments is a catch-all category for hazard information not previously covered or needing reinforcing.

Just the fact that an MSDS document is provided with the product should be an incentive to read the information on the Safety Information sheet.

Where a multi-color finish is being applied as part of a show restoration, one of the tricks is knowing where the factory put the two-tone color lines. Photo courtesy of Jean Allen.

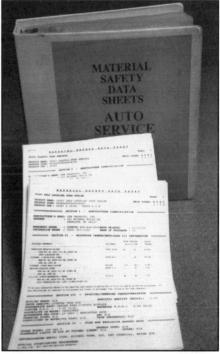

By law all chemical products that contain hazardous substances must be supplied with a Material Safety and Data Sheet (MSDS). Commercial shops are required to maintain copies of the MSDS for the products they use. Hobbyists are advised to familiarize themselves with the MSDS information.

doors, hood, trunk seams and seals, gas tank filler lid, along masking edges, from wheel wells, and every crack or crevice that can hold sanding dust or debris
- wipe down all surfaces to be painted with wax and grease remover or Windex
- sweep and wet down the floor of the painting area to remove and suppress dirt and dust
- make sure spray area filters are clean
- gather proper painting clothing, including disposable painter's coveralls. Before entering the paint booth to spray the color finish, blow off your clothing with an air gun. Wear a painter's hat to prevent loose hair from falling into the paint.

With all preparations completed you're ready for finish painting, which is the most exciting part of the refinishing sequence because color changes everything.

Do-It-Yourself Guide to CUSTOM PAINTING
Selecting or Matching a Finish Color

The enormous variety of colors we see around us are actually variations or hues of four basic colors: blue, red, yellow, and green. Telling your refinishing supplier "I want to paint my Road Runner Superbird Yellow," won't get the right color unless the supplier's chart shows the specific hue of yellow used on that car.

Coming up with a correct match for an original color or deciding on the right color for a car can be sufficiently complex so that you'll want to make the color selection early in the refinishing process — likely before laying on the first primer coating. Otherwise, you could find yourself ready to apply the final finish and still debating on the car's color scheme or needing time to research and find a mixing formula for the car's original color.

A friend who owns a classic LG-45 Lagonda Rapide roadster (made in England) stripped the car to its bare aluminum about 10 years ago and the car still sits unpainted. Bob can't make up his mind on the finish color. In the meantime, he's looked at other restored Rapides, but none of the colors appeal. They're dark, the green-black British Racing Green seems a favorite, and Bob thinks the car needs a lighter color to accent its sculpted lines. He's inclined toward yellow, but hasn't decided which hue.

If Bob were to ask his refinishing supplier for "yellow paint" for his Lagonda, he'd be asked "which yellow?" meaning which manufacturer's color for what year and car would he like mixed and in what finish system: single-stage color, base coat/clear coat, or tricoat/multi-stage color? If he hadn't already selected a color, he might say, "Sort of a light yellow." Since what one person might think a "light yellow" represents can be shades different from another person's color, it helps to have at least a basic understanding of how color shading works. Then, at least you will know the foundational values, or dimensions, of the color you have in mind. Describing the color in these terms will help the refinishing supplier find paint samples in the range you are seeking.

MAKING COLOR CHOICES

The enormous variety of colors we see around us are actually variations or *hues* of four basic colors: blue, red, yel-low, and green. Think of these four basic colors on a wheel with blue at the top in the 12 o'clock position, red at the 3 o'clock position, yellow at 6 o'clock, and green at 9 o'clock. Mixing can occur only between colors that precede and follow each other on this wheel. For example, yellow (at the bottom of the wheel) can mix with red to produce reddish tints of yellow, or orange if the colors are blended evenly; or yellow can mix with green, producing tints in the direction of lime. Moving to the top of the wheel blue can mix with green, producing tints toward aqua, or with red, giving to a color in the direction of violet. Colors do not mix with those in opposing positions on the wheel. So, blue at the top of the wheel does not mix with yellow at the bottom, nor does red in the 3 o'clock position mix with green in the 9 o'clock slot. While companion colors can be blended to produce an enormous variety of hues, to create a full range of colors we have to consider two other dimensions: *value,*

Changing a color's value makes it lighter or darker. British sports cars often wear a green so dark as to be almost black. This MG-C is painted a much lighter green with a near neutral (neither light nor dark) color value.

Increasing the richness or chroma results in a color that's unmistakable. When I asked my wife what she thought of my freshly painted Studebaker pickup, she said: "It's green."

which is the color's lightness or darkness; and *chroma*, which is the color's richness or intensity, the purity of its hue.

As we change a color's **value,** we can make it lighter by moving it the direction of white, or darker by moving it toward black. British Racing Green, the color my friend rejected for his Lagonda Rapide, has a value so dark that in dim light the color actually appears to be black. Only in bright sunlight can the color's green hue be seen. In contrast, a popular 1950s color called "Sea Mist Green" is so light that it looks like what its name describes, a white sand beach with just a hint of green. In dim light, the green hue fades almost beyond recognition. A color with a neutral value (neither light nor dark) would be like my Studebaker pickup that I brought home from the paint shop and asked my wife what she thought of the truck's new appearance. Her response, "It's green!" In its neutral value, the color is unmistakable.

We increase the richness or **chroma** of a color by eliminating shades of darkness or lightness (influences of black or white) and by letting the pure color express itself. Sometimes pure colors seem too bland, like my green Studebaker. Adding a clear coat for increased gloss or reflective effects such as pearls or metallics to a highly chromatic color can produce a paint that is stunning in its intensity. Candy

colors with their added dimension of translucence are an example.

Considering these three dimensions, hue (the color blend), value (the color's lightness or darkness), and chroma (the color's intensity) will help you select the finish paint color that looks best on your car. Just like clothing colors on people, there's a "right" color for each car and others that just don't make it. The silver metallic finish on my Peugeot 405 MI-16 sports sedan, for example, is the right color for that car. Peugeot also offered my MI-16 in light and dark shades of blue and red, as well as black and beige. I've seen these cars in those colors and even though the MI-16 is a very low production model, the more pedestrian colors with their ability to blend in easily with the traffic make the car look common. Silver, in contrast, seems to highlight the car's well-proportioned styling. Not coincidentally I'm sure, silver is shown most prominently in the sales brochure.

Just as people feel "confirmed" when their clothing selections are also featured in the displays, so too we can reinforce our "color sense" by looking at the cars selected for magazine ads and sales brochures. The designers of these promotional pieces have learned to recognize colors that look best in certain settings, which with a car includes the body style and other factors such as the bulk or lightness of a

Sometimes you'll recognize the "right" color from an ad or a photograph. The white and red color combination on this 1972 pickup, matched by the stripes on the buildings, gives these trucks a stand-out look.

design. Sometimes, you can adopt the "right" color you've seen in an ad or on the street to your car. But be aware that other factors besides the color's appeal in the ad or street setting have to fit with your car, too. For example, Chevrolet used a very attractive Ochre (a burnt yellow) on its 1971-72 Cheyenne series pickups and Blazers. This color seemed to fit the personality of those vehicles, harmonized as it was by simulated wood grain trim and black or white two-toning on the roof or top. That same color would look downright foolish on a modern Tahoe whose image of bulk and masculinity is best served by the suit color of a Secret Service body guard.

Matching the exterior color with the interior isn't much of a problem if the seat coverings are black vinyl as on this jeep. Usually, though, the exterior and interior colors have to be coordinated.

Paint from a different mix or changing the type of paint can create problems in the color match. On this jeep, various sections of the floor have been painted from different paint mixes; also some panels are painted with basecoat/clearcoat and others are single stage finish. The color differences are apparent.

LIMITATIONS ON COLOR CHOICES

The preceding discussion of the color dimensions and ways to select a suitable color for your car has assumed that you have free reign in the color choice — as is likely the case for those building street rods and sometimes with restoration. More often, however, the color choices for a new finish are limited. You may need to match the color to upholstery and interior colors that are not going to be replaced. Maybe you are spot repairing an exist-

ing finish. Or perhaps you want to keep the car original for showing and judging purposes.

A car's exterior color has to be coordinated with the interior. If the interior is being replaced it can be color-coordinated to the exterior, allowing the widest range of choices in the exterior color. But if the finish color needs to harmonize with an existing, or pre-selected interior, you'll need to consider the color dimensions presented earlier. For example, if the interior color is a shade of green, then the exterior should harmonize, not clash, with that color. A harmonizing color could be a darker or lighter shade of green or a mix with either blue or yellow, the primary colors that blend with green. Modern cars generally have neutral interiors allowing wider exterior color choices. When changing an exterior color, consideration also needs to be given to repainting inner door facings and trunk and engine compartments, areas where the exterior color is visible.

MATCHING THE CAR'S ORIGINAL COLOR

Spot refinishing requires very accurate matching of the existing exterior color, which may have changed in all three dimensions (hue, value, and chroma) due to fading and other conditions that can affect the paint's color. To match an existing finish, you'll start by identifying the color. If the car still wears the factory finish, or a repaint of the factory color, you'll look at the paint code on the car's body I.D. tag for the color information. On newer cars, body I.D. tags can be found in various locations, often inside the engine compartment on the bulkhead (or firewall), sometimes in the trunk, driver's side door pillar, or driver's side door liner. Your refinishing supplier should have a list of body I.D. tag locations and interpretations for the paint code and paint type numbers.

Note: With later model GM cars (excluding Saturn), the body I.D. tag is likely to have both a two-digit paint code and a four-digit paint number preceded by the letters WA. This WA prefix number should be used, rather than the two-digit paint code, to specify the

finish color. GM used some of the two-digit paint codes to represent completely different colors, so ordering the finish color from the two-digit paint code when a WA number is also available, could risk the supplier's mixing a batch of the wrong color.

Once the color is correctly identified, any variances have to be recognized and taken into consideration. Color variations and their causes are discussed in the next section.

Restoration to factory standards also calls for identifying and matching the car's original color. As with newer cars, the paint code is found on the body number plate (usually a metal plate riveted to the cowl underneath the hood, but sometimes to the left front door hinge pillar above the lower hinge). This plate typically contains coding for the car's year of manufacture, styling series, and body type, along with the paint and interior colors. While the refinishing supplier may have color information, including mixing formulas, for paint numbers from cars of the 1960s and '70s, colors from earlier eras may lie outside the paint manufacturer's data base. For these cars, you'll need other resources to identify and match the original finish colors (many 1950s cars had two, even three, body colors).

Resources for determining the original colors of older, collectible cars include:

- Books in the Catalog of American Car ID Numbers series published by Cars&Parts magazine and distributed by Classic Motorbooks International contain deciphering information for body plate codes, including interior and exterior colors. Books in the *ID Number* series cover U.S. built cars from the 1950s, '60s, and '70s, as well as Chevrolet and Ford light-duty trucks from 1946 to 1972.
- Original paint chip samples (where available). For some collector cars, such as Model A Fords, the original paint color chips have been accurately reproduced and are readily available. In other cases, original paint chips may be available from literature vendors, either as pages from older paint manufacturer's books or as dealer litera-

ture. Keep in mind that original color samples are likely to have faded. Due to photo reproduction and printing variables, magazine ads should be regarded as approximations of original colors, not an exact color match.

- A Color Spectrometer as a means of identifying original colors. These electronic color sensing devices and corresponding color matching services are provided by major automotive paint manufacturers and are available through refinishing suppliers and collision repair centers. The color sensing device not only recognizes the gradients of the finish color, but also produces a mixing formula for the new paint.

In some cases, the color name (from the data plate code) may be all the information the refinishing supplier needs to mix the paint, since the painting manufacturer may have converted older nitrocellulose lacquer or synthetic enamel mixing formulas to newer single or base coat/clear coat finishes. However, the refinishing supplier will have to access the manufacturer's data base for the conversion mixing formula. Often, a mixing formula for an older color in a modern paint will not be available. That's where some evidence of the original color (paint chips or a true color example somewhere on the car body) is needed. Having the color sample, it may not be necessary to use a color sensing device to produce a mixing formula. If the color sample matches closely enough to a current paint the new paint color can be substituted with no noticeable change. If no color match can be found, then the color spectrometer offers an accurate means of producing a mixing formula for the color.

COLOR VARIABLES

The difficulty in matching an existing or older finish comes from variances in the color. Color shifting is common with older finishes due to fading and changes in the paint's pigment. But a relatively new finish can also be at variance from the color mixed according to the manufacturer's formula. Sometimes the variance occurred at the body assembly plant where the car was orig-

inally painted. To help refinishers match paint that is off by a known variance, PPG, Sherwin Williams, and other major automotive paint manufacturers publish color deck books that show the true color (mixed according to the car manufacturer's formula) and variances to that color. Using this book, the closest color match for the car's finish can easily be selected. Formulas for the variant color are printed on the back of the chip, or are available on microfiche or from the paint manufacturer's color data base. These color variance books are published for all major manufacturers, including General Motors, Ford, Daimler-Chrysler, Honda, Nissan, Toyota, Mazda, Subaru, Saab, BMW, Volvo, and Volkswagen.

Beyond variances that may occur at the body assembly plant, color mismatches can occur for one or more of the following reasons:

- The painter assumes "black is black." When refinishing or spot painting a black car, it is as important to make sure you've got the right mixing formula as with any other color. The black paint you're trying to match may have a subtle tint of yellow, brown, red, or violet. Comparing the black on the car with the painting manufacturer's black variance color strips will help make sure you've got the right mixing formula.
- Painting conditions can affect the color. Both temperature and

humidity can cause the color to shift darker or lighter. However, these variables work oppositely of each other (decreasing humidity tends to make the color lighter, as does an increase in temperature), so extremes in both conditions tend to cancel each other out. Likewise, spray gun settings, the condition of the spraying equipment, amount and type of solvent used, and distance and speed of the spray gun can all lighten or darken the color.

- With metallic paints, whether or not the metallic flakes are dispersed evenly with the pigment can lighten or darken the color.
- We're looking at the color under the wrong light. Probably all of us have experienced the weird colors certain cars appear to project at night under street lights. In this lighting condition, red looks orange and green looks black. About the only color that looks somewhat true is white. If you select a color match under artificial light, don't expect to see the same color in sunlight.
- Not all of us share the same color acuity. Color matches need to be made by someone who sees the true color. My Dad, who suffered from partial color blindness, mistook a gray blue for a bright blue and quite contentedly bought the wrong color paint.

Just as black isn't black, white isn't white. Even "neutral" white can be influenced by changes in the color's value.

Metallic paints give sparkle to the finish, but since metallics are created by adding specs of aluminum, a strong metallic effect also diminishes the paint's brightness by adding overtones of gray.

VARIATIONS OF "NEUTRAL" COLORS

Just as black isn't black, white isn't white. The white GM has used on its light-duty trucks from 1955 until present is tinted with black, making it a very distinct color, especially if spot painted with a generic white. Be sure when asking for a color that may sound universal (white, black, silver) to specify the make, model, and year of the car or truck, and then also ask if the painting manufacturer has variance chips for that color.

You'll find codes for the original colors on the car's body plate. If you're restoring a car for showing, the body plate color codes may be a determining factor in the vehicle's purchase, as was the case with this rare Surrey Jeep whose body plate showed an eye-catching original paint scheme of pink and red.

SPRAYING CONDITIONS AND PAINT COLOR

Shop variables such as temperature, humidity, and ventilation can produce noticeable changes in color. Higher temperatures tend to lighten the color while colder temperatures make the color darker. Lower humidity lightens the color while high humidity makes it darker. Painting in a well-ventilated shop or spray booth tends to make the color lighter while an enclosed shop with little ventilation makes the color darker. As noted, changes in temperature and humidity often cancel each other out. However, raising the shop's temperature also lowers the humidity (because heated air is dryer), and changes in both conditions could combine to noticeably lighten the paint. If shop ventilation is increased in the process, the color could be driven even lighter.

With spray gun settings, a smaller fluid tip lightens the color while a larger tip darkens the paint. Likewise, adjusting the gun to constrict material flow lightens the color while more painting material darkens the color. The air tip works conversely: An air tip with few openings makes the color darker while an air tip with more openings lightens the color. Fan width has the same effect: Wider fan — lighter color, narrower fan — darker color, as does air pressure at the gun. Increasing air pressure lightens the color while decreasing pressure darkens the color.

Variations in the distance the spray gun is held from the surface being painted and the speed of the gun also affect the color. Increasing the distance lightens the paint while bringing the gun closer darkens the paint. The speed at which the gun moves across the panel has the same effect: A faster sweep can lighten the color while a slower sweep can darken the color. As with temperature and humidity, gun distance and sweep speed can combine to make a minute color shift more noticeable. Flash time allowed between coats can also affect the color, long flash time lightening the color and short flash time making the color darker.

These adjustments and variations are helpful to keep in mind when creating custom effects, such as stripes, scollops, splashes, or flames, since they allow a color to lighten or darken without altering the paint.

COLOR SHIFTS WITH METALLIC PAINTS

When metallic paints are sprayed without stirring or agitation, the metallic particles can concentrate at the bottom or top of the paint film. When metallic flakes are concentrated at the bottom of the color finish, they're likely to be vertically oriented, making the color look darker. When the flakes are near the surface of the paint, they're likely to be horizontal, increasing the reflection and lightening the color. Since metallics are created by adding specks of aluminum, a strong metallic effect also diminishes the paint's brightness (or intensity) by adding overtones of gray.

Most of us have probably noticed that metallic colors often look much darker when viewed from an angle and brighter when looked at straight on. The darkening of a metallic's color in a side view is called "flop" and is due to the reflective angle of the metallic flakes. Even careful stirring won't have much effect on this visual color change. Flop is best combated by adding a flop adjuster to the metallic base coat. The flop adjuster additive not only helps give a uniform appearance to the color, regardless of the angle from which the car is viewed, but also helps ensure the metallic flakes are thoroughly covered in the clear coat where light bodied base coats are used.

HOW OUR EYES SEE COLOR

Our eyes register an object's color by the wave length of the light reflected from the object. A red car, for example, reflects only the red portion of the color spectrum. In natural sunlight we see the object's true color because sunlight contains all of the primary colors, allowing reflection of the color's exact hue. Artificial light, in contrast, does not project the full color spectrum (incandescent light concentrates in the yellow and red portion of the color spectrum), so the reflection is not the true color. Under artificial light a red car looks orange, the color at the red/yellow boundary and the strongest portion of

One advantage of building a custom, you can use any color you choose.

artificial light's color spectrum. If you're looking through a paint chip book to match an existing finish, you need to be looking at the colors in natural sunlight.

COLOR MIXING AND ADJUSTING

Although you'll likely be involved in selecting the car's color or colors (even if only by deciding that the car be repainted its original or existing color), mixing the color and any adjustment to ensure an accurate match needs to be done by professionals who have both the equipment and knowledge to precisely match a color within the three dimensions of hue, value, and intensity. If you are spraying the color finish yourself, as discussed in the next chapter, then it will be your responsibility to carefully monitor shop and spraying condi-

tions to make sure that variables in these conditions don't affect the color.

If you're using a base coat/clear coat system for the color finish, you'll encounter an additional color challenge. If you've never sprayed base coat/clear coat paints before, you'll be shocked to see the base coat projecting a flat, off-hue color. Only when the clear coat is applied will you see the true color. With a base coat/clear coat system, attention to spray gun settings and shop temperature/humidity conditions, as well as proper gun technique — possible causes of the color variables discussed earlier in this chapter — are essential to producing an on-target color. What a stress relieving sight it is to see the true color emerge with the clear coating.

Although traditional finishes were single-stage lacquer or enamel, today collectors are favoring base coat/clear coat systems for their durability and high gloss. Photo courtesy of Mike Cavey.

In the past, when a painter applied a color finish he concerned himself with making sure the finish coating was free of drips and runs and had good gloss. Today's painter carries these concerns and many more. First, the painter has to decide on the finish system. To some extent, that selection may already have been made, as the paint system used with the topcoat has to be compatible with the undercoat. Also, if the painter is making a spot repair, the topcoat system has to match the paint already on the car. Since there are several topcoat systems to choose from, let's look at the options. Unless the car is to have a dazzling multi-color effect, in which case a multi-stage color system may be selected, the color system choices for regular colors and metallics are: single-stage color, base coat/clear coat, single-stage color with clear overlay (also called "color with clear").

SINGLE-STAGE COLOR SYSTEM

When a finish consists only of the color coating it's called a single-stage system. Traditional lacquer and enamel paints are of this type. With these paints, the color coating is the last step in the refinishing process. Since lacquer is rapidly becoming obsolete, the painting systems most likely to be used for single-stage color are acrylic enamel and acrylic urethane. Professional refinishers typically prefer acrylic urethane for this paint system's compatibility with OEM finishes and the toughness of the urethane coating. Hobbyists, however, may be better served by acrylic enamel, since this paint system does not require a catalyst (though a hardener or catalyst may be an option in some systems). The absence of a catalyst suggests that the paint is isocyanate free and therefore safe for the hobbyist wearing a respirator to spray. Acrylic urethane systems do require a cata-

lyst and consequently are likely to contain hazardous isocyanates. Anyone contemplating using an acrylic urethane color system should refer to Chapter 2 on Painting Safety for necessary equipment and precautions when spraying isocyanate paints.

A single-stage color finish would be applied in the following settings:

- When spot repairing an existing single-stage finish
- When repainting a car or truck which had this type of finish from the factory
- Where the painter lacks the skills and equipment for applying a base coat/clear coat finish

Single-stage color finish has the advantage that it is relatively easy to apply — even an inexperienced painter can expect good results if he/she carefully follows the mixing and spraying directions. However, it also has disadvantages, the main one being diminished gloss. This doesn't

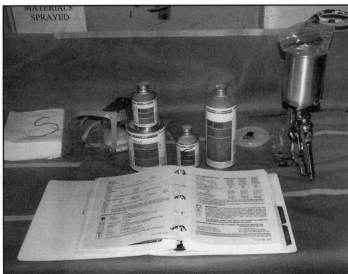

Panel lips around the hood and trunk as well as door jambs are often painted first to assure coverage of these "hidden" areas.

mean single-stage color looks flat. You can expect a glossy finish, but single-stage color doesn't shine as deeply or as brilliantly as a base coat/clear coat. Another disadvantage, the color coating lies exposed to harsh airborne chemicals. In a two-stage finish, the color is protected by the clear coat.

To offset these drawbacks, paints in some single-stage color systems can be covered with a protective clear coating.

APPLYING A SINGLE-STAGE COLOR FINISH

When the color finish is not being covered with a clear coat, thickness or film build of the color coating is critical to the paint's durability and appearance. Too little paint may cause the finish to peel or fade. A thin color coating is also easily rubbed through in the buffing/polishing process. The recommended thickness for a single-stage color finish is 2 1/2 mils. Since 1 mil is 1/1000 of an inch, or .001 inch, the measurement probably seems too small to imagine. For comparison, plastic food wrap is about 1 mil in thickness. To achieve the recommended 2 1/2 mil coating, you'll need to apply 2 to 3 wet coats (the data sheets for some single-stage color products call for 3 to 4 wet coats).

Assuming all preparation steps are complete through the primer sealer stage and the undercoat and topcoat paint systems are compatible, you will mix the color product according to the manufacturer's instructions. Acrylic enamel is typically mixed 2 parts color to 1 part reducer. Note that this mixing ratio is by volume, not weight. Although the proper mixing proportions are most accurately achieved using a measuring beaker, Phil Noder, a professional refinisher featured frequently in this book's photos, relies on a "pork and beans" can that is segmented in thirds by ridges. Phil jokes, "If anyone throws out my old bean can I'm lost." However, the segments conveniently match the mixing proportions and, as Phil says, "just fill my spray gun cup."

If the acrylic enamel color system offers the option of being mixed with hardener, this additional component changes the mixing ratio. Likewise additives, such as a color blending solvent, require recalculating the mixing ratio. With an acrylic urethane system, metallics may have a different mixing ratio than solid colors and will require both a compatible reducer and hardener. Always refer to the mixing instructions for the specific configuration within the painting system being used.

Air pressure settings at the spray gun are likewise found in the product data information. Common settings are 40-50 psi at the gun for conventional spraying; 5-10 psi for HVLP. **Note:** Spot repairs may call for lower (30-35 psi) settings with conventional spraying.

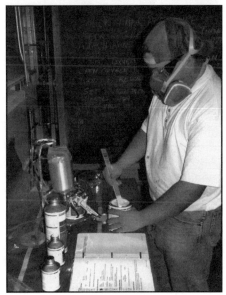

Mixing should follow precisely the instructions for formula and sequence that are given in the product description sheets.

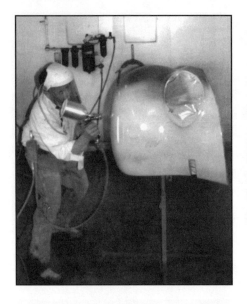

Air pressure settings at the gun are as critical as the paint mix. All relevant spraying information is found on the painting product information sheets.

Small parts like these headlight rims and air vent doors are also often painted separately.

Standard gun distance is 8 to 10 inches from the surface being painted. After each wet coat allow 15-20 minutes of drying time. Refer to the Product Data sheet for the recommended number of wet coats. With metallic colors, the Information sheet may call for a mist coating immediately after the last wet coat, sprayed at a greater gun distance (10-12 inches). With spot repairs, a blending additive is recommended for mist coating over the edge of the repair area and onto the surrounding finish. Other additives may be used to combat fisheyes or to enhance gloss. These will be discussed later.

On older cars and trucks, removable parts like fenders are often painted separately so the undersides can be finish coated as well.

BASE COAT/CLEAR COAT SYSTEMS

With new car manufacturers and refinishers alike, the favorite finish approach is base coat/clear coat. This two-part finish system originated in Germany in the 1970s as a response to paint damage being caused by chemical pollutants in the air. Initially, the purpose of the clear coating was to protect the color finish. Painting manufacturers now formulate their base coat/clear coat systems for advantages beyond protection from chemical damage, though this feature remains one of the advantages of a base coat/clear coat finish. Additional advantages include richer gloss and option of high pigment "glamour" colors, which are not available in single-stage color systems.

A base coat/clear coat finish would be applied in the following settings:

• When spot repairing an existing two-stage finish
• When a high gloss finish is desired
• Where protection of the underlying color coating is needed, either to keep a richly pigmented color from fading or to seal the color against atmospheric chemical pollution.

The "shine" of a base coat/clear coat finish exceeds even the legendary "19 coats of hand-rubbed lacquer" seen on yesterday's show car. Anyone seeking to match or exceed the gloss of a fragile lacquer finish will opt for a base coat/clear coat color system. Those whose vehicles will be parked for extended periods out-of-doors (or inside but uncovered) will likewise select base coat/clear coat.

Although more complicated to spray than a single-stage finish, base coat/clear coat color systems can be successfully applied by an amateur who, 1) understands the technique and 2) follows "to the letter," every detail of the paint system's mixing and spraying instructions.

APPLYING THE BASE COAT

Thickness or film build is also a critical factor in two-stage color systems. However, the painter now has to be concerned with thickness of both the base coat and the clear coat. The paint isn't just laid on until it "looks right." The base coat is typically kept thin (between two and four medium wet coats). The goal is to apply just enough paint to establish the color. Professional automotive refinishers talk about spraying the base coat "to hiding," meaning the undercoat is completely hidden by the color finish. You may recall the discussion in Chapter 11 about adding a color tint to the primer sealer coating. One purpose for tinting the undercoat is to assist the base coat with hiding, and is especially beneficial with light finish colors. The recommended thickness for the base coat layer is one mil.

The paint is mixed according to the manufacturer's specifications and poured through a filter into the gun cup.

In preparation for finish painting, an air hose gun is used to blow dust off masking as well as all painting surfaces.

To achieve success with the base coat, you'll need to make sure the reducer matches shop temperature and painting conditions, and you need to carefully follow the paint manufacturer's specifications for spray gun setting, application, and dry times.

Reactive reducers (solvent with catalyst) are available for shop temperature and humidity conditions ranging from cold to hot and dry to humid. Using a reducer that is too slow or too fast (for conditions colder or hotter than actual) can delay or speed the base coat's drying effect. Slowing the drying time can result in drips or runs or the solvent may penetrate the undercoat causing sand scratches to show through the finish. Speeding up the drying can produce dry spots and with metallic paints can cause disorientation of the metallic particles. Since the base coat has a dull appearance, dry spots might be overlooked but will show up as shadows under the clear. Not a desirable effect! Problems with metallic paints are likely because it's natural to try to compensate from the rapid drying of a too fast solvent by holding the spray gun closer to the painting surface. Choosing the solvent most closely matched to spraying conditions helps eliminate all these potential problems.

Be sure to follow the painting manufacturer's mixing specifications for base coat and solvent. Typically, solid colors are mixed 1 part paint to 1 1/2 parts reducer (reduced 150%), while metallics are mixed 1 to 2 (reduced 200%). A fisheye eliminator may be added to the base coat, but a flexible additive (for rubber and flexible plastic parts) is typically added to the clear, *not* the base coat. Refer to the mixing instructions for the specific base coat for the painting system being used. Remember to stir the mixture thoroughly before spraying.

Typical air pressure settings are 35-45 psi at the gun for conventional spraying; 10 psi maximum for HVLP, but check the manufacturer's specifications for the base coat product being applied. Remember to keep the film build thin. Recommended base coat thickness is usually two medium coats, but sometimes an additional coating is required to achieve consistent color ("hiding"). Because the coatings are applied medium dry (as opposed to wet), perhaps as little as 5 to 10 minutes flash time may be needed between coats. Note the dry times in the product specification sheets and don't recoat until the previous coat has dried to a "flat" appearance.

Base coats are not designed to dry glossy. The flat finish you see as the base coat dries will remain until the clear coat is applied, at which point the finish will acquire a deep, penetrating gloss. If you're not familiar with the base coat's flat finish, you're likely to think you've made some sort of fundamental error in the coating's application. As long as you've avoided causing sags or runs in the paint, haven't

The surface is then wiped with a tack cloth to pick up any remaining dust or other residue.

exceeded the desired thickness, and didn't spray the base coatings too wet or too dry, you've achieved success. If you notice any runs or sags, these can be sanded out using 500 grit sandpaper usually after 30 minutes of drying time. Runs and sags are typically caused by applying the coating too thick and too wet or not waiting the required tack time between coatings. After sanding any trouble spots smooth, you'll need to recoat.

The base coat's flat finish can also cause anxiety about a correct color match. Unless you have experience with base coat/clear coat finishes, you'll look at the dried base coat and think the refinishing supplier missed one of the steps in the color formula. Like gloss, the paint's true color will

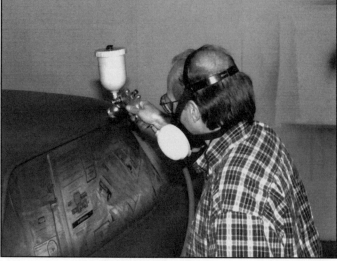

The finish painting sequence starts on the car's roof, then proceeds to the hood and trunk with the lower areas of the doors and fenders following.

Care needs to be taken to make sure that all surfaces, including the undersides of drip moldings, are thoroughly covered.

emerge with the clear coat. If you want to make certain the color is correct before spraying a repair area or the whole car, apply the base coat and clear coat to a small out-of-the-way spot. If when viewed under natural light the color doesn't seem absolutely correct, have the refinishing supplier add the missing tint to the base. Remember, you can't trust artificial light to give a true color reading. If you're looking at the color spot under incandescent or fluorescent lighting, you can expect the color to shift toward yellow and red.

APPLYING THE CLEAR COAT

You'll typically apply the clear coat right in sequence with the base coat. For some base coats, the recommended dry time before clear coating is 10 minutes times the number of coats (meaning the dry time could vary from 20 to 30 minutes depending on whether 2 or 3 coats were applied). Other products may recommend waiting only 10-15 minutes after the last color coat. In all cases, follow the dry time for the base coat you are using as specified on the Product Information sheet. If you don't apply the clear coat right away, you'll need to note the recoat window for the base coat product you've applied. The recoat window will be listed in the product data — 24 hours is typical. If

you delay clear coating until after the paint's "recoat window" expires, you'll need to scuff sand and add another coating before spraying the clear.

The clear coat should be twice as thick (2 to 2 1/2 mils) as the base coat, requiring two to three full wet coats (with some products four coats may be recommended if the finish is to be polished). Be sure to follow the manufacturer's recommendations on dry times between coats. For some products, prolonging the dry times could cause the finish to lift. Not allowing adequate dry time could cause runs or sags in the clear. If drips or sags occur, the damage can be repaired (typically after 24 hours), but the repair will have to be recoated.

Where the refinishing manufacturer offers a variety of clear coat products, make sure the clear coat and base coat are from compatible systems. Make sure the activator or reducer matches shop conditions at the time of spraying, and follow mixing instructions and spray gun settings exactly as they are stated on the product information or data sheets. When spraying rubber or flexible plastic parts, the flex additive is mixed with the clear.

COLOR WITH CLEAR

This third refinishing option sounds the same as base coat/clear coat, but it's not. Essentially what you're doing

is applying a single-stage color and covering it with clear. Color with clear is different from base coat/clear coat in that the color coating is substantially thicker than the clear — which is applied as a protective overlay. With base coat/clear coat the build is reversed — a thin color coating and thick clear. Color with clear might be applied in the following settings:

- on complete re-sprays when a clear coating's protective characteristics are desired
- to add depth and gloss to a single-stage color; metallics, especially, benefit from a clear coating
- to retain gloss after polishing

Likely, this finish approach would not be used with spot repair.

APPLYING COLOR WITH CLEAR

The color coating would be applied as described in the single-stage color section above. The clear can be applied two ways: as a 50/50 mix in the last color coating or as an overlay. With either approach, it's essential that the clear and color products be compatible. Product data sheets for clear coat products will list compatible bases. Lacquer coatings, especially, can be problematic.

When spraying the clear as a 50/50 mix with the last color coating, the color and clear products are mixed independently (using the same reduc-

On commercial vehicles, like this panel truck, the interior also often needs to be painted.

On bodies that are going to be two-toned, the primary color is applied first, then areas to be covered with the contrasting color are scuff sanded.

er and catalyst to avoid problems of compatibility) in accord with the ratio listed on the product information sheet. When both products are mixed to spraying consistency, equal proportions of the two products are combined for the final coating. Applying clear in this way usually eliminates problems that might occur with a separate clear coating.

Note: Mixing clear with the last color coat does not work with products that are part of a base coat/clear coat system. The base coat in that system needs to dry before the clear is applied.

Spraying clear as an overlay to a single-stage color creates essentially the same effect as a base coat/clear coat finish and therefore is seldom done except to enhance gloss with custom colors that may not be available in base coat/clear coat paints. With this approach, make absolutely certain that the base color and clear overlay are compatible.

BLENDING FOR SPOT REPAIRS

Although blending solvents have greatly simplified the process, merging the new finish on a spot repair into the larger panel can be tricky. You don't want to have the spot repair come to an abrupt edge, like a friend once did when spot painting an MG roadster. This fellow simply masked around the repair spot, applied primer, then the finish. The color matched, except the repair spots were glossy whereas the rest of the finish had dulled from sunlight and lack of care. What made the repair job look absolutely awful was the seam ridges around each repair spot, making the new paint stand out like plaid patches on a blue suit. The goal with spot repair is to blend the new paint into the surrounding finish so smoothly that there's no evidence the car has even been repainted. Although the overall approach is very similar, the actual blending technique differs between single-stage color and base coat/clear coat.

Blending single-stage color. Prepare the surrounding finish by cleaning (which means washing and wiping down with a wax and grease remover product, as would be done to prepare a substrate for priming), then sand with 1200 to 1500 grit wet sandpaper. Now spray the repair area to hiding, meaning 2-3 medium wet coats or until a uniform color is achieved. The traditional approach for single-stage color has been to increase the solvent in the last coating or spray a final mist coating of pure solvent to melt the overspray into the surrounding finish. Most refinishing manufacturers now offer blending solvents that achieve the same effect without risk of damage by the topcoat solvent to the old finish. However, these special blending solvents are not necessarily compatible with all types of finishes, so be sure to tell your supplier what finish paint you are using and, if possible, the type of finish you're repairing. When the final paint coating dries, you can lightly polish the overlay to eliminate any visual sign of repair. **Note:** Chapter 17 describes the polishing process in detail.

Blending base coat/clear coat. If the old paint is oxidized, it's very important to completely remove the "dead" surface layer; otherwise, the blending overlay may not adhere. Of course just "cleaning up" an oxidized finish where the old paint blends with

Although blending solvents have simplified the process, merging a new finish on a spot repair can be tricky, especially on a basecoat/clearcoat finish.

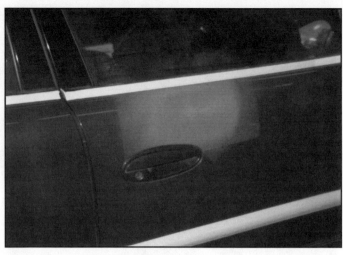

Scott Taylor uses a spot repair technique that doesn't require blending solvent. Scott covers both the repair and blending area with clear basecoat, which has a cloudy appearance. Next he applies the color basecoat, then the clear. Light polishing finishes the repair.

new is not going to create satisfactory results. Instead, the oxidation layer should be removed from all areas of old finish by microsanding and polishing. Be sure to thoroughly wipe down the blending area with wax and grease remover.

Apply base coat to the repair until you've achieved good color coverage (until hiding). On the second or third coat, extend the base coat slightly over the edge of the repair area. On the first clear coating, spray only to the edge of the repair area. Apply a dust coat of blending solvent along the edge of the old finish. Now spray the second coat of clear and extend this coating out over the blending solvent. Apply another dust coating of blending solvent along the overlap area. If a third coating of clear seems necessary, spray out over the blending solvent as previously, then polish the edge when dry.

Scott Taylor's base coat/clear coat blending technique. Scott's Body Shop in Rogers Heights, Michigan, uses a different technique that doesn't require blending solvent. After preparing the old finish and undercoating the repair area, Scott covers both the repair and blending edge of the old finish with clear base coat, which has a milky appearance. Next, the color base is applied to the repair. The clear coat is then applied over both the repair and edge of the old finish previously coated with clear

base coat. Light polishing finishes the repair. The technique works, producing impossible to detect color blending from repair to old finish.

COUNTERING PROBLEMS WITH THE COLOR FINISH

Unlike primer coatings where problems can be sanded out and covered in the next coating, problems in the color finish can be a major setback, possibly requiring the finish be sanded and re-sprayed. For this reason, it's good policy to review possible problems and their solutions before applying the color finish. That way, hopefully, you can avoid any problems and the added time and expense correcting them is likely to entail.

In their order of likelihood, possible problems include:

Dust or dirt particles in the paint (also insects if spraying is done in an open shop). Don't try to pick out dust or dirt (or an errant insect) while the finish is still wet. Instead, wait until the finish dries (typically 24 hours). With solid colors or clear coat, wet sand with 1200-1500 sandpaper then polish. Note that wax and grease remover works well as a sanding lubricant. Metallics should not be sanded, but polished only.

Sags or runs on vertical surfaces. Essentially, the paint was applied too thick, too fast. Depending on their severity and location, sags and runs

may be removed by micro-sanding and polishing. Note that runs or sags in the base coat cannot be removed after the clear coat is applied.

Streaks or mottling in a metallic finish. Here the application was wrong. The problems are big and there's no simple solution. Possible spraying errors include: air pressure set too low at the gun; the spray gun held too close or gun movement too slow; reducer too slow for shop temperature; the spray gun not kept consistently parallel with the painting surface; or insufficient flash time between coats, including clear coat. Metallics are especially sensitive to improper spraying technique.

Orange peel — the finish has a rough texture, resembling the skin of an orange. Air pressure at the spray gun is set too low, the gun held at the wrong distance, or the paint is improperly mixed with reducer.

Lack of gloss — the finish looks dull or dry. Air pressure at the gun is set too high or paint buildup is inadequate. With clear coats, insufficient film build with the base coat can also cause a poor bond with the clear coat. Too much solvent is mixed with the paint or the solvent used is too fast for shop conditions.

Fisheyes — tiny circles permeating the paint. The likely culprit for this condition is silicone, usually from a wax coating that wasn't properly removed, or from the products with contaminat-

Covering the new finish with light-weight plastic protects the fresh paint.

ing silicone being used in the shop. Silicone, which is widely used in rubber protectorants and lesser quality waxes, is the refinisher's curse. Avoid using products containing silicone on your new finish and ban them from your shop. Oil in the air supply line is another cause.

PROBLEM SOLVING ADDITIVES

Some problems can be countered with painting additives. These include:

Fisheye preventer — used over preparation surfaces that display small cratering due to silicone contamination. Although fisheye preventer helps assure a smooth finish, it is not to be used as a silicone antidote or to eliminate proper preparation. Fisheye preventer is not added to the base coat in a base coat/clear coat finish, but the clear coat only.

Flop adjuster — used with metallic paints to establish consistent appearance, whether the finish is viewed face on, or from the side. Add to color coat only, not clear.

Blending solvent — helps avoid dry edges on spot refinishing. Can be used with single-stage as well as base coat/clear coat finishes.

Although most refinishing projects will use the paints and application techniques described in this chapter, specialty finishes are gaining popularity. These visually tantalizing glamour finishes are described in the next chapter.

TWO-STAGE REFINISHING TECHNIQUE FOR REPAIRED PANELS
by Robert Zweng - Manager, Banka's Collision, Inc.

With trim and bumpers reinstalled, a new finish gives a car a "freshly-minted" look.

TOOLS REQUIRED:
- Dual-action sander (D/A)
- Paint spray guns
- Block sander
- High-speed polishing wheel
- Spray gun cleaning brushes

SAFETY EQUIPMENT
- Chemical-resistant, light-weight, disposable coverall
- Safety glasses
- Rubber gloves
- Filtered breathing mask

MATERIALS NEEDED
- 150, 320, and 500 grit sandpaper
- Wax and grease remover solvent
- Masking tape and paper
- Tack cloth
- Two-part catalyst primer
- Two-part epoxy sealer
- Base coat paint
- Clear coat
- Catalyst and reducer
- Rubbing compound and polish

PROCEDURES:
WARNING: Rubber gloves and protective clothing must be worn when using chemicals. Failure to wear rubber gloves and protective clothing may cause skin irritation or long-term skin rashes.
WARNING: A filtered breathing mask must be worn at all times during refinishing (spraying procedures). Failure to wear a protective mask may cause lung problems.

- Wash repaired panel with wax and grease remover solvent.
- Feather-edge repaired area with dual-action sander tool (D/A) and 150 grit sandpaper.
- Feather out farther using D/A with 320 grit paper.
- Mask adjacent panels up to 36 inches.
- Prime sanded area with two-part catalyst primer and allow one hour to dry.
- Block sand primered area with 320 grit paper.
- Use D/A and 500 grit paper and sand entire panel.
- Wash panel with fast drying wax and grease remover.
- Spray two-part epoxy sealer to entire panel and allow 15 minutes to flash.
- Spray base coat onto entire panel. Allow 15 minutes to flash. Apply second coat and let panel dry 15 minutes.
- Clean surface of panel using tack cloth.
- Spray approximately 1.5 mils of clear coat on entire panel. Allow 10 minutes to flash. Reapply 1.5 mils of clear coat and allow panel to dry thoroughly (12 hours).
- Clean equipment.
- Rub out and polish panel to remove minor imperfections.
- Remove masking materials from adjacent panels.

Do-It-Yourself Guide to CUSTOM PAINTING

Custom Paints and Creative Designs

Metallic paints give the finish reflective glitter. This street rod also wears a design effect called scallops (sometimes spelled scollops), which is a variation of flames where the streaks are spear-shaped.

Today, custom painters choose from a tableau of glamour and exotic finishes, from iridescent pearls and color-shifting chameleon paints to bright translucent candy colors. The trend in custom finishes has moved away from the gaudy and toward the subtle. While a custom finish is likely to follow a minimalist theme — using the same color on all painted surfaces, including the grille and bumpers — the unifying common denominator among show finishes is quality. Flawless would be an apt description. An observer might comment on the finesse of the car's overall appearance — every detail blending seamlessly with every other. Observe some of the better custom cars being built today and I think you'll agree that this assessment applies.

When a custom design is bold, it's likely to be <u>very bold</u> — no half-statements as we enter the New Millennium. Bold means exciting, different, not following anyone else's path. But bold won't cover for shortcomings in quality

and even a bold design should be clean and uncluttered, free from anything that doesn't belong or looks out of place. Even when a custom finish or creative design is bold, everything should work together to create a unified image.

In the past, a finish with "pizazz" started with a paint containing metallics or bolder metal flakes. Today metallics and flakes may be combined with iridescent pearls, candy colors, and chameleon paints, adding not only sparkle, but also a rainbow radiance — an effect that is multi-dimensional, yet subtle. Quality, clean, subtle, and integrated: these four characteristics represent the goals most sought after in a show car finish.

CREATING A STAND-OUT CUSTOM FINISH

Step 1. Pick a stand-out color. Besides all of the standard colors, custom colors are available from both major paint manufacturers and specially paint companies. Ask your refinishing

supplier to see the latest color chips. Look at several paint manufacturers' samples, including custom finish specialists like House of Kolor (see the listing in the Resource Appendix). Refer to Chapter 12 for color selection tips.

Step 2. Decide whether you want to embellish the paint with metallics, flakes, or pearls. Each can be added to virtually any paint formula. Metallics, which are made from tiny flakes of aluminum, add reflective glitter. Flakes, which are larger than metallics, give an intense sparkle. Pearls, which today are made from specially coated mica, are translucent, allowing light to pass through so that the pearl's iridescent color seems to shimmer on the surface of the paint. By the way, nothing says you can't choose a straight color without metallic or pearls. You may find a custom color that doesn't need glitter or subtle color shifts to express the car's image.

Step 3. Decide whether you want to make a bold statement, in which case your choice may be a rich, reflective candy color. Translucent and richly tinted, candy paints give the appearance of having laid a coat of cellophane over the car's finish. If painting the entire car a bright candy color seems too bold, consider using candy on a panel or as part of a design.

Step 4. Decide whether you want to be both bold and subtle by choosing a chameleon paint. These deceptive color shifting finishes are as attention grabbing as they are expensive. A chameleon finish presents itself as several different colors, teasing viewers as the car instantly transforms from one color hue to another.

Step 5. Go for bold and add wild with a glow-in-the-dark phosphorescent. Rather than give the whole car a nuclear powered look, better to limit the phosphorescent paint to a special effects graphic.

Notice that these steps focus on the finish. We'll look at design options later in the chapter.

APPLYING CUSTOM PAINTS

Metallics, flakes, and pearls are additives usually for the base coat, but sometimes also for the clear coat. The additives are most often mixed with solid colors, but can also be added to candy colors and other special effects paints. Metallics don't necessarily require a clear coat and are commonly used with single-stage colors. To give greater iridescence or sparkle, pearls and flakes are sometimes placed in a midcoat paint applied between the base coat and the clear coat.

Candy colors require a tricoat, also called a "multistage" finish. Rich, translucent candy colors have been used in custom finishes since the 1950s — and are the earliest example of a tricoat finish. In their original formula, candy colors were a midcoat paint applied over a lacquer base and coated with a lacquer clear. Although candy colors are still available in acrylic lacquer (House of Kolor still formulates its "Kustom Kandys" in lacquer), these custom paints are more widely available in modern urethane and polyurethane enamels.

Just as light passing through a candy sucker seems to make the candy glow,

The first step to a stand-out custom finish is selecting an exciting color. Custom colors are available from both major paint manufacturers and specialty paint producers like House of Kolor. Color-changing chameleon paints (called Kameleon by House of Kolor and Harlequin by PPG) can produce bold, exciting effects. Poster courtesy of House of Kolor.

so too a candy finish projects a rich "glowing" color. To create the candy effect, a silver, gold, or black base, either solid color metallic, or in some cases containing pearls, is covered with 1 to 4 light coats of the candy color paint. The midcoat can vary in thickness; however, increasing the number of mid-coatings darkens the color. Think of the midcoat build as looking into a relatively clear pool of water. The deeper the water, the darker the images

appear to be at the bottom. Since the color changes with each additional coating, the painter needs to be alert and stop when he has achieved the desired candy effect.

When you're selecting the candy color, ask to see the manufacturer's color chart showing the color tints produced by the different base coats. The chart will help you coordinate the candy color and base coat to create the desired color effect.

Custom painting isn't limited to vehicles; creative colors and designs also look great on boats.

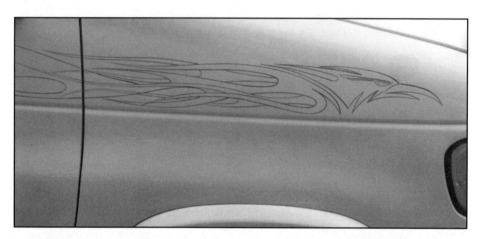

Pinstriping revived in the 1950s, largely in response to the enormous talent of a California customizer named Kenneth Howard, more popularly known as "Von Dutch." In their intricacy and free-form design, these thin, pinstriped flames that originate as feathers from an eagle's head represent the Von Dutch influence and style.

Sometimes a slight amount of the candy color is added to the initial clear coat. Two to three coatings of clear are typically applied. Many custom painters will use a high solids clear to give the paint a look of crystal — as though the color resides in a glass coating. One example of a high build clear is a product called "2 Plus 2," available from Restorer's Choice. (See Resource appendix.)

Chameleon paints get noticed. Everyone wonders how the finish changes colors. At first they think their eyes have tricked them, then they take another look and discover that the finish has changed color yet again. The visual effect of a chameleon finish is not the same as pearls. With pearls you have to look at the car at just the right angle to see the iridescent sparkle. With chameleon paints, the color change occurs regardless of the angle from which you're viewing the car — and the shift is dramatic: not a tint, but a completely different color.

Chameleon paints are applied as a base coat underneath a clear. Since chameleon paints are expensive, they're often used in designs and graphics.

Phosphorescent paints do just what the name implies — they absorb light and glow in the dark. To create the phosphorescent effect, a powder additive is mixed with clear. Like the chameleon effect, the phosphorescent glow works well in flames and graphics.

SPRAYING TRICOAT FINISHES

Candy colors and other special paints that are applied in a midcoat require a different spraying technique than the "across and down" spraying pattern commonly used with single-stage as well as base coat/clear coat paints. Since each additional candy color coating changes the color's shading, you can't spray one panel (a front fender, for example) and then move onto the next (the door). Some overspray is bound to land on the adjoining section of the car, so coating one panel or section before moving onto the next is certain to create a zebra effect with darker stripes where the panels or sections join with lighter color in between. Two spraying techniques can be used to avoid this light/dark color band problem. The first technique is to run each spray gun sweep the entire length of the car. This approach requires lots of foot work. The other technique is to spray across the car in a 45-degree "cross hatch" pattern. The 45-degree pattern allows you to apply a consistent build as you work your way down the car. At the front and the rear, the 45-degree pattern would extend over the hood and trunk. Though both patterns produce equal results, different painters will prefer one over the other. For the less experienced painter, the "cross hatch" 45-degree pattern is probably easier to spray.

To find the effect you're trying to create, it's best to practice on an old hood or trunk, some large panel destined for scrap. Be sure to note the number of midcoats applied to achieve the desired color, since you'll need to apply the same number of coats to match the color on the car.

Because a tricoat finish is thicker than normal, it's best to begin with properly undercoated bare substrate. Applying a complete candy color finish over existing paint is likely to result in a paint build that's thick enough to crack.

REPAIRING TRICOAT FINISHES

While a creative painter can use a midcoat paint to create dramatic color effects, satisfactorily repairing a tricoat or multistage finish can be a challenge for the professional and a nightmare for the inexperienced painter.

The problem comes in trying to determine the number of midcoats. Since each midcoating shades the color, it's necessary to know the number of coats to achieve a color match. Professional refinishers have developed a strategy to "back out" a tricoat finish to determine the number of midcoats required to duplicate the color, but success in matching an original multistage finish requires lots of skill and finesse. Since tricoat finishes are very difficult to repair, they are recommended mainly for show cars. On cars that are driven, a multistage finish might be applied in a graphic design or to a decorative panel.

CREATING DESIGNS

With rigid patterns fading from popularity, free-form designs are taking hold. Today's custom and show car designs are exercises in imagination and creativity first and demonstrations of painting expertise second. Examples of rigid patterns are stripes and various other geometric shapes. Their fading popularity comes from the pattern's being too predictable — ultimately just a contrasting color with few or no surprises. Free-form designs reflect the creator's imagination. Prime examples are shapes that transform into something else: Like an eagle Jeff Main created for his van where the feathers from the eagle's neck transform into long, slender flames.

If you have a professional create the design, you'll give some ideas of what you'd like, and the designer will either sketch out a concept for your approval or counter with ideas of his/her own. Since you're hiring the designer's artistic instinct as well as his/her skills and technique, ideas the designer suggests may be better than your own.

Ralph Starek, a talented automotive custom painter and design artist in Traverse City, Michigan, tells of a Ford "Splash" (Ranger pickup) owner who brought his truck to Ralph's studio for a custom touch. The "Splash" owner said he'd like Ralph to paint a set of flames. To Ralph's artistic sense, flames didn't fit the "Splash" motif. "Why not create a splash design instead?" Ralph asked as he snipped a splash shape from a sheet of paper and held it up to the side of the truck. Now the owner could visualize the design Ralph had in mind. Of

Today's custom and show car designs are exercises in imagination and creativity. Hiring an artist to paint the design not only assures professional work, the artist is likely to have more creative ideas for the design. Poster courtesy of Starek Designs.

course it complimented his truck's image perfectly, whereas flames would have confused the image.

When he saw Ralph's creative application of the splashes, the owner was overwhelmed by the design's effect. He expressed his thanks in a letter to Ralph that reads in part:

"When I see the truck for the first time each day, I get the feeling that I am a five year old seeing an elephant or giraffe for the first time, a feeling of complete awe."

That statement captures well the emotion you hope a design will spark.

If you decide to create your own design, you've got three options.

Option 1. Buy a ready-to-apply and paint stencil. This is obviously the easiest way to give your car professional-looking creativity, but don't be surprised if a car with an identical design pulls up beside you at a show or cruise. House of Kolor has created a "Bag o' Flames" kit intended for use on most cars and light trucks. The kit includes the flame

Ralph Starek, a talented automotive custom painter and design artist in Traverse City, Michigan, tells of a Ford "Splash" (Ranger pickup) owner who brought his truck to Ralph's studio for a custom touch. The owner said he'd like a set of flames. "Why not create a splash design instead?" Ralph asked as he snipped a splash shape from a sheet of paper and held it up to the side of the truck. Photos courtesy of Ralph Starek.

BAG O' FLAMES

House of Kolor is pleased to announce the release of a new aftermarket product, "Bag O' Flames." This unique kit offers an excellent opportunity for custom enthusiasts and professional painters alike, and fits most trucks and cars.

The kit includes a complete set of patterns for hood and fenders. Step-by-step instructions (with photos) are included to make this product easy to use. Jon Kosmoski has included suggested blending techniques that will help you in your painting process.

Retail Price: $31.45

One of the options when painting a design is to buy a ready-to-apply and paint stencil. House of Kolor's Bag O' Flames stencil kit can be adapted to most cars and trucks, even motorcycles. Poster courtesy of House of Kolor.

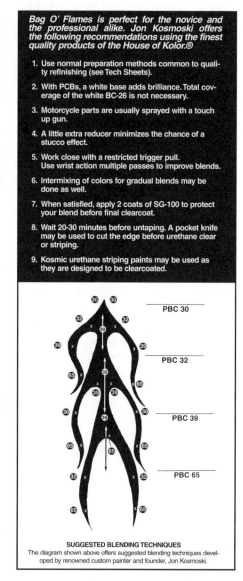

Bag O' Flames is perfect for the novice and the professional alike. Jon Kosmoski offers the following recommendations using the finest quality products of the House of Kolor.®

1. Use normal preparation methods common to quality refinishing (see Tech Sheets).

2. With PCBs, a white base adds brilliance. Total coverage of the white BC-26 is not necessary.

3. Motorcycle parts are usually sprayed with a touch up gun.

4. A little extra reducer minimizes the chance of a stucco effect.

5. Work close with a restricted trigger pull. Use wrist action multiple passes to improve blends.

6. Intermixing of colors for gradual blends may be done as well.

7. When satisfied, apply 2 coats of SG-100 to protect your blend before final clearcoat.

8. Wait 20-30 minutes before untaping. A pocket knife may be used to cut the edge before urethane clear or striping.

9. Kosmic urethane striping paints may be used as they are designed to be clearcoated.

	PBC 30
	PBC 32
	PBC 39
	PBC 65

SUGGESTED BLENDING TECHNIQUES
The diagram shown above offers suggested blending techniques developed by renowned custom painter and founder, Jon Kosmoski.

The Bag O' Flames stencil provides the flame tips, which can be applied in a variety of patterns. Illustration courtesy of House of Kolor.

Design shops can create patterns on a computer and print the pattern as a stencil for transfer onto the car.

Personalized designs such as these spears are drawn freehand, then taped and painted.

patterns for hood and both front fenders, as well as complete instructions for applying the stencil and color blending tips for painting the flames.

Option 2. Have a design shop create a custom pattern, or series of patterns, with a computer and print a stencil on adhesive-backed paper. If you'd rather the design be removable, have it printed on vinyl which can be painted if desired and removed when the vehicle is sold. If you're going to paint the design on the car, you'll attach the stencil then peel off the sections revealing the design. Using a computer simplifies the creative process by being able to copy images from clip art as well as a wide range of artistic fonts for lettering. With a stencil from a computer, it's also easy to create an identical design for both sides of the

vehicle, if symmetry is desirable.

Option 3. Create your own design and transfer it to the vehicle. This approach gives you the greatest latitude for creativity, but is likely to be the most time-consuming, especially if you're going to try to make the design the same on both sides of the vehicle. Creating a custom design typically follows these steps:

- Draw the design. Sometimes you'll draw the design free-hand on the vehicle, other times you will draw the design first on paper, then transfer it to the vehicle.
- Mask the design. Masking, too, can take a couple of approaches. You can cover the surface where the design will be painted with adhesive frisket paper and cut out the

design with an X-acto knife (this approach saves additional masking), or you can mask the design with tape and paper.

The design process also has three parts or stages.

Stage 1. Establish the motif for the design. This is a creative stage. If you're naturally artistic, you'll probably have no problem coming up with ideas. Artistic or not, it's often helpful to look at other people's designs — either on cars you see at shows or in magazines. When you see a design you like on a car, take photos both close-up and full view. If you keep a scrapbook of photos and clippings from magazines, you'll have lots of design concepts to spark your imagination.

Stage 2. Transfer the design to the vehicle. This is a technique stage. As

Creating an elaborate, stand-out design as seen on this drug education car requires creativity, artistic talent, and knowledge of technique.

Patterns such as racing stripes can be taped and painted, or as in the case of this Camaro, created by applying a vinyl applique.

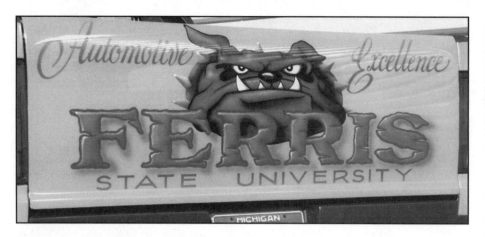

Custom painting often combines several design elements, lettering, drawing or illustration, and patterns such as flames.

Unlike hand-painted lettering which fades and is difficult to remove, stencils can be used to create lettering that looks hand painted and can be airbrushed, but can also be easily removed for changes, updates, or when the lettered vehicle is sold. In this sequence, Ralph Starek is applying lettering stencils to a client's truck.

To keep the stencil positioned as he removes the backing, Ralph applies a "hinge" of masking tape at about the midpoint of the stencil.

Next, he smooths and adheres the first half of the stencil with a squeegee.

Now Ralph removes the masking tape "hinge" and peels back the rest of the stencil backing.

Using a squeegee, Ralph smooths the rest of the stencil.

With the stencil thoroughly adhered, he removes the clear overlay.

The second stencil applies the same way. Ralph has already measured and marked the stencil's location.

The second stencil is adhered and the overlay pulled off.

The finished lettering looks professionally painted and can be airbrushed for color tinting or pinstriped for outlining as has been done with the lower stencil set.

mentioned above, several methods can be used to place the design on the vehicle. These are explained in more detail in the next section.

Stage 3. Paint the design. This is an artistic stage. Until it's painted, the design exists only in concept. Painting brings the design to life. This stage is artistic because it calls for an artist's sense of proportion, shading, and color. When a custom design fails, this is were the failure occurs.

DRAWING DESIGNS

As mentioned in the options above, designs can be drawn on a computer and printed onto a stencil, or drawn on paper and transferred to the car, or drawn on the car itself. For lettering as well as all sorts of artistic effects, computers have overwhelming advantages as creative tools. Additionally, computers eliminate repetitive tasks, save hours in masking, avoid unevenly spaced lettering, and give access to an enormous variety of fonts as well as artistic images either through commercially available font and clip art collections, or by scanning original designs. The computer equipment to produce custom lettering or designs is readily available from shops that may specialize in printing signs but advertise their services as creating custom designs.

Stencils can be applied dry or wet. With lettering, Ralph Starek prefers to put the stencil on dry because it goes on faster. First, he marks the location on the vehicle using a water-based marker. Then he aligns the stencil and tapes it in place using professional automotive masking tape, not the "cheap" masking tape from a discount mart. Next, he places a piece of masking tape at the midpoint of the stencil as a hinge. Removing the tape from one side of the stencil, he pulls off the backing and adheres the stencil to the vehicle. The moment the stencil touches, it sticks so the positioning has to be right. Trying to peel off the stencil to reposition it is likely to tear the material. The hinge helps with proper positioning since it holds the other half of the stencil in place as a guide. With one side attached, he removes the tape and backing from the remaining portion and sticks it in place. That done, he smooths the stencil with a rubber squeegee.

To apply a stencil wet, Ralph mixes a lubricating solution consisting of one pint of isopropyl alcohol (available from pharmacies), a squirt of dish soap, and water to fill a quart plastic spray bottle (available from home improvement stores). He sprays the pre-sanded surface where the stencil will go with the soap-alcohol-water solution, then positions the stencil. This time the stencil can be moved slightly or removed if needed for repositioning. When Ralph has the stencil where he wants it, he squeegees out the water and air bubbles. (This same technique also works well for attaching decals and appliques.) As soon as the solution has dried, portions of the stencil can be removed to paint lettering or a design.

Lettering or a design drawn first on paper (to create a template) can be transferred to the vehicle using graphite paper (which looks like a thicker form of old-fashioned carbon paper). Just place the graphite paper under the template and retrace the design with a soft lead pencil. The graphite paper will leave the design's outline on the vehicle. The design can then be masked using 1/8 in. fine line masking tape or painted directly using an airbrush. (Airbrush technique is described in the next chapter.)

To draw or mask a design directly on the vehicle, you need to have the concept you're creating well-visualized in your mind. Although some custom painters will draw their designs with a Stabilo pencil or a China Marker, Ralph Starek uses a soft lead pencil. The pencil tracing, he says, is easily covered by paint. When laying out a design in tape, Ralph says you need to be looking a foot or two ahead, pulling the tape with one hand and pressing it down with the thumb of the other hand. Trying to attach the tape inch by inch as you go along will result in jagged edges instead of smooth flowing curves.

Whichever approach you use, common design options include perennially popular flames, scallops (which are similar to flames, but geometric rather than freeform in shape), drips, splashes, and "retro" or trick styling features. Examples of retro and trick designs could include painting and airbrushing '50s style chrome trim onto a modern car or a car's signature — the Viper's scoop, say, onto the side of an SUV or pickup used as a Viper's tow vehicle.

PAINTING THE DESIGN

Obviously you don't want to got to the trouble of putting a design on a faded or damaged finish. If the finish needs microsanding or polishing to restore its lustre, do that first, along with any repair work the finish may need. Otherwise, if you're putting the design over a sound or freshly painted finish, scuff the area to be covered by the design with

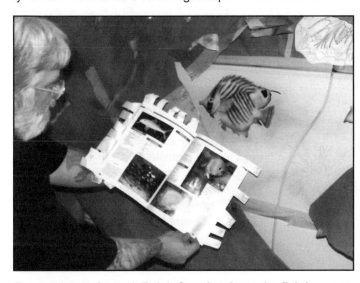

To create a reef mural, Ralph Starek selects the fish he wants to paint from a photo book.

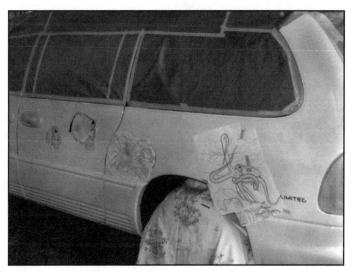

Next, he outlines the shapes and tapes them on the vehicle.

Using graphite paper (like old-fashioned carbon paper) Ralph traces the design onto frisket paper to create a stencil.

Drawing on the stencil, he darkens and fills in details of the design.

Scotchbrite pads or 600 grit sandpaper. In scuffing up the surface, you've got two options:

1 Scotchbrite or sand the area to be covered by the design before tracing and masking. You'll need to clear coat the entire surface, not just the design, but the advantage of this approach is that the overall clear coat will soften or remove any abrupt ridges at the edges of the design.

2 Scotchbrite or sand only the area covered by the design. Here you'll mask and tape the design first, then scuff up only the area inside the masking. This approach saves time, but since only the unmasked area will be clear coated, you'll see and feel ridges at the edges of the design.

Whether you sand the entire panel or just the design, be sure to clean the surface thoroughly with wax and grease remover.

If the design is on a stencil or frisket paper, use an x-acto knife to cut out the design or reach under the cutout portions of the stencil and pull them away. This will expose the areas you're going to paint. Try to avoid cutting the paint, but if you do don't fret. Painting the design will fill in the cuts. Again, wipe exposed areas with wax and grease remover. Mask the finish at least two feet away from the stencil using automotive masking paper. Newspaper is porous and not suitable for masking an automotive finish.

Although you can paint the design a contrasting solid or candy color, or with any of the special effects paints described earlier — metallics, pearls, flakes, or chameleon — often you'll blend two or more related colors for a color shift effect. This color shift is commonly seen in flames where a light shade is used at the start of the flame and a darker shade at the tip, imitating fire which is hottest at the lightest color.

To paint a color shift, you'll need not only the major colors that will appear in the design, but in-between shades as well. For example, if you're painting flames and plan a color shift from yellow to orange to red, you'll need not three colors but five, with a yellow-orange and an orange-red for the transitions. Color blending works best if you have more than one spray gun. Then you can load the different colors in different guns and avoid the delay of emptying, cleaning, and refilling the gun to spray the next color.

To spray the color shift, begin at one end of the pattern and spray the first color. Carry the gun beyond the blending point. Now spray the second (transition) color, starting ahead of the blending point so that the colors overlap. Continue this pattern with the remaining colors. If the color shifts look too abrupt, you may need to respray the pattern in reverse sequence making the color transitions as smooth as possible.

You can also paint a color shift pattern using the spray gun technique in place of the in-between colors. This time you'll turn the spray gun air adjustment way down for the blending points so that the gun mists the paint. Holding the gun a greater distance than normal from the spraying surface (18 in. to 2 ft.), you can wand the gun over the blending areas, backing way off on the trigger to just lightly dust on the paint. Increasing gun distance and decreasing pressure lightens the color, so if your design shifts from light to dark, you'll want to make the blends at the front of each new shade or color in the pattern.

Modern designs often use shadowing to create a three-dimensional look — the design seems to stand off the surface of the car. Shadows are painted with an airbrush and the shadowing technique is described in the next chapter. The shadows are often airbrushed after the masking is removed.

For protection and a smooth finish, the painted design is clear coated then polished. If the design has lots of paint ridges, lightly wet sand to remove the sharp edges, then clear coat. Wet sand the clear and apply another coating. The surface will now look and feel smooth.

MARBLEIZING AND SPLATTER EFFECTS

Patterns like stripes or scallops often use special paint effects for added creativity.

Ralph has airbrushed the fish and is ready to remove the stencil.

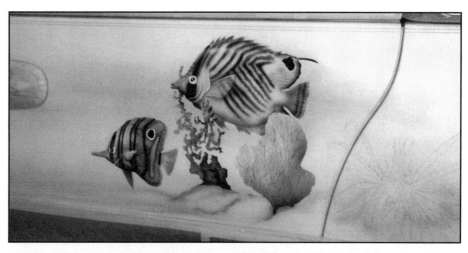

Portions of the stencil are reapplied as masking when painting additional reef details.

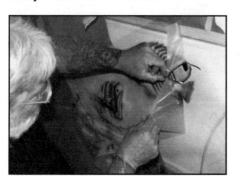

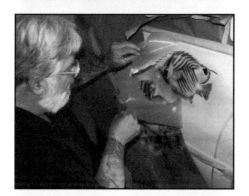

HOW RALPH STAREK PAINTS FLAMES

Having mentally created the design, Ralph establishes the external shape with 1/8 in. fine line masking tape. He then sprays an outline inside the tape with an airbrush. When the paint dries, he masks the outline with 1/4 in. masking tape and lays another layer of 1/4 in. tape over the crack between runs of tape. Now Ralph sprays the flame color. If he decides to add highlights and shadows, the highlight (lighter) shading is on the top, while the shadow (darker) color is on the bottom. Ralph locates his light source upper left and highlights and shadows his designs to match natural light effects (highlights appear upper left, shadows lower right). After painting the flame colors, Ralph peels off all tape except the outside edge (original outline) and clear coats the design. "I pull the last tape while the clear is still tacky — as tacky as I dare," Ralph says. "This lets the edge of the clear lay down tight. The next day I lightly sand the edge and hit it with a buffing wheel. You can still feel a slight edge, but it's not abrupt."

Marbleizing, which grains the paint to simulate the fissures or polished marble, is relatively simple to create. You'll need a black base, House of Kolor marbleizer paint, and a plastic grocery bag.

Step 1. Mask the design.

Step 2. Apply the black base.

Step 3. Shoot the marbleizer heavy enough so that the paint starts to run.

Step 4. Crimp up a plastic bag and imprint the bag (squish against) in the paint. The paint will set up fast, so you'll want to make the imprints in quick succession. The more "hits," the lighter the effect since the bag pulls off paint.

Splattering gives a random creative effect, like the artwork of Jackson Pollock or a Chimpanzee. You'll need a foam roller, toothbrush, kitchen fork, or palette knife.

Step 1. Mask the design.

Step 2. For the background, roll on lettering enamel with a foam roller (gives the paint texture).

Step 3. Create a splatter design by standing back a few feet and flinging paint against the background. The tool you use can be a stiff brush, a palette knife, or a toothbrush for a light splatter, or a fork for a string effect. Fling by dipping the tool in various colored paint containers, then jerk the handle in a sharp sideways or downward motion. On a vertical surface, the splatters will run, which may be part of the effect. Choice of colors for the splatters is part of the design pattern.

Custom painting is often embellished by airbrushing and pinstriping. These techniques and more of the designs they can be used to create are described in the next chapter.

Ralph carefully peels back the stencil to reveal his design.

Do-It-Yourself Guide to CUSTOM PAINTING
Airbrushing and Pinstriping

Metallic paints give the finish reflective glitter. This street rod also wears a design effect called scallops, discussed previously in Chapter 14.

The most versatile tool for custom painting is an airbrush. Some readers may have familiarity with airbrushing from model building. When our son Anthony was an avid modeler, he discovered that to create realistic paint schemes on his models (camouflage for his military vehicles and some aircraft, or glossy factory color or custom paint on his cars and trucks), he needed an airbrush. His first airbrush was an inexpensive kit from a hobby shop that included a single-action airbrush, a couple of paint containers, a short length of air hose, and a can of propellant. For modeling, the kit worked quite well, though the propellant cans quickly became a nuisance as they always seemed to run out in the middle of a paint project. One Christmas we bought our son an air brush compressor. Now he could paint his models without interruption.

Airbrushing allows the same control on real cars and trucks that it does on models. Of course you wouldn't paint the whole finish on a real vehicle with such a miniature tool, but an airbrush is ideal for creating all sorts of special effects. It can draw pencil thin lines or mist a fairly wide area with very little overspray. For custom painting that includes flames, scallops, or any other special effect, an airbrush and some degree of mastery of technique is a must.

AIRBRUSHING EQUIPMENT

Our son's single-action airbrush worked fine for his modeling. It was easy to use and control on the small surfaces. But for custom painting on a car, a single-action airbrush has limitations. The name "single-action" means that one button controls both the air and paint flow. Push the control button, which sits on the top of the airbrush shaft just above the connector for the air hose, and paint flows. Release the button and the paint stops. What could be simpler?! It's no different than triggering a regular paint spray gun. But with an airbrush you often want another dimension of control and that's the width of the spray pattern, which is variable from a thin line to a fan pattern. With a single-action airbrush, you vary the spray pattern by turning a dial (called the fluid control knob) just behind the tip. I've seen experienced airbrushers twiddle this knob as they're painting (to increase or decrease the flow of paint and thereby vary the pattern), but the two-handed coordination while painting looks awkward and makes transitions between patterns difficult. However, for the novice who wants to use an airbrush in limited ways — to outline letters or a design for example — an inexpensive single-action airbrush will do the job and keep the learning phase relatively short. You can even start as our son did using propellant cans for the air supply.

For more control and a greater range of painting technique, you'll

Beginners to airbrushing will want to purchase a kit, which includes several paint bottles, assorted paint nozzle and needle assemblies, a six-foot length of air hose, and basic tools for servicing the airbrush. Photo courtesy of the Eastwood Company.

You hold an airbrush just like a pencil or a pen. Watching airbrushing and following practice exercises on an instructional videos are great ways to learn proper airbrushing technique. Photo courtesy of the Eastwood Company.

want to purchase a double-action airbrush. An instructor in custom painting was more direct. "Tell 'em that's the only one to buy," he said. What is the difference? With "double-action" the button also varies the amount of paint, meaning the spray pattern. On a double-action airbrush, when you push down on the button, you get only air. Push down and pull back and you get both air and paint. The farther back you pull the button, the more paint you get. So if you want just a narrow pattern to outline a shape, you press and pull the button just a "whisker." When you want to broaden the line, you nudge the knob a little farther. (The distance you hold the airbrush from the painting surface also affects the spray pattern.) Working the control in both directions takes a little longer to get comfortable doing, but the increased control and flexibility of the double-action over the single-action airbrush is like the difference between fuel injection and a carburetor.

Besides single or double action, airbrushes also differ by whether they place the paint cup at the top, bottom, or side. Airbrushes that place the paint cup at the top or side are gravity feed — just like the modern type spray guns. The advantages of this type of airbrush are similar to those of gravity feed spray guns: they're easy to clean, handle, and maneuver. Other airbrushes place the paint container at the bottom. These are siphon or suction feed — like the older style automotive spray guns. As their advantage, siphon feed airbrushes offer a larger paint container for painting a greater area before refilling. Gravity airbrushes have very small paint containers, which require frequent refilling.

Generally, a gravity feed airbrush is used for work that is intricate — like a design — where ability to control the gun and see exactly where the nozzle is pointing are important, and colors are likely to be changed frequently. A siphon feed airbrush would be selected where a relatively large area needs to be painted before changing colors — like outlining or painting the tips on flames.

Although you can "power" an airbrush with a portable air supply (a tank that you fill periodically from an air compressor) or cans of propellant, the best air source is an oil-less, 110 volt airbrush compressor. Often, you'll find the compressor included in a "deluxe" or "professional" airbrush kit. Prices for a complete airbrush kit and compressor range from $150 to $300 — relatively inexpensive when you consider an airbrush's many uses. With the kit you may also get several paint bottles (very handy for quick color changes), assorted nozzle and needle assemblies, a 6 ft. length of air hose (allowing free movement of the airbrush with the compressor somewhat out of the way), a small tool kit for the brush, and in many cases a beginner's lesson guide. Airbrush lessons are also available on video tape, but as with any tool, mastering airbrush technique takes practice, which can be done on a sheet of plywood, cardboard, scrap automotive panels, or models.

AIRBRUSHING TECHNIQUE

You hold an airbrush just like a pencil or a pen, the shaft cradled against the middle finger knuckle with the thumb pressing against the shaft, holding it in place. This grip leaves the index (first) finger free to operate the control button. Turning the wrist easily moves the brush in a rotational as well as sideways or up-and-down motion.

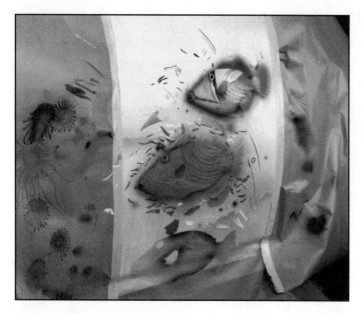

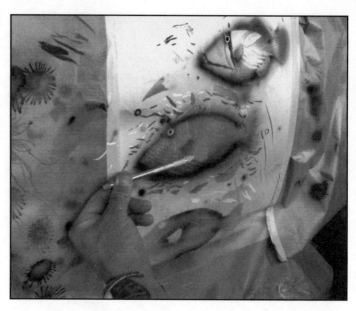

The following sequence shows airbrushing artist Ralph Starek creating a portion of a reef mural that will appear on a scuba diving instructor's van.

Here Ralph covers a fish's fin with a small piece of masking.

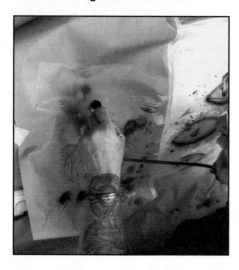

When he needs to clear the airbrush Ralph sprays against a layer of masking he has placed beside the design he's painting.

To get used to the airbrush's operation and feel, and to gain control of the air and paint flow, you'll need to practice. You can use a sheet of paper or a piece of cardboard as your practice surface. Begin by painting a series of dots. This will give you a feel for the pressure and action of the control button. If you have a double-action airbrush you can practice increasing the size of the dots by pulling back farther on the control button. With a single-action airbrush you could draw a series of dots one size, then increase the paint flow by opening the fluid control knob and draw the next series of dots another size. You can also practice holding the airbrush close to the painting backdrop and then pulling it away, observing changes to the spray pattern that result.

When you're comfortable with the airbrush's feel and action, practice painting a series of lines. You'll need to hold the airbrush quite close to the painting surface for the spray pattern to appear as a narrow line. Concentrate on controlling the airbrush so that the lines are straight and consistent in width. This practice will help prepare you to outline lettering or shapes. After you feel comfortable with consistent width lines, practice painting lines of increasing width. With a double-action airbrush, you can make the lines wider by pulling back on the

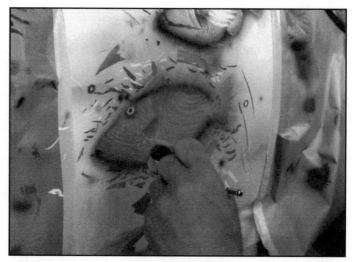

He airbrushes a shadow to give the fin a realistic three-dimensional appearance.

control button. With a single-action tool you'll need to twirl the fluid knob.

From dots and lines you can progress to drawing shapes, especially ovals and circles. Don't worry, you don't have to draw perfect circles freehand — you'll either be tracing or outlining circles that have already been drawn or painted on the car. Next you can practice shading, a technique that adds realism by giving shapes a three-dimensional look. You can practice shading a circle by laying or taping a circle template (piece of paper or cardboard with a round hole cut out) over a fresh area of your practice surface. Lightly spray the circle's entire circumference but darken one section (typically the bottom) by applying more paint. As you extend the shading you'll notice that the circle begins to look more like a three-dimensional sphere with the shading on the underside, away from the light. Shading requires an artist's awareness of an image's light source and consequent shadows.

As light shines on objects it creates highlights, a horizon line, and shadows. Highlights, or lighter shades of color, typically appear at the top where the sun would strike the object or design most directly. The horizon line represents the point where the sun fades into shadow. As you observe objects in sunlight, you'll notice that this horizon line is more a transition point than an actual line — a subtle shift of shading from light to dark. Shadows are the darker shades, representing areas light doesn't strike directly. As you begin to notice light's different effects in the three zones (highlights, horizon line, and shadows), you'll be able to use your airbrush to imitate effects and make your designs (whether lettering or flames) more realistic. Instructional videos are available from The Eastwood Company and other sources that can help you learn shadowing and other airbrushing techniques.

"TRICK" EFFECTS

An airbrush is an extremely creative tool, making possible almost any design or effect the artist can imagine. Among the more fascinating effects are optical illusions — painted designs that

appear so realistic they're mistaken for the object they represent. An example is fake chrome. The popularity of retro styling (as seen in the "new" Beetle and various show cars) has led some custom painters to include popular Fifties chrome motifs (such as Buick "portholes") on a more recent car. As Ralph Starek explained, chrome is reflective, so to paint chrome's imitation you use the colors that chrome reflects — typically blue from the sky, light blue or white for the horizon line, and a darker color such as burnt umber, sand, or brown for the ground. You won't see silver in painted chrome. Capturing the chrome effect requires an artist's eye for color and shading and a degree of skill in airbrush technique, but the result is both dazzling and playful — is it real or isn't it?

A more easily achieved "trick" effect is fake woodgraining, which Ralph has used effectively as a backdrop for lettering, signage, and logos. If the wood effect is small, it can be done almost entirely with an airbrush, but if large, a regular spray gun would be used for the base color. Follow these steps to create artificial woodgraining.

1. Spray the base color. Creative possibilities include a candy apple red or tangerine, light browns, or oranges and browns together. Since realism isn't essential, you can choose colors for their effect.
2. Using a two to three-inch brush, paint a darker color over the base coat. With this step you're imitating the woodgrain lines, so you may want to cut back the bristles for a rougher look. You'll also vary the brush strokes to suggest woodgrain's irregular lines and patterns.
3. Using an airbrush and a sheet of cardboard with holes cut in different shapes and sizes, spray "knot holes" in random locations on the woodgrain.
4. Airbrush the rest of the design, which may include a business name or logo.
5. Optionally, use the airbrush to outline and shadow the wood pattern.
6. Clear coat the design. Clear coating will darken the colors slightly.

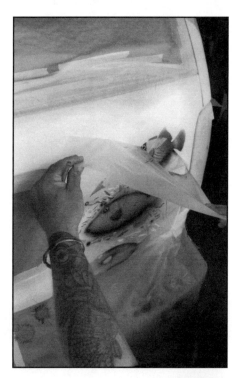

With the painting completed, Ralph carefully peels the masking away from the design.

The fish are not only lifelike, Ralph has given them personality besides.

Watching an instructional video is an easy way to learn how to airbrush custom graphics and designs. Photo courtesy of The Eastwood Company.

An easily achieved "trick" effect is fake woodgraining, which can be used as a backdrop for lettering, signage, and logos. Photo courtesy of Ralph Starek.

AIRBRUSH PAINTS

Traditionally, airbrushing used lacquer paints. Today, airbrushing is done with 1 Shot lettering enamel and water-based paints. Suppliers for these products are listed in the Appendix. Lacquers are discouraged for two reasons: 1) even though lacquer is among the least toxic of automotive paints, you're inhaling the paint at close range while airbrushing, and 2) urethane clears are not recommended over lacquer color. Non-toxic water-based colors are the most popular choice. The ease with which mistakes are corrected and their instant drying are other reasons for the popularity of water-based colors.

However, it's very important to make sure no water accidentally splashes on the design before the colors are covered with clear coat.

Airbrush colors even include metallics and pearlescents. You can buy the paints individually, but to get started you'll probably purchase a kit or color set. Generally, you'll apply the darker background colors first, the lighter foreground later. With this sequence, if there's some overspray in

Ralph Starek's airbrushing talent can be seen in this flamboyantly painted Drug Abuse Resistance Education (D.A.R.E) car.

the foreground colors, it's not likely to be seen against the darker background. One of the best ways to keep up-to-date with products, designs, and techniques is to browse issues of magazines dedicated to airbrushing like *Airbrush Action*, which can be viewed on the web at www.air-brushaction.com.

Paint consistency is important both for flow and to prevent the airbrush from clogging and sputtering. You should follow the paint manufacturer's mixing instructions, but to prevent clogging it's best to start thin and add paint to the mixture if needed. An airbrush is a very delicate tool; if the tiny internal passages become clogged with paint, your painting experience will quickly become a painting nightmare.

AIRBRUSH CLEANING AND CARE

Always flush the airbrush with solvent between colors and immediately after using. Flushing should be done two ways: 1) regular flushing where you spray solvent through the nozzle until the spray is clear of color, and 2) back flushing where you cover the tip with a clean cloth and press the control button. Stopping the flow of air and solvent from the nozzle forces the material back into the paint cup. A good cleaning regimen alternates between spraying solvent through the nozzle and back flushing. The combination helps loosen and remove any obstruction. You can also use back flushing to remove obstructions while painting.

Common airbrush problems are "splattering," caused by letting off on the control button too abruptly and "spitting," which is caused by dried paint in the air passages — a result of inadequate cleaning. Splattering is corrected by practicing airbrush technique. Spitting can be more severe. Start by cleaning and flushing (with the back-and-forth pattern of spraying clean solvent through the nozzle and back flushing). If spitting continues, remove the tip and clean the head, but do not attempt to disassemble the airbrush. Tiny internal parts are easily damaged. If internal cleaning is needed, you should have the airbrush professionally serviced.

Airbrushed lettering can create bold, creative designs.

PINSTRIPING

The idea of embellishing automotive finishes with delicate hand painted lines and patterns isn't new. Striping was even used to decorate buggies and wagons prior to the automotive age. Early cars often had elaborate striping patterns on body and fender reveals, front frame arms, and wheel spokes. The practice continued through the 1930s, with men using brushes at the factory to deftly spin stripes on wheels and paint outline patterns on body moldings. The practice faded in the postwar Forties, largely because of production schedules and the diminishing pool of talented stripers.

Pinstriping revived in the 1950s, largely a result of the enormous talent of a California customizer named Kenneth Howard, more popularly known as "Von Dutch." I remember reading a story about Von Dutch in one of the Fifties pocket-sized rod and custom magazines. According to the story, Von Dutch had such fine artistic

When one of Ralph Starek's customers asked if he painted garages, the client wasn't thinking about the exterior.

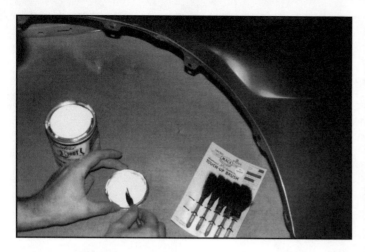

The best way to learn pinstriping is to practice on a damaged or discarded body panel or fender.

control that he could draw perfectly round circles by hand without use of a compass. Von Dutch discovered this ability, the story related, in a high school drafting class. The instructor, non-plussed by a student who could spin circles freehand, insisted that Von Dutch use his drafting tools. Somewhat rebellious, Von Dutch refused, and failed the class. The sting of that failure, the article implied, led to Von Dutch applying his drawing talent to automobiles and elaborate pinstriping designs.

PINSTRIPING TOOLS AND TECHNIQUE

Freehand pinstriping uses a special dagger brush that holds the quantity of paint needed to lay down long, unbroken lines. While pinstriping can be mastered by anyone with a steady hand, the technique requires practice. You can purchase pinstriping brushes from a number of sources, including The Eastwood Company. The dagger brushes come in a variety of widths and sizes from "00" Very Fine to size "4" with striping tips ranging in width from 1/8 to 1/2 in. Bold. If you're contemplating a variety of pinstriping styles, you may want to purchase several sizes. Although lacquer paints can be used, the better choice is slower drying 1 Shot enamel or similar lettering and striping paints, which are preferred because of their easy flow for eliminating brush marks and durable, high gloss finish. With the paint, you'll also need a compatible

thinner or reducer. Eastwood offers a pinstriping kit that includes a range of brush sizes, two choices of 1 Shot paint, and an instructional video.

Actual pinstriping technique has three parts: preparing the painted surface to be striped, mixing the paint and loading the brush, and applying the stripe. An advantage of striping with lettering enamel, as long as the surface is clean, is you don't need to scuff up the paint for adhesion. For cleaning you can either use a quality wax and grease remover or ordinary Windex (without ammonia). But you should also wipe the surface with an anti-static cleaner, such as PPG's Multi-Prep, especially when striping

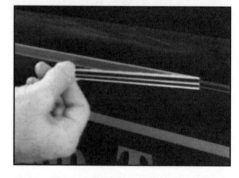

For those who don't trust the steadiness of their hand to draw a long, straight stripe, masking kits are available to create a stencil for the stripe, which is still painted by hand using a pinstriping brush. Photo courtesy of The Eastwood Company.

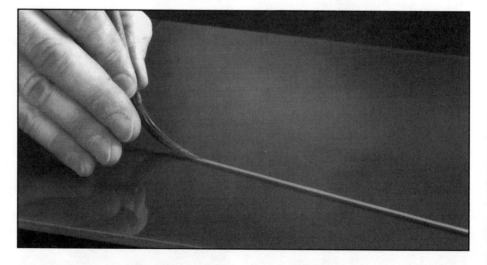

Hand painting lines and patterns is an old art, pre-dating automobiles, yet remains popular today. Freehand pinstriping uses a special dagger brush that holds the quantity of paint needed to lay down long, unbroken lines. Photo courtesy of The Eastwood Company.

plastic parts. Otherwise, rubbing the finish during cleaning can build up enough static electricity to suck the paint off the brush as you approach the surface.

Different colors of lettering and striping enamel can be mixed for just the right hue. You'll mix the paint in a small plastic cup (usually no larger than about half-pint size) and add the recommended amount of reducer. 1 Shot products have their own reducers formulated for normal, high, and low temperature conditions. As with other paints, it's important to use the right reducer.

Naturally, you'll need to practice pinstriping technique before trying it on a car. The simplest strokes are straight lines, which can follow the beltline crease along the body sides. On older cars or customs with hood louvers, striping can accent the cutouts. Other strokes follow curves or make patterns, often imitating the complex interweave of spears and circles that originated with Von Dutch.

To pinstripe with any degree of success, you've got to hold the brush with the proper grip. Both single-handed and double-handed grips are used — single-handed for straight lines and double-handed for curves and designs. The single-handed grip places the brush handle between the thumb and index finger, resting the handle's shaft against the fleshy bridge. The other fingers form a support base, both for steadiness and to keep the tip at a consistent angle as it's pulled along the surface. Varying the angle will narrow or widen the width of the strip, so it's important to hold the brush absolutely steady, and the entire hand gets put to work doing so.

You'll see different variations of the two-handed grip. Some hold the brush with one hand and use the other for steadying and as a pivot. Others press the brush between both thumbs and forefingers and use the little fingers like outriggers on a canoe or training wheels on a bike to steady the brush on long strokes or as pivots on turns and curves. Your best source of grip and hand technique is a demonstration video, available from The Eastwood Company and others. You'll see all stages of brush action and get ideas for

designs that you may want to practice and paint on your car. Of course practice is the next step after watching the video. Unless you're a "natural" like Von Dutch, you'll spend a number of hours practicing before you feel ready to actually lay down stripes on a car.

If you're striping a reveal or raised molding, which are com-monly found on car bodies of the Twenties through the Forties, you can use the molding's upper or lower edge as a guide for your hand. But if you're laying down a long stripe on a car without the raised reveals, you'll probably need to make your own guide which can be done using a strip of fine line tape. If you're accenting a body crease, you can keep the line straight just by following the crease. The tape shouldn't be a masking for the stripe, but a guide for your hand, so it needs to be the guide your fingers follow. Running the brush tip against the tape risks thinning the stripe. If you don't have a crease to follow, you may want to make measurements from a window edge or bottom of the door, and follow the markings as you lay the tape, pulling the tape to make sure it's taut as you press it in place.

Where laying down a straight line by hand seems daunting, you can use stencil tape. In this case you lay out the tape the same way you would if you were making a guide (as described above) then peel off the stencil covering. Pinstriping tape comes in various widths for narrow or wide stripes or multiple stripes of different widths and possibly different colors. Using tape, you can paint the stripe with an artist's brush (you don't need a pinstriping brush as you're not concerned about pulling the entire stripe with one fill of the brush).

Concerns when using striping tape are to:

1 Clean the surface before applying the tape. Dust, lint, hair, whatever, trapped under the tape could allow paint to seep through the stencil.

2 Make sure the tape is exactly where you want it before peeling off the clear covering; you won't be able to adjust the stencil once the covering is removed.

3 Press the tape securely in place. Paint could seep under loose spots.

4 Apply the paint in slow strokes; otherwise you might splash paint outside the stencil. The level of care increases if the stencil allows for more than one stripe and you plan to paint the stripes different colors.

For those who are brush phobic, stripes can be laid down smoothly and cleanly with a Beugler tool that rolls on the paint. The tool can be purchased with a variety of roller heads for varying width stripes. Photo courtesy of The Eastwood Company.

The van's owner is a scuba diving instructor who uses her business name "Suzie Seahorse." The designer "monogrammed" the seahorse on the driver's door. Photos courtesy of Ralph Starek.

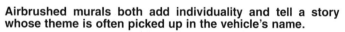

Airbrushed murals both add individuality and tell a story whose theme is often picked up in the vehicle's name.

Rick Hall created this unique cab-over-engine pickup using the nose from a ton-and-a-half truck on a shortened mid-50s Chevrolet pickup chassis. The flames paint theme adds character to Rick's one-off creation. Photo courtesy Rick Hall.

You'll remove the tape as soon as the paint has set but before it fully dries. Waiting until the paint dries risks pulling off some of the stripe with the paint that's hardened on the tape. Pull the tape smoothly and evenly away from the stripes. If any of the tape touches the still tacky paint it could blemish the stripe.

For those who are brush-phobic, pinstriping can also be done with a tool that rolls on the paint. You may have seen this tool demonstrated at car shows and swap meets. The tool, properly called a Beugler Mechanical Pinstriper, paints curves and designs as easily as straight lines; however, you'll have to use the same kind of control techniques for freehand work as you would with a brush. For lines, the Beugler tool can be used in combination with a magnetic guide strip that keeps the stripe as straight as you've laid the strip. Like a brush, the Beugler tool requires practice. You'll also find watching a demonstration video (available from The Eastwood Company) helpful not only to see how to fill the tool with paint and maintain it after use, but also for tips on proper grip and various patterns the tool can create.

Whether by brush or Beugler tool, pinstriping is a highly versatile art, as useful for outline lettering and patterns like flames as it is for creating designs or running lines.

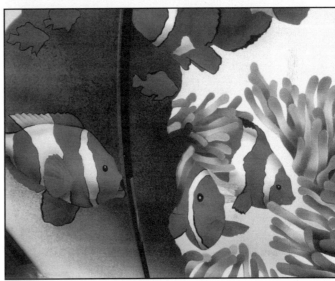

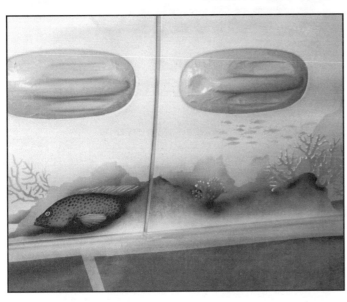

The finished reef scene shows the creative effects an accomplished airbrush artist can produce. Photos courtesy of Ralph Starek.

Finesse Pinstriping Inc.

P.O. Box 541428 Linden Hill Station
Flushing, New York 11354-7428

THE STRIPER® Stencil Tape
Size Chart

With these 41 different sizes, anybody can repair just about any pinstripe job that comes into the shop or generate extra business by doing complete car paint pinstriping. Our tape leaves the cleanest and sharpest lines, nothing even comes close! Additional sizes available upon request.

Actual Sizes of Results:

F-00
3/16"
1/4"
1/16"

F-0
3/16"
3/16"
1/16"

F-1
5/32"
5/32"
1/16"

F-2
5/32"
1/8"
1/16"

F-3
1/8"
5/32"
1/16"

F-4
1/8"
1/8"
1/16"

F-5
3/32"
5/32"
1/16"

F-6
3/32"
1/8"
1/16"

F-7
1/16"
1/8"
1/8"
1/8"
1/16"

F-8
5/32"

F-9
1/8"

F-10
3/32"

F-11
1/16"

F-12
1/8"
3/16"
1/8"

F-13
1/8"
1/8"
1/8"

F-14
1/8"
3/32"
1/8"

F-15
1/8"
1/16"
1/8"

Finesse Pinstriping provides stencil tape in a wide range of patterns and strip widths. The patterns are even more flexible because with a multiple strip tape, the user can choose to paint some or all of the stripes. To select a desired pattern, it helps to observe stripes used on cars you consider attractive. Normally, you'll apply the stripes along the body creases or accent lines in the styling. Striper chart courtesy of Finesse Pinstriping.

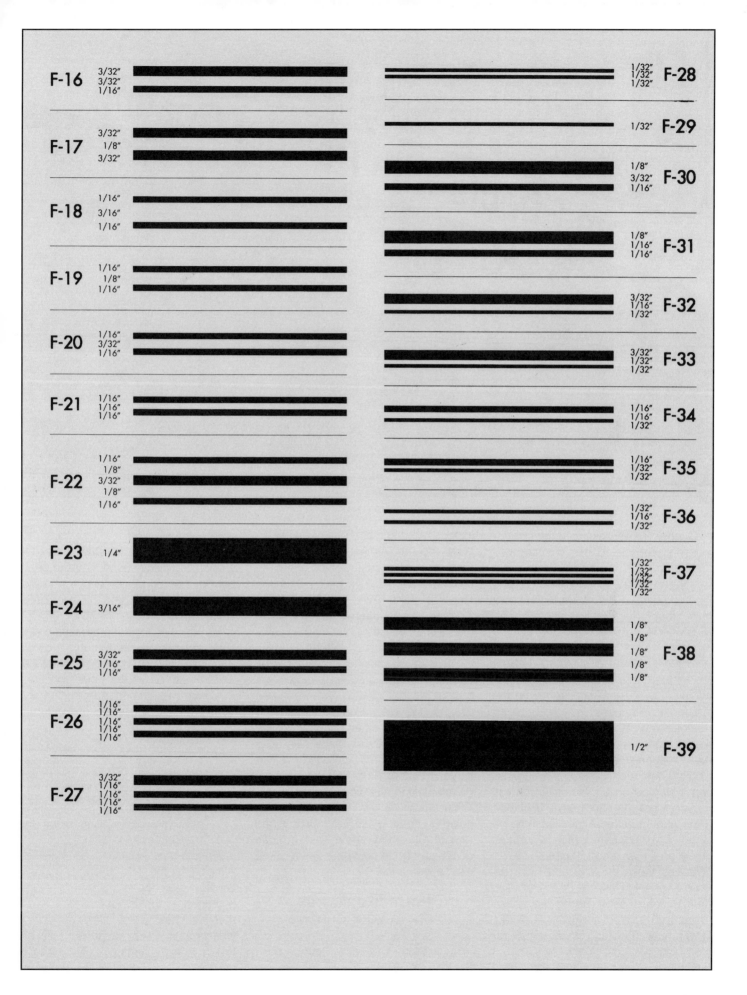

F-16   3/32″ 3/32″ 1/16″

F-17   3/32″ 1/8″ 3/32″

F-18   1/16″ 3/16″ 1/16″

F-19   1/16″ 1/8″ 1/16″

F-20   1/16″ 3/32″ 1/16″

F-21   1/16″ 1/16″ 1/16″

F-22   1/16″ 1/8″ 3/32″ 1/8″ 1/16″

F-23   1/4″

F-24   3/16″

F-25   3/32″ 1/16″ 1/16″

F-26   1/16″ 1/16″ 1/16″ 1/16″

F-27   3/32″ 1/16″ 1/16″ 1/16″ 1/16″

1/32″ 1/32″ 1/32″   F-28

1/32″   F-29

1/8″ 3/32″ 1/16″   F-30

1/8″ 1/16″ 1/16″   F-31

3/32″ 1/16″ 1/32″   F-32

3/32″ 1/32″ 1/32″   F-33

1/16″ 1/16″ 1/32″   F-34

1/16″ 1/32″ 1/32″   F-35

1/32″ 1/16″ 1/32″   F-36

1/32″ 1/32″ 1/32″ 1/32″   F-37

1/8″ 1/8″ 1/8″ 1/8″   F-38

1/2″   F-39

Do-It-Yourself Guide to
CUSTOM PAINTING
Custom Effects with Powder Coating

Chapter Three described the powder coating process. In this chapter we'll look at what you can do with powder coating to create custom finishes and special effects. So it's back to the shop, this time for a creative session with Eastwood's HotCoat™ powder coating system.

The original line of standard HotCoat colors has expanded to include specialty colors for custom effects. Top on the list for "infinite uses" is a color called Almost Chrome, which Eastwood's marketing manager John Sloane describes as the nearest to real chrome of any coating he's seen. John isn't exaggerating in his description. Almost Chrome is exactly what the name says. My friend Rich wanted to see Almost Chrome on a set of runners for a GM tune port fuel injection. His shop specializes in installing these engines and Rich has tried a variety of finishes on the runners, from uncoated beadblasting (they're aluminum) to painted and chrome plated. The runner tubes don't disassemble for polishing. Chrome looks nice, but it attracts a bit too much attention and

looks gaudy on these "brainy" engines. Rich thought Almost Chrome might have the right gloss — not too bright like chrome, not too dull like plain aluminum. He was right. Even as the Almost Chrome powder-coated runners sat in the baking oven, they gleamed — shiny like chrome, but not so glittery.

The instructions said Almost Chrome had to be clear coated. Eastwood offers a clear powder coating. We wondered whether the clear would diminish the gloss and what other changes to the appearance it would make. We also wondered about the application. It had to go over the Almost Chrome, which meant baking the first coating twice. What would be the effect? The clear powder coating slightly diminishes Almost Chrome's shine, but it adds depth, giving the coating a softer, more satin appearance.

PARTS TO BRIGHTEN
WITH ALMOST CHROME

Applications for Almost Chrome powder coating include numerous smaller

engine, suspension, and trim parts that might otherwise be chrome plated. On suspension pieces especially, the bright powder coating could even be considered superior to chrome for several reasons:

1. The electroplating process weakens steel parts through a condition called "hydrogen embrittlement." Of all the parts you don't want weakened, suspension and steering pieces are at the top of the list.
2. Electroplating is dangerous and environmentally hostile, whereas powder coating is safe and environmentally friendly.
3   πChrome plating is expensive while powder coating using the HotCoat system is cheap.

Wheels are another candidate for Almost Chrome. The coating is unquestionably superior to paint and avoids hydrogen embrittlement, which is as much a risk when chrome plating wheels as it is with suspension pieces. Where Almost Chrome really "shines" is on diecast trim. Let's not get confused.

112 *Do-It-Yourself Guide to Custom Painting*

Almost Chrome isn't real chrome, so you wouldn't want to powder coat diecast from a restoration show car. But for a "driver" or a custom, Almost Chrome turns distressed diecast into one of the car's most embellishing features without the exorbitant expense of restorative chrome plating. When coating diecast trim, be sure to follow the prebaking tips outlined in Chapter 3.

Recently, as I approached a "highboy" roadster to admire the car and its builder's work, I realized that most of what was chrome plated could have been coated Almost Chrome. The cost savings would have been substantial and the difference in appearance would have been negligible, providing all brightwork was consistently Almost Chrome. Larger items like the front axle would need to be commercially powder coated, or HotCoated and cured using Eastwood's infrared cure system. Or some combination of Almost Chrome and real chrome-plated items could be retained, with the plated pieces tinted with translucent powder coatings for a uniform warm brightness instead of the sharp reflection of real chrome.

A caution about Almost Chrome or any powder coating finish: Be sure to follow to the letter the application and baking instructions, as described in the HotCoat system manual and in Chapter 3 of this book.

The day Rich powder coated the fuel injection runners, we invited a friend to watch. Our friend is retired, which means his time is his to do with as he pleases, but he also keeps a tight tether to his wife's meal schedule. In our haste to show off the results — so that our friend wouldn't be late to dinner — we apparently cut short the curing time.

The powder will melt at around 100 degrees F. Baking at 400 degrees F and allowing a 15 to 20 minute curing time is necessary to build the coating's resistance to chipping, chemicals, and bonding. Bake at a lower temperature and/or cut short the curing time and problems can occur. Eastwood reports problems with spider cracking; we created a coating with zero resistance to lacquer thinner. Rich had decided to paint the plenum above the runners with a "rattle can." A few shots of overspray landed on the Almost Chrome. "Piece of cake," Rich thought, "I'll wipe this off with lac-

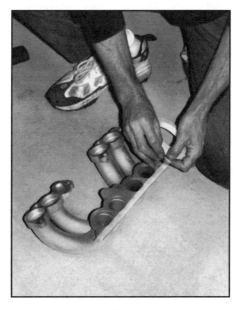

Runners from a GM tune port fuel injection seemed an ideal candidate for Almost Chrome powder coating. To keep the coating off mating surfaces, the runner ports and mounting flanges had to be masked with special high temperature masking tape.

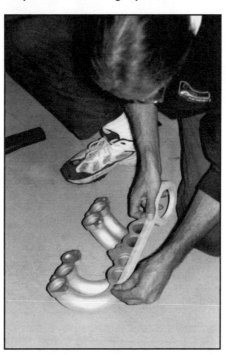

The masking is carefully applied one strip at a time, each strip having a slight amount of overlap.

quer thinner." Wrong move, the thinner turned the clear coating over the Almost Chrome into little "gummie balls." Not a pleasant sight! Be sure your oven holds the required baking temperature, follow the baking time schedule, and allow full curing. Resist opening the oven during curing. Let the part cure in full heat for the full length of time. Otherwise, your

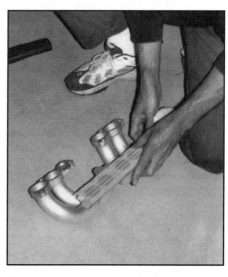

The process continues until the runner ports are completely masked.

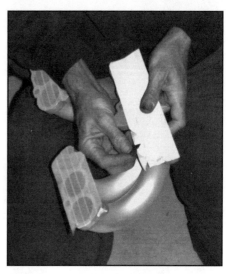

An x-acto knife or razor blade is used to cut the masking to the contour of the part.

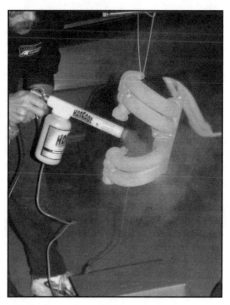

Now the runner set is sprayed with the Almost Chrome coating.

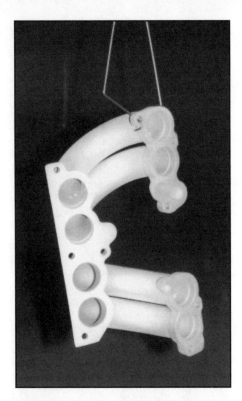

Powder coating is so easy that the most complicated part of the process is rigging a support stand to hold the part while the coating is applied.

Next, the Almost Chrome plating is placed in an oven to bake

Baking transforms the dull powder to a gleaming chrome appearance.

Almost Chrome has to be clear coated, so as soon as the runner set had cooled, it was placed in the spraying box and recoated.

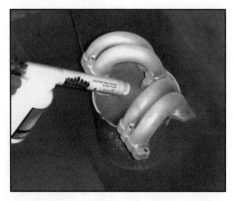

The clear coat is also a powder.

After baking the clear coating, the Almost Chrome had lost a little of its sparkle, but still could pass for chrome plating.

powder coating won't have the strength and chemical resistance that are the coating's bragging rights.

COLOR TINTING WITH TRANSLUCENTS

If the plating on a diecast trim piece is still sound, you can color tint the part with a translucent powder coating. You'll find that the baked and melted powder adheres to chrome much better than paint. And you're certainly not limited to coating diecast. In fact, the opposite is the case with diecast being the least desirable base; the reasons for this are discussed in Chapter 3. Another place to look for translucent-over-chrome applications is inside the engine compartment where plated engine accessories like the air cleaner and valve covers could easily transform into highpoints of color. Think, too, about powder coating the master cylinder reservoir cover. Though plated, these covers eventually corrode. Powder coating would not only seal out rust, but provide an easily cleaned finish. If you don't want to highlight this functional device, you could powder coat the master cylinder cover — or both the reservoir casting and cover if the master cylinder is disassembled for rebuild — with natural-looking powder colors like Cast Iron for the casting and Argent Silver for the cover.

While the HotCoat system's limitation is the size of the baking oven, this constraint doesn't apply to commercial powder coating. For a custom car, you might decide to have bumpers commercially powder coated either a tinted Almost Chrome or a Translucent color that compliments your car's finish. Metal interior pieces also make good candidates for powder coating. Don't try powder coating plastic parts as they won't survive the baking process. Metal door handles and window cranks, as long as they're free of plastic knobs or springs, won't be harmed by baking.

You can create some "fun" effects with powder coat translucents, like reflective blue hubcap spinners. For maximum effect, the translucent coatings should be applied over chrome, polished metal, or an Argent Silver powder coating base coat. Whereas solvent-based paint would require primer coatings over bare metal, powder coating adheres to bare metal, so a polished finish works fine as a base. If you want to preserve the polished finish as is, without tinting with a translucent, you can coat the metal with Gloss Clear powder, the same coating used over Almost Chrome. Likely candidates for polishing and translucent or clear coating include various aluminum under-hood parts like water pumps, water inlets, and performance intake manifolds.

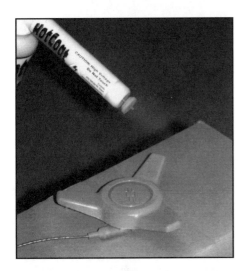

The spinner and air cleaner cover went into the baking oven together.

If the plating on a diecast trim piece is sound, you can color tint the chrome with a translucent powder coating. The translucent powder adheres much better than paint and gives the part a "candy color" look. The item being coated is a Chevrolet hubcap spinner.

Another place to look for translucent-over-chrome applications is inside the engine compartment where plated engine accessories like the air cleaner and valve covers could easily be transformed into highlights of color.

Both emerged glittering in their translucent-over-chrome coatings.

WRINKLE COATING FOR A PERFORMANCE LOOK

Engine valve covers take on a whole different personality when powder coated with a Black Wrinkle finish. Frankly, I was amazed with the difference. Rich had an early Corvette cast-aluminum valve cover hanging in his shop that he'd cleaned so it was ready for powder coating. The casting had a crack around one of the tie-down bolt holes, so it was strictly a display item. "Let's see what Black Wrinkle does to this valve cover," Rich said as he suspended it from his powder coating stand and wafted on the Black Wrinkle. When he finished he wrapped a shop towel around an index finger and carefully wiped the powder coating from the casting fins and Corvette lettering. This "trick" is one of the neat abilities of powder coating and difficult if not impossible with paint. A friend who was observing the process commented, "Wouldn't that be easier with a Q-tip?" Rich agreed, but the shop towel had been handier. Also, with the towel he had more fresh surface to absorb the wiped-off powder. What'll happen if he slips, I wondered, and wipes off some of the powder on the casting. Just as I'd uttered the thought, the slip occurred. "No problem," Rich said, "I'll just touch that up with the gun." With the HotCoat system, control is so precise that you can touch up a small mishap without recoating the whole part.

The Corvette valve cover looked good going into the baking oven, but it looked great coming out — the ribs and Corvette script in aluminum, the rest of the cover in black. This wipe-off treatment would work with other parts and coatings. However, wrinkle finishes have long been used in performance settings and they convey that image. Of course you can have a wrinkle coating commercially applied, but now you can create a "dead ringer" wrinkle effect in your own shop with the HotCoat system at almost no cost. If you want to have fun, you can "wrinkle" a plain valve cover and

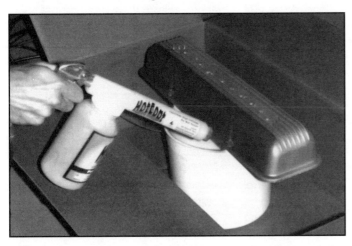

Valve covers take on a whole new personality when powder coated with a black wrinkle finish.

The Corvette valve cover looked a little too plain in all black.

To highlight the Corvette names and the cover's distinctive fins, Rich Jensen wiped the powder coating off the raised surfaces. This "trick" is easy with powder coating and difficult if not impossible with paint.

For curing the powder coating the oven needs to be preheated to 400 degrees F., so it's hot. Rich wears heavy leather gloves to prevent burning his hands or fingers.

Cleaning the gun canister between coatings is extremely simple and mess-free. Just pour the unused powder back into its container and blow out the residue with an air hose nozzle.

The Corvette valve cover looked good going into the baking oven, but it looked great coming out.

The black wrinkle coating makes a clear Performance statement.

attach a more exotic engine maker's nameplate — then see who notices the switch. I've seen this done on a GM small-block V-8 with fuel injection installed in a Jaguar XJS. The installation was hygienic; the engine didn't look out of place. And with Black Wrinkle valve covers wearing Jaguar emblems, it takes a minute or two to recognize the swap. Some people probably never notice.

Black wrinkle also makes a muscular-appearing backdrop for custom instrument panels — just be sure the panel material is metal. Plastic won't withstand powder coating's 400 degree F. melting and curing temperatures. Wrinkle finishes were rather common in the Forties and Fifties on instrument panel facings

for light and heavier duty trucks as well as hot rods and cars modified for racing.

MIXING AND TINTING POWDER COLORS

While powder doesn't mix and tint like paint, it is possible to mix small amounts of tinting base or powder from darker or lighter colors in with a standard color to alter the color's shade. You'll want to mix the powder well and test the color on a scrap part, because while it's possible to mix a small amount of Black with Medium Green to produce a shade of Hunter Green, it's also possible that the mix will give a variegated color. In some instances, the variegated — streaked or spotted — finish may be desirable for a custom effect. Still, it's best to mix a small amount and see what it produces rather than waste material and effort on a finish that isn't what you expected or wanted and isn't easily removed.

The point: Powder has more color flexibility than you might think. However, this flexibility doesn't extend to mixing opaque colors with opaques, unless you're looking for a speckled "salt and pepper" effect. Mixing translucents with translucents or translucents with opaques yields an almost liquid-like homogenous mix. Translucent black (called Black Tint) can be mixed with any of the powders to achieve a wide range of gradation. Since it's impossible to see what the mixture, or indeed any powder, will look like until it's cured, you'll want to sample your concoctions first on a piece of metal scrap or some item you're not going to use on your car. If your wrenches are hardware store variety, rather than professional tools, you could try the powder mixes out on them. Most "generic" wrenches have adequate tolerances to accommodate the .003 -.004 in. powder build without affecting the size.

Chrome Smoke, which is Almost Chrome with a tint of black, adds another twist to powder's bright coatings. While Almost Chrome doesn't blend seamlessly with real chrome, parts coated with Chrome Smoke make a nice contrast with reflective brightwork. Since Chrome Smoke has brightness without glitter, it may be a desirable alternative to plating on bumper guards and other trim pieces.

Suspension and driveline parts, including brake drums are ideally suited to powder coating.

If the drum lining is going to be turned on a lathe, the entire drum can be powder coated without masking.

While powder coating has many applications for detailing engine compartment and chassis parts, not all engine and chassis items can be powder coated, usually because they can't be baked. In restorations also, you're often challenged with detailing parts that were originally cadmium plated, a coating no longer available. With these parts you'll use specialized detailing paints, usually provided in aerosol (rattle) cans, which include:

Gold cadmium — a "system" of four tints that overlay to create the multi-colored reflective cadmium look. Brake parts (boosters, calipers) are a common application.

Silver cadmium — not a silver paint but a single-step specially formulated acrylic lacquer coating containing the bluish-silver tent of silver cadmium plating. Generator pulleys and hood safety latches are examples of items originally plated in this coating.

Carb renew — available in both silver and bronze, a paint coating formulated to imitate factory plating.

Hammertone — useful for both restoration and custom cars. This glass and aluminum impregnated paint imitates coatings used on European cars especially.

Spatter color trunk paints — multi-color "spatter" finishes are found commonly in trunk linings of cars from the 1960s and '70s. A sealer coating is required.

While powder coating has many applications, not all engine and chassis parts can be Hotcoated, usually because they can't be baked. For detailing this disk brake caliper, Eastwood Company offers a detailing paint system that imitates the cadmium plating.

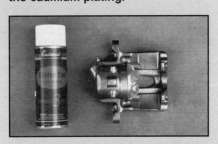

The cadmium system consists of four tints that overlay to produce a multi-colored reflective look.

Tip: You'll get a finer mix and better mixing if you place the spray can in a jar or bucket of warm (not hot) water before shaking and spraying.

The detail paints in this list are available from The Eastwood Company.

If you want to see what powder coating looks like in a metallic, you can add a small amount of Prism powder (the mixing ratio is 1 part Prism additive to 40 parts powder). The Prism additive contains multi-colored flecks, not just aluminum, so it gives a combination pearlescent and metallic effect, which is quite dramatic when added to dark colors, especially black.

OTHER APPLICATIONS

Spotting a stack of brake drums, I said to Rich, "Why don't we powder coat one of these?"

"They all need to be powder coated," Rich answered. "My son and I picked those drums out of a metal heap at the salvage yard. They're going to be 'played' in a high school band concert."

The brake drums, I found out, had been selected for their pitch — which explained their seeming random sizes. Their "music" would be a cacophony of noise at the end of a concerto decrying war and destruction.

Whether for a band or a car, brake drums look great powder coated. If your aim is factory finish, you can powder coat your car's brake drums semi-gloss black, that is unless you want to take one more step back and coat them "cast iron." For the band, Rich thought the drums should be coated a variety of translucents. These colors (probably all the same, not mixed) would also dress up a street rod and could add "spice" behind a set of custom wheels. Assuming the drums have been completely cleaned and sandblasted, and that the linings will be turned, there's not

even any masking. If the car has disk brakes up front, the hub part of the rotors can be powder coated as well.

Metal nameplate scripts and emblems can also be customized and "dressed up" with powder coating. For example, if the nameplate script overlays a metal plate, you could powder coat the plate, wipe the powder off the script, and have a two-tone chrome and translucent nameplate. Just be sure you're working with metal, not plastic as is used on modern cars.

Powder coating's uses and special effects are virtually endless, limited only by the size of the baking oven and your ingenuity. And keep in mind, if the powder coating surface isn't as mirror smooth as you'd like, the coating can be compounded and buffed following the steps described in the next chapter.

Do-It-Yourself Guide to CUSTOM PAINTING

Final Steps

We've got the car (or the parts) painted. What remains to be done? At least three steps: 1) removing the masking, 2) polishing the finish, and 3) replacing emblems and trim. The masking needs to come off promptly, within 24 hours of finish painting. Leaving the tape in place longer risks leaving behind residue — which can be cleaned off, so this is not the big problem — and lifting the new paint. That's the real concern. Removing masking may seem simple, but there's a technique.

UNWRAPPING YOUR PRIZE

In the eagerness to see what a new finish really looks like, there's a temptation to rip off the masking. I've seen it done; I've even done it myself. If you've taped over a fresh finish for two-toning or a custom paint effect like flames, the tape needs to be pulled promptly — manufacturers recommend as soon as the new paint is tack free — within about 45 minutes of the last coating. Otherwise, you should

remove the masking within 24 hours. The longer the tape sits in place, the greater the chance of the tape's wanting to bond permanently with the surface it's adhering to. As one refinisher puts it, let the tape get wet and sunshine bake on it and the glue will turn to "gumbo." Think of the fun you'll have removing that! There's also the risk that as the paint hardens some of the overspray on the tape and masking will have bonded firmly enough with the finish coat to chip the masking edge. Best to remove the tape and masking within the appropriate time window.

As you pull the tape, peel it backwards, away from the fresh paint. Pull the tape slowly, rolling up the masking as you go along. Bending the tape backwards on itself as it peels off helps keep the paint edge even. Go slowly, that way if you notice the tape starting to lift you can cut the edge smooth with a single-edged razor blade or sharp x-acto knife. Where you're removing masking from designs, begin at the widest sections

of design and work toward the narrow parts, keeping your razor blade or knife handy to make sure you don't peel off the tip of a flame, say.

With two-tones and custom designs, where removing the masking leaves a sharp edge, the tape border can be lightly sanded and clear coat applied to the two-tone or the custom design. The edge or ridge of the masking line will be unnoticeable and barely felt under the clear coat. Another alternative with custom designs is to airbrush or pinstripe the edge. Airbrushing with a shadow effect will give the design a three-dimensional look, while pinstriping will sharpen the outline, eliminate any raggedness from the tape, and — if a slightly contrasting color is used — add boldness to the design.

POLISHING FOR MIRROR SMOOTHNESS

One of the reasons lacquer finishes were so well suited to amateurs or hobbyists, was that you could spray with almost any kind of equipment and

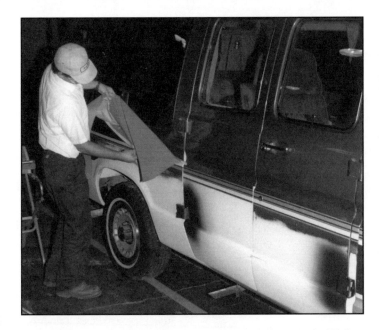

To remove masking tape peel it backwards, away from the fresh paint.

Masking tape on panel seams and crisp edges prevents polishing from cutting through the thin paint build in these areas.

as long as you laid on enough paint, you could rub out the defects and polish to a mirror gloss. This was, in fact, the painting technique commonly used by old car restorers I hung around with in the 1950s. Surprisingly, despite the enormous advances in painting technology, polishing steps similar to those used with lacquer still apply to today's catalyzed, base coat/clear coat finishes. The differences lie in the materials used for the polishing steps and the necessity that the finish be applied correctly. Today's polishing can remove minor defects and enhance gloss, but it won't fix a coating that's been improperly sprayed or mixed. The days of "fog it on and rub it smooth" are gone.

Lacquer was rubbed smooth with a combination of coarser grit "rubbing" and finer grit "polishing" compound, often by hand. Today the polishing sequence often begins with progressively finer microgrit sandpapers followed by machine polishing with "finishing systems" of graduated polishes and glazes. The purpose of the polishing set can be to remove defects, but its ultimate purpose is to create a mirror smooth, extremely high gloss finish.

COMMON FINISH DEFECTS

Even with all the technology — HVLP spraying systems, filtered paint booths, ultra-fast drying paints — the problems that have been the bane of refinishers over the years still exist. Runs, dirt and insects, orange peel, and fisheyes can still blemish a final finish. It's not just amateurs who are embarrassed by runs and sags. Experienced painters can have these blemishes happen to them too, especially if they're using new products and haven't sprayed a practice panel to get a feel of the coating's tack time and drying characteristics.

Dirt in the paint can have many sources, the most common being failure to thoroughly blow dust out of door jambs and crevices, not remasking after priming and sanding, not wearing proper painting garb designed to resist dust, and clogged spray booth filters or fans made inefficient by overspray buildup on the blades. Proper preparation, following the steps outlined in Chapter 11, is the best antidote to dust and dirt in the finish. If insects are a problem it's because you're not spraying inside a filtered enclosure. Spraying in an open shop any season when insects are about is sure to trap some tiny creatures in the paint.

Some orange peel is common, even in professional finishes, and will be removed by polishing. However, you want to reduce the degree of orange peel, which results from the paint not flowing out properly before it dries. If orange peel is extreme, the finish may need to be sanded and recoated.

Common causes of a rough orange peel texture include:

- improper spray gun adjustment (too little pressure or too wide a fan pattern) or holding the gun at excessive distance from the painting surface
- painting in high temperature conditions or using the wrong temperature reducer
- exceeding recommended flash time on recoats; earlier coats dry and absorb solvent from the fresh finish coat
- incorrect paint/reducer mix
- paint mix not thoroughly stirred.

Surfaces on the edges of the masking should be compounded and polished by hand.

Unlike lacquer finishes that can be compounded and polished any time over the life of the paint, modern two-part catalyzed paints have a short buff and polish window — often measured in hours, not days or weeks. This means you'll compound and polish the finish before remounting bumpers and trim.

A finish that is nearly defect free can be brought to a bright luster by compounding and polishing.

Fisheyes that look like water or oil has gotten into the paint are usually the result of silicone contamination. Although careful cleaning of the surface before painting with wax and grease remover should remove any silicone residue, the problem can occur from silicone residue in recycled lacquer thinner used for cleaning spray guns or oil contamination in the

air supply. The answer to silicone in the gun cleaner is to use a quality gun cleaner product and rinse with reducer before painting. Contamination of the air supply can be avoided by daily purging the air compressor tank; making sure the compressor uses special compressor oil, not motor oil; and installing a four-stage oil and water separator, desiccant dryer in the painting air line drop. Beyond these steps, fisheye eliminator can be added to the paint.

REMOVING DEFECTS

The finish needs to air dry at least 24 hours at 70 degrees F. before beginning the micro-sanding/polishing process used to remove defects and smooth the surface. The first step is to wash the finish thoroughly with soap and water. A good cleaning removes any water soluble particles as well as dust and dirt. Now that the finish is clean, it can be inspected noting the extent and seriousness of the defects. As mentioned above, extreme orange peel, fisheyes, runs, or dirt may require sanding and recoating. Hopefully, the defects are minor. Your approach will be directed by the condition of the finish.

PPG has established the following rating chart to determine the material needed to remove the defects.

Level 1   Moderate orange peel, minor sags and runs, dirt nibs
• Use 1000 to 1200 grit micro-sandpaper or compound

Level 2   Minor orange peel, small dirt nibs, overspray
• Use 1500 grit

Level 3   Overspray dust (or on an older finish, swirl marks and light oxidation)
• Use 2000 grit

Level 4   Finish is virtually defect free, just needs enhancing
• Use only a mild non-abrasive polish. PPG recommends its DRX 3000 Professional Finish Enhancer.

(Finish rating levels from PPG Refinish Training Manual)

The sanding grits recommended in the PPG chart are starting points in a graduated wet sanding sequence. The principle of micro-sanding and polishing is always to start with the mildest grit that will remove the defect, then proceed through successively milder grits of sandpaper or compound to 2000, followed by polishing. So, starting from level 1, the sanding grits would progress from 1000 or 1200 to 1500, then 2000. The sequence uses each successively finer grit to remove sand scratches and finish scuffing left from the previous step.

Note that wet sanding with fine micro-grit sandpaper should only be used with solid colors or metallics that have been clear coated. Single-stage metallic paints may be lightly compounded, but should not be sanded.

Unlike lacquer finishes that can be compounded and polished at any time over the life of the paint, modern two-part catalyzed paints have a short buff and polish window, often measured in hours, not days or weeks. Since the product information sheet may state the minimum drying time before polishing, but not the maximum time, you'll want to check with your refinishing supplier for the recommended "polishing window" (time during which polishing should occur) for the finish paint you're using.

Larger defects like insects and dust nibs that protrude from the paint surface can be cut off with a sharp single-edged razor blade. Be careful not to cut or scrape the paint. The motto of defect removal is to be as gentle with the finish as possible.

MICRO-SANDING AND COMPOUNDING

Unless the finish is exceptionally smooth and defect free, you'll now begin the graduated wet sanding process using extremely fine grit sandpaper, available either from your refinishing supplier or Meguiars. The micro-sanding process is done largely by hand using a sanding block. Pressure should be light with care taken not to sand through creases and seams. A higher quality dual-action (D/A) sander with very smooth sanding action can be used to smooth large, flat panels such as the hood, trunk, and roof. While micro-sanding uses gentle grit sandpaper, it's still important not to be aggressive. Sand only enough to remove the blemish. As the finish smooths, progress to the next milder sandpaper, until you reach 2000 grit.

As an alternative to micro-sandpaper you can use a sanding compound with moderate speed (1500-2500 rpm) buffer. Work the compound in a circular motion with enough pressure to remove the blemish, but not to cut too deeply into the finish. Do not compound in direct sunlight or on a hot surface. As with sandpaper, always start with the least aggressive grit that will remove the blemish and progress to milder grits to erase swirl marks from earlier compounding.

POLISHING

Now we've reached the last step in the finish enhancing process. If the finish was largely defect free (Level 4 on the PPG chart), the micro-sanding /compounding steps might have been

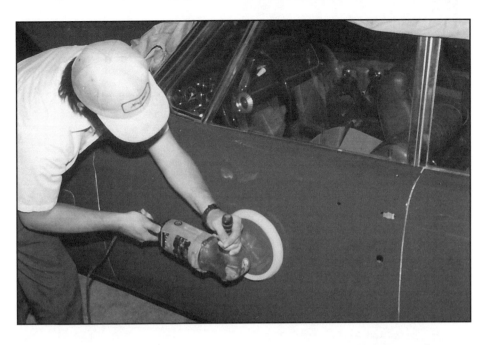

Polishing is done a small area at a time, using a circular, overlapping motion.

skipped with polishing following directly after washing and cleaning the new finish. If the finish required micro-sanding and/or compounding, then polishing follows the mildest (2000) grit.

While compounding is usually done with a low RPM (1200-1500 range) power buffer, polishing can be done with an inexpensive orbital polisher, also used for applying cleaners and wax to the finish. Besides low cost, an orbital polisher is also beneficial for the polishing step because the orbital tool is less likely to leave swirl marks and its double handle design makes it easier to control. A word of caution with either tool — power buffer or orbital polisher — let the weight of the tool apply the pressure; don't press the tool's polishing pad aggressively against the finish.

Lacking a power tool, polishing can also be done by hand, but the hand process is much more time-intensive and it's more difficult to apply a consistent pressure. An orbital buffer costs in the vicinity of $100 and is useful in the finish care process.

With buffers, wool pads are used for compounding. Foam pads are used for polishing. Orbital polishers come with cotton terrycloth bonnets that can be washed and reused.

Guidelines for polishing include:
- **S**hake the polish container well before applying polish to the pad or finish.

- Use a slow buffing speed and keep the tool moving.
- Apply light pressure. On horizontal surfaces, let the tool's weight apply the pressure.
- Polish a small area (about 2 ft. square) using a circular, overlapping motion, then proceed to the next. Don't try to polish across an entire panel or section of the car.
- As imperfections disappear, lighten the pressure and polish for gloss.
- Polish away from, not into, panel edges or body lines.

Polishing should be done with finishing system products from your refinishing supplier, or products specially formulated for that purpose from a quality car care supplier like Meguiars or One Grand.

REPLACING EMBLEMS AND TRIM

With the finish enhancement steps completed, it's time to replace items removed from the car for painting. These can include trim, emblems, ornaments, bumpers, and mirrors. Sometimes fenders are painted separately and have to be remounted, often using welting to fill the seams. Whether the items are large or small, they have to be replaced carefully to avoid scratching the finish.

Before replacing trim, you may want to straighten any dents and restore

Probably many of us have seen pictures or actual forests where trees are dying from acid rain, but if the devastation isn't occurring in our back yard, we're inclined to think that acid rain falls somewhere else, not on our driveway or our cars. The exact opposite is true. The dying forests are no doubt receiving a higher concentration, but if you're almost any place other than Lake Baikal in Siberia, you can be sure the rain falling literally on your back yard is acidic. How acidic is the question.

But you say, I live in rural Nebraska, or Northern Vermont, or sunny Arizona, away from factories and smokestacks, how can the rain that falls on my plain be acidic? Currently in the U.S., 30 million tons of sulphur dioxide and 25 million tons of nitrogen oxides are released into the atmosphere each year. When these compounds combine with water vapor they form sulfuric and nitric acid. On the scale of 0 to 14, distilled water has a reading of 7, or a neutral pH. The lower numbers reflect acidity, higher numbers a basic condition. Rain that shows a pH of 5 is 100 times more acidic than that with a pH of 6. In New Jersey, for example, rainfall has an average pH of 4.3 — 10 times more acidic than a solution of acid and water. Rainfall this acidic can be highly destructive of automotive finishes.

Damage from acid rain isn't difficult to detect. What you'll see are spots that look like water has dried on the paint, causing minor discoloration. In more extreme cases, the spots may have a white ring and a dull center. In the next stage, the acid actually pits the finish. The discoloration varies with the finish color. Spots on a blue finish may appear white, on a white finish spots may appear pink or purple. Metallics are especially susceptible as the acid eats through the outer coating and contacts the aluminum flakes embedded in the finish.

Single-coat enamel and lacquer finishes are most vulnerable. Clear coating offers protection against discoloration, but not the ring etching or pitting.

Preventing Acid Rain Damage

Sealed storage in a Carbag (described in the next chapter) offers the best protection against acid rain, but isn't practical for cars that are driven. Your best protection there is prevention, which consists of washing the car with a soap solution frequently enough to prevent dust build up, and after exposure to rain. Dust contributes to acid rain damage because it contains airborne chemicals and pollutants which, when dissolved by the rain water, may increase the acidic coating. Periodically, you may want to neutralize the finish by washing with a solution of baking soda and water in a ratio or one tablespoon of baking soda to a quart of water. Be sure to rinse thoroughly. Beyond that, maintaining a quality wax coating and following the car care regimen described in the next chapter are the best prevention steps.

Repairing Acid Rain Damage

After washing and neutralizing the finish, following the steps described above, you may be able to eradicate acid rain discoloration and etching by compounding and polishing, as outlined earlier in this chapter. If the damage is more severe, micro-sanding may also be required but you'll need to check the paint depth to make sure you don't risk sanding through a clear coat layer or color coat. (A device for measuring paint depth is described in the Finish Repair section of the next chapter.) If micro-sanding, compounding, and polishing removes the damage, you're "home free." Now if you follow a frequent cleaning and periodic waxing regimen, and store the car under a car cover when parked inside, you'll be able to protect the finish from further damage.

If the acid rain has eaten through either the clear coat or color coatings, repair is going to require repainting following the preparation steps outlined in Chapter 7.

Besides acid rain, damage can occur from bird droppings, tree sap, and industrial fallout. Of the latter, tiny airborne iron particles can be the most destructive because if they penetrate the paint they can set up a corrosion battery — igniting rust in the base metal and eventually lifting the paint. Iron particles often can't be seen, but they can be felt by rubbing your hand along the finish. You won't actually feel the metal slivers, but the finish will have a gritty touch that will feel more abrasive than dust.

Caution: If you sense metal particles in the finish, don't polish or buff; you'll drive the metal into the paint. Instead, clean thoroughly with a chemical treatment designed for industrial fallout. Ultimately, the antidote to all these conditions is a proper car care regimen as described in the next chapter.

the metal's brightness. These repair and restoration steps are described in the next section. Sometimes you'll notice rust on the backside of the trim pieces, either stains of rust from the trim's touching against a paint blister, or actual rust on the steel fasteners. All traces of rust need to be removed, either by wiping or soaking with a liquid rust remover chemical or by scraping and abrading. If the rust is left on the trim, it will spark a corrosion battery wherever contact is made with bare metal.

If the clips for the trim are broken, show rust, or are weakened, they should be replaced. Trim fasteners for most domestic cars are available from sources listed in the Resource Appendix. On modern cars trim is typically held in place by glue. Your refinishing supplier will have the correct glue for this application.

With trim that clips in place through holes in the sheet metal, it's good practice to squirt a dab of silicone sealer into the hole before inserting the fastener. The silicone seals the hole from moisture and helps prevent the fastener from abrading the thin paint coating from the edges of the hole, exposing a potential corrosion battery. Silicone also works well to hold emblems in place. Usually, nameplate script and emblems have studs on the back that insert through holes in the panels. The studs are typically fastened with nuts and washers or clips. A healthy squirt of silicone sealer into the hole will often hold the script or emblem securely without the fastener — making it much easier to remove the emblem in the future and eliminating the sometimes awkward step replacing the clip or nut. If you're uncertain as to whether silicone alone will hold the script or emblem securely enough, you can, of course, also replace the fastening device — leaving the silicone to seal the hole.

STRAIGHTENING AND POLISHING BRIGHT METAL TRIM

On older cars the bright metal trim is usually stainless steel. On more recent cars the trim may also be aluminum or chrome-plated plastic. Trim that has lost its luster, may be dented or scratched as well. While you can send bright metal trim to a service that specializes in straightening and polishing these decorative pieces, you can also do this work yourself at considerable savings. You'll need an electric motor, a set of buffing wheels, and an assortment of polishing grits and buffing compounds. The expense of setting up a buffing/polishing station can be minimal if you have a spare electric motor. If you need to buy the motor as well as the buffing and polishing products, you'll still be money ahead of the per-piece cost for professional straightening and polishing.

To straighten the trim, you'll need to work out any dents or gouges in the metal using a hardwood dowel, bolt, or small trim hammer. To straighten a dent, work from a circular motion from the outside in, applying minimum force so as not to stretch the metal, and using a metal dolly as backing. When the surface feels and looks flat,

Holes for nameplates and emblems should be sealed with silicone. Sometimes the silicone alone will hold the emblem in place. Where the emblem is going to get a lot of road vibration, as would be the case with this fender-mounted nameplate, fasteners should be clipped to the mounting studs inside the fender.

You can send bright metal trim to a restoration service for straightening and polishing, or you can do the work yourself at considerable savings. To polish bright metal trim you'll need an electric motor, set of buffing wheels, and an assortment of polishing grits and compounds. Photo courtesy of the Eastwood Company.

Dents in the trim can be straightened with a special sharp-bladed hammer.

When the surface looks and feels flat, rub a fine file across the surface. The file marks will show any high and low spots that need more straightening.

Once the dent is straightened, the metal can be polished.

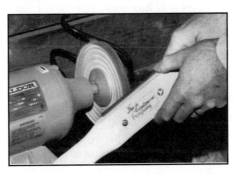

The polishing wheel can be cleaned between grits with a metal rake.

Polishing uses progressively finer grits to remove scratches and bring the metal to a bright glistening shine.

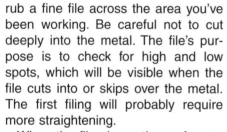

Flexible trim pieces need to be held firmly to prevent twisting and distorting by the polishing wheel.

If door weatherseal has been removed for painting, new rubber will have to be glued in place.

rub a fine file across the area you've been working. Be careful not to cut deeply into the metal. The file's purpose is to check for high and low spots, which will be visible when the file cuts into or skips over the metal. The first filing will probably require more straightening.

When the file shows the surface to be essentially smooth, you'll remove the deeper file scratches and hammer marks by sanding. This can be done by hand, starting with 220 grit wet/dry sandpaper and a wooden or rubber block and progressing to less coarse grits. If you're straightening several trim pieces, you'll probably want to speed up this process with an expander wheel mounted on an electric motor. The combination of the expander wheel and various grit sanding belts allows this sanding step to proceed at almost a production pace. To prevent deep scratches, each time you change sanding belts, you need to rotate the parts a right angle (90 degrees) for sanding with the next milder grit.

Once hammer marks and the scratches have been removed by sanding, the trim piece can be polished to a high gloss. The desired polishing/buffing station consists of a double arbor motor with a coarse buffing wheel installed on one end of the shaft and a softer wheel on the other. This avoids having to change wheels between buffing steps.

Beginning with a rough wheel and coarse grit (a sisal wheel works well for fast, aggressive cutting, along with an emery grit) the trim piece should be buffed in small sections until all areas have been worked. Avoid holding the piece in one spot for long; an aggressive grit and harsh wheel can warp or twist a slender trim piece or even cut holes through the metal. Coarse buffing is followed by an intermediate spiral wheel and milder grit, then finish polishing with a soft loose section wheel and a coloring compound to bring the metal to high luster.

Besides bright metal trim, aluminum parts like alternator housings and intake manifolds can also be buffed

and polished to a chrome-like finish. Hand-held grinders can be used to polish small recesses on these parts that can't be reached by the expander wheel. Aluminum or brass items that have been polished to a gleaming finish need to be protected from tarnishing and oxidation by a light clear coat — either with a solvent-based paint or powder coating.

Plastic parts like tail light and parking light lenses can also be brightened by buffing. Typically, original plastic lenses will have a dull look caused by tiny scratches. A soft spiral wheel followed by a finish buff with a flannel wheel and special plastic buffing compound easily removes scratches, restoring the plastic to a shiny, new look. A caution: When buffing plastic, be careful not to remove part numbers or other detail features.

For those who would like to see the polishing/buffing process done before trying it themselves, a video titled "The Art of Buffing" is available from The Eastwood Company.

HOW TO BUFF WITHOUT SWIRLS USING THE WIZARDS®
FINISH CUT™ BUFFING SYSTEM
by John Schlumpberger, Founder and CEO, Wizards Products

1) Start with a clean surface. You cannot expect to remove swirls if dirt or compound dust and residue (from coarse compounds) are pulled into the work area.

2) If wet or D/A sanding is required to remove dust nibs or texture, always finish off with an American grade 1500 or 2000 grit paper. Coarser grits will work okay on certain paints, especially on fresh (not wet) paints and clears. Note: Japanese and European papers are not rated the same as American. They are coarser than the numbers rated from American manufacturers.

3) Apply Finish Cut™ compound #11040 generously to one spot on a panel, NOT ribbons or specks all over. Finish Cut™ is a water-based system that requires little more product than the more difficult to clean up, scratchy, oil-based compounds. Also, keep in mind that you won't be using a second or third product for this step.

Buff one area before continuing.

4) Position the Finish Cut™ Wool Blend Pad £11203 onto the Finish Cut™ compound. If the pad is new it would be best to spur the pad to help break it in (spur outside if possible). Misting the new pad with water, waiting a minute and then spurring will minimize linting. More compound may be required to break in the new pad the first time it is used.

5) Apply adequate pressure and product to remove scratches. Do not whip the buffer back and forth over the entire panel. Work a small area at a time; move on only after the scratches have been removed. Run buffer at around 2000 rpm if possible and spur the pad as needed. This process gives the best initial cut and moves it into a high gloss polishing stage. Slowing down on back and forth movement does not take longer. It produces superior results without going over the surface with two or three different compounds, leaving scratches that are covered up with heavy oils.

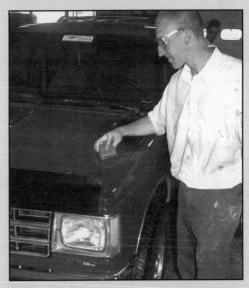

Wet sanding may be needed to remove dust nibs or texture.

6) Your best tool is your eyes. Look at your work from different angles and complete one area before continuing (adding more product as needed).

7) For dark colors, or the ultra finish, take the yellow foam cut pad #1120-4 using the same Finish Cut™ compound #11040 and buff (working smaller areas) to eliminate all slight marks that the wool pad may have delivered. This is the key to that super shine and small scratch removal. Some softer clears may polish up nicer with the white foam pad #11205. Both foam pads will finish nicer as they "break in" and soften up after initial use with products.

8) Wash off any excess compound and residue using Wipe Down #01220, then inspect. This system (following the above-mentioned steps with the Wizards® products) will provide a show-quality finish without hiding scratches with masking oil.

9) To protect and provide an "awesome" shine, apply Shine Master™ Polish and Breathable Sealant #11033 to the surface using the Gray Foam Finish pad #11206. Use just enough to cover the surface; unlike compound, more of this is not better. Shine Master™ can also be hand applied with a damp or dry cloth. However, do not squirt the polish on half the hood and spread it out. It will dry faster, go further, and work better by applying evenly and thinly.

As noted in the acid rain discussion from the previous chapter, the most important step to preserving a car's finish is frequent cleaning. This doesn't necessarily mean you're going to run the car under a hose every second or third day. It does, however mean taking steps regularly when the car is in use to keep dust and grime off the finish and then periodically washing the finish with quality cleaning products that will lift off grime and pollution, but won't destroy the protective wax coating.

KEEPING THE FINISH CLEAN

Regular cleaning is best done without water, for the simple reason that when a car is washed (or driven in the rain), some water seeps past the window seals and runs down inside the doors. Also, moisture combined with dust that has settled on the finish penetrates into body seams. If the moisture contains acids (as is commonly the case with rain water) and the dust has other airborne chemicals, the goo that has now settled into those tiny crevices

makes a perfect breeding spot for rust. Even though you carefully wipe the finish with a Turkish towel or chamois, you won't mop up all the moisture, and what remains is in those inaccessible spots where damage can begin to occur. If you wash your car with a pressure spray at a coin-op car wash, then you've really blasted water underneath the weather seal, and into body seams and crevices. Worse, you may have washed your car with recycled water — a bath rich in corrosive chemicals. For regular cleaning, dry-washing is the better way.

DRY WASHING

Assuming the car only has a light dust coating, it can be cleaned by wiping exterior surfaces with a hand mop called the California Car Duster. (See Resource Appendix for supplier address). As a rule, it's not advisable to dust a dry finish. When moved across the surface, the tiny dust particles, which may contain caustic chemicals from industrial pollution, can scratch

the paint like sandpaper. The California Car Duster works to remove dust because its 100 percent cotton strands are treated with a baked-on paraffin wax that picks up the dust rather than brushing it around. A true California Car Duster (as opposed to imitations) can be used for years and won't scratch the paint. Simply shake before and after using and store the duster in its protective sheath. Depending on conditions, the duster might be used on a daily basis.

Even when the finish becomes dirty, it can still be dry washed using a cleaner product called Dri-Wash 'n Guard. This cleaner uses emulsifiers to lift dirt and grime from the finish. When you wipe the dried film, you remove the grime without scratching the paint. It may sound impossible, but the product works, not only cleaning but leaving a protective coating of wax and sealant coating that gives the finish a deep shine. You won't find Dri-Wash 'n Guard on the shelves of the car care department at discount marts or auto parts stores. It is sold, along with other spe-

Regular cleaning is best done without water. Assuming the finish has only a light dust coating, it can be cleaned by wiping with a cotton mop called a California Car Duster.

It's best to wash your car yourself in your driveway or apartment parking lot rather than running it through a high pressure car wash. At home you can use a lower pressure spray and control where you direct the water.

cialty car care products, through independent sales consultants who are best contacted through the distributor, Enviro-Tech International. (See the resource appendix.)

For those living in arid areas, or who are simply environmentally conscious, both dry wash products mentioned above have another benefit — cleaning your car without using precious water.

WET WASHING

It's best to wash your car yourself, in your driveway or apartment parking lot, rather than running it through a car wash or taking it to a coin-op car wash. The bristles on the car wash brushes can be harsh on the finish and the high pressure spray can drive past weather seal and send grime into crevices. At home you can use a lower pressure spray and control where you direct the water.

One of the biggest mistakes people make washing their cars at home is picking a bright, warm sunshiny day. A car should always be washed in shade, in cooler temperatures (early morning or late afternoon) with cool or lukewarm water. Hot water not only melts any wax coating but can "shock" thermoplastic finishes like lacquer and acrylic enamel and cause microscopic fractures in the paint. Washing in direct sunshine causes the water to dry before you have a chance to wipe down the finish. If your water supply is "hard," meaning it has a

high content of minerals, you'll see "water spots" on the finish that may require abrasive cleaning to remove. Even if the water is "soft" the sun's rapid drying is likely to bake some chemical residue on the paint's surface. The best approach is to park the car in shade, allow the finish to cool, then wet down with a rinse before washing.

Washing should begin at the roof, then proceed across the windshield to the hood and rear window to the trunk. The sides of the car, doors, and fenders, follow these large horizontal surfaces.

A second major mistake people typically make in washing their cars is using dish or laundry detergent for the soap. Household soaps are too harsh. Think of it; they're designed to remove grease and oil and will just as efficiently remove any protective coating on your car's finish. The soap to use is a car wash product from a quality finish care supplier like Wizards Products, Meguiars, or Gliptone. Cleaners like Wizards Wash, Meguiars Car Wash and Conditioner or Soft Wash Gel, or Gliptone's Wash N Glow Car Soap are concentrated for thick suds, and provide gentle, but thorough cleaning action for all vehicle surfaces, including grimy hubcaps and wheels. If you've been washing your car with a household cleaner, you'll be amazed with the difference the quality car care products make. With a proper wash product, the water will "sheet up," flowing off the car

in a more fluid cleaning action. When you're finished washing, the wax coating will still be on the paint but with renewed shine. You won't have to wax after every washing. Wizards also recommends its Wash product as a lubricant for wet sanding.

When washing, apply the soapy solution with a large car wash sponge or sheepskin mitt and keep the surface well lubricated with water and soap at all times. As you work your way down the sides of the car, you should spray up under the fender wells to rinse away grime and possible road salt. Make sure to spray along the inner fender lip

After rinsing, the finish should be wiped dry with a chamois.

Chrome trim is also kept clean and looking bright by washing and polishing—using either professional polish products or simply Windex.

Cleaning and detailing extends underhood as well as exterior surfaces.

around the wheel well. Often the water will drive some of the grime up onto the finish. Be sure to rinse off any residue before washing this area with a sponge or mitt.

Washing shouldn't require pressure. Road tar, smeared insects, and other blemishes that don't wash off easily should be cleaned with other products. Windex works great for insects, as does WD-40, which will also remove grease and tree sap. Both Wizards and Meguiars offer safe, non-abrasive clay system cleaning products for removing contamination including paint overspray (sometimes picked from highway maintenance on overpass bridges),

chemical fallout, tree sap, tar, and bug smears. Meguiars calls its tough contaminants cleaner Smooth 'n Clean. Wizards calls its competitive product Clay Mate.

Note: Don't wait for washing to remove bird droppings. Remove the splatter as soon as you first see it by moistening with water and wiping with a paper towel. When dry, apply a cleaner wax like Wizards Mist-N-Shine or Meguiars Cleaner Wax to ensure the spot hasn't left any lingering contamination. Bird droppings will eat through the finish and will require repainting.

When the car is clean, rinse off all the soapy water. Use a low pressure

spray close to surface to wash off residue, not a hard spray. Rather than allowing the rinse spray to air dry on the finish, you should use a chamois, either natural or man-made, to soak up the water. A soft squeegee can also be used, but a chamois works better to avoid streaking. A natural chamois is an actual skin from an animal by the same name. Artificial chamois are less expensive and if good quality are nearly equally absorbent. Rinse the chamois frequently during wiping and wring dry. Since a good chamois is relatively expensive, you'll want to keep the cloth in good condition for many years' use. Proper care includes periodic washing in mild detergent and hanging the cloth where it can dry.

After drying with a chamois, the car gets a final wipe down with 100% cotton terrycloth towels. Use these towels just for drying, not for other cleaning steps that could contaminate them with grease or grit. When you're finished wash the towels with bleach and detergent, but without a fabric softener. When you place the towels in the dryer, add an anti-static sheet so they'll be soft and fluffy on the next use.

CLEANING A DULL FINISH

If the finish has been neglected, it may require cleaning in addition to washing. You'll know whether the cleaning step is needed if the finish turns dull after drying — indicating sur-

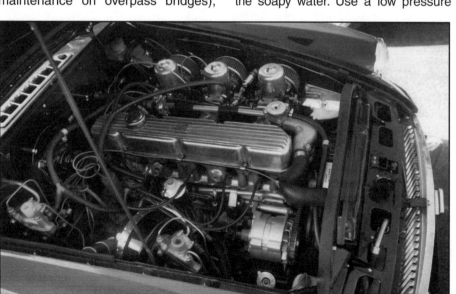

Regular cleaning will keep the engine compartment looking as tidy as the topside.

face oxidation that has microscopically roughened the paint's surface, eroding the gloss. If the oxidation is slight, it can be removed with a cleaner product like 3M's One Step Cleaner Wax or Meguiars Deep Crystal System Paint Cleaner. If your car's finish is a base coat/clear coat, be sure to use a cleaner that won't damage the clear. Look for "clear coat safe" — or words to that effect — on the product label.

The cleaner's purpose is to smooth the surface, restoring the paint's "reflectivity," meaning gloss. If oxidation is severe, you'll want to use a more aggressive cleaner, or possibly give the finish a light buffing using a mild polishing compound like Wizards Finish Cut. While some cleaners may also contain wax, protective waxing should be a separate step.

WAXING FOR LONG-LASTING PROTECTION

Finish waxes come in two forms, liquid and paste. Which is best to use? What's best isn't the form but the content. Liquid or paste, you want to choose a product that is rich in carnauba — a natural plant-derived wax that creates a hard, heat-resistant coating. Of course the car wax manufacturers know the value of carnauba, which in pure form is somewhat expensive, so you'll find "carnauba wax" hawked at flea markets and "carnauba" on the label of products that contain very little of this important ingredient. That's why it's important to purchase quality car care products from reputable suppliers. When these products say "carnauba," you know you're buying the real thing.

The liquid waxes are usually easier to apply, largely because the carnauba has to be diluted to be suspended in the liquid. To put a shine on the finish in less than an hour's time, liquid waxes are great, but the shine and protection aren't going to last like a paste wax. The best wax to use is a quality paste product like Meguiars Deep Crystal System Carnauba Wax, One Grand's Pure Carnauba Blitz Wax, Mother's California Gold, or Gliptone's Carnauba Paste and Cream Wax.

You can apply the wax (liquid or paste) with a slightly dampened section of cheese cloth, small piece of

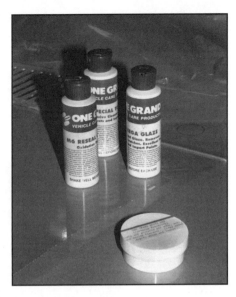

Dull, chalky finishes can often be restored with compounding products like Wizards Finish Cut.

Finish waxes come in two forms, liquid and paste. Which is best depends on the content. You want to choose a wax product that is rich in carnauba, a natural plant-derived wax that creates a hard, heat-resistant coating.

Liquid waxes are easiest to apply. Using a quality liquid wax like the Meguiars and Wizards products shown here and a power buffer, you can give your car or truck's finish a deep shine in less than an hour.

100% cotton terrycloth towel, or the foam applicator that may have come with the wax product using a back and forth motion. Laying the wax on thick won't necessarily give more protection or a deeper shine. If you cleaned the finish before waxing, the wax coating can be light. If the finish didn't seem to need the cleaning step, you may want to apply two light wax coatings. When the wax dries, you can buff it to a shine by hand using cotton towels, or with an orbital buffer — or rub the wax by hand and polish to a gloss with the power buffer. When you've finished polishing, spend a few more minutes wiping dried wax from panel seams, chrome, and weather seals. Cotton swabs have the right size tip for cleaning wax around nameplates and emblems. A quality paste carnauba wax should give protection and gloss for 3-6 months.

Gliptone product chart:

Product	Size	Name
GT1764	64oz.	Emerald Clean™ Degreaser
GT1722	22oz.	Emerald Clean™ Degreaser
GT1922	22oz.	Total Tire™ & Rim Cleaner
GT0113	13oz.	The Original Carnauba Paste Wax
GT0913	13oz.	Platinum Paste Wax with Teflon®
GT1822	22oz.	True Blue™ Professional Tire Shine
GT2022	22oz.	Body Gloss™ w/Carnauba (spray n wipe)
GT0364	64oz.	Wash-n-Glow™
GT0616	16 oz.	Pro Buff™
GT0216	16oz.	Original Carnauba Cream Wax
GT0716	16oz.	Pro Glaze™
GT1208	8oz.	Liquid Leather Cleaner
GT1108	8oz.	Liquid Leather Conditioner
GT0508	8oz.	Vinyl, Rubber & Plastic Protector
GT0816	16oz.	Clear Coat™ Car Wax
GT0416	16oz.	Show Gloss™
GT1016	16oz.	Platinum Cream Wax w/Teflon®
GT0316	16oz.	Wash-n-Glow™

Gliptone is one of several companies offering a full line of car care products. Product chart courtesy Gliptone, Inc.

RECEIVING YOUR PERSONAL CAR CARE PRESCRIPTION

Especially helpful in making sure the finish care regimen covers all the steps are the "Paint Care System" products from Meguiars. The Meguiars Deep Crystal System, for example, includes all three important finish care products: Step 1, Paint Cleaner; Step 2, Clear Coat Safe Polish; and Step 3, Carnauba Wax, either liquid or paste. Meguiars also offers a unique service: a free Personalized Car Care Prescription. Available by mail, phone, or over the internet, the prescription is based on a series of easily answered questions about the present condition of the car's finish, desired finish goal, the amount of time you're willing to invest to meet that goal, where the car is parked, how often the finish is washed, and most common finish care problems. The prescription doesn't just recommend products; it explains each finish care step, why to do it, what to use, and how often. Based on answers given to the questions, the prescription also rates the likely environmental impact on your car's finish on a scale of fair to very severe. The prescription form can be accessed on the web at www.meguiars.com, by mail at Meguiars Rx. Dept., Box 17177, Irvine, CA 92614-9933, or by phone at (800) 545-3321. The online response is instantaneous. Mail response can take up to 4-6 weeks.

MAINTAINING WAX PROTECTION

Since the wax gloss and protection will slowly decline, you'll want to revitalize the finish between waxing cycles using a gloss enhancer product like 3M's Perfect-It, Wizard's Mist-N-Shine, or Meguiars' Quick Detailer. These products would be used following a rinse and wash.

TOUCHING UP AND REPAIRING PAINT DAMAGE

Small nicks and scratches that are the inevitable result of daily driving need to be repaired to prevent further damage to the finish. If the chip hasn't broken through the primer, you can fill in the color with a few drops of touch-up paint, available in small bottles or spray cans from auto parts stores and new car dealerships. The touch-up paint can be dabbed into the spot with a small artist's brush or even a toothpick. (Sometimes the touch-up paint has its own nail brush-like applicator.) Just filling the chip leaves out two important steps. First, the chip should be cleaned to remove loose paint and any rust. Second, you can hide the repair if you fill the chip above the level of the finish, then micro-sand and polish the area around the repair.

Chip repair kits by Pro Motorcar

Products (see resource appendix for address) contain a glass fiber brush to scrub the repair spot and a paint thickness gauge to use in determining the extent to which a finish can be buffed and polished to remove scrapes and other surface damage. Both of these items are essential for a quality repair. The kit also contains complete instructions for the repair process. It does not, however, include the touch-up paint which you need to purchase separately.

With the chip hole scrubbed clean, paint is dabbed into the hole until the build-up protrudes slightly from the surrounding surface. You'll probably need to do the build-up in several applications, allowing drying time between the dabs of paint. If the finish is base coat/clear coat, you'll need to complete the build-up with several layers of clear. With a clear coat you'll build the color slightly below the level of the finish; the clear will supply the additional build. Be sure to give the color time to dry before dabbing on the clear. Properly done, the process could take a couple of days.

When the paint is dried, the spot is wet sanded flat using an ultra-fine micro-sandpaper wrapped around a small soft rubber sanding block. Finally, the spot is polished to remove sand scratches and restore gloss with a very fine polishing compound like Wizards Finish Cut. The result should be a repair that's nearly invisible. Beyond the cosmetic benefit, you've sealed the spot against potential rust.

For scrapes, the repair method is compounding and polishing as described in the previous chapter. You'll need the paint thickness gauge from the Pro Motorcar Products kit to make sure you don't buff through the finish trying to remove the scrape.

PROTECTING THE FINISH DURING STORAGE

Since sunlight will also deteriorate the finish, it's important to cover the car or truck when not in use. Car covers also shield the finish against dust, which can include industrial chemicals. You'll find a wide variety of covers from inexpensive nylon or plastic throw-over wraps available in discount marts to better quality, but generic sized, to higher quality and custom fit. The better

A well-cared for finish should be covered when the car is not in use.

Batteries can be preserved during storage with a product called the Battery Tender that is guaranteed not to overcharge.

(more expensive covers) are tailored to your vehicle — so that they match not only the length, but also the contours. They are also constructed from material that can "breathe," which is important to prevent moisture from being trapped under the cover and condensing on the vehicle. Higher quality covers have softer flannel linings to prevent scratching the finish.

Although you'll see cars parked outside snugly covered, there's a risk that wind whipping the cover can mar or scratch the finish. It's best to have the car parked under a car port or in the garage. Even inside, a cover is advisable to protect the finish against sunlight, dust, and chemicals.

For periods longer than a few days or weeks, a car's or truck's storage needs go beyond protecting the finish. It becomes important to seal the interior, underbody, and mechanical elements against moisture and the rubber against ozone and ultraviolet light. A car cover, which primarily protects the finish, is inadequate for this overall protection. What's needed is to encapsulate the vehicle in a sealed storage bag called the CarJacket.

Before storing in a CarJacket, both the interior and exterior should be thoroughly cleaned.

For long term storage, cars and light trucks should be sealed in a CarJacket (MotoJackets are available for motorcycles). The CarJacket zips conveniently in place and seals the vehicle against moisture as well as harmful sunlight. Illustration courtesy of Pine Ridge Enterprises.

PREPARING FOR LONG-TERM STORAGE

Whenever a car won't be driven for an extended period (several months or more), a series of preparation steps need to be taken to help forestall deterioration that can occur even in a dry environment. Top on the list is changing the oil. Although the oil ceases to circulate through the engine during storage, vital parts such as bearings remain covered with a thin oil film. If the oil is contaminated with acid, this film also contains traces of acid that can eat into bearing surfaces and other fine-tolerance parts. The way to prevent possible internal engine damage is simply to change the oil.

Likewise, anti-freeze develops an acidic pH over time. The long standing recommendation has been to flush and refill a car's anti-freeze every three years. If flushing and refilling the cooling system is too much of a hassle, then the answer is Evans Coolant, a non-glycol-based product that is *not* mixed with water.

Modern gasoline breaks down rapidly. For shorter storage periods (a few months) the gasoline can be treated with a fuel stabilizer. For longer storage the gasoline should be drained. The battery should also be disconnected and removed. Be sure the hand brake is off.

Never put a car away dirty. Always clean the finish and apply a quality protective wax. Along with washing, treat the chrome and other bright metal as well as rubber window moldings, weather seal, and tires with protective coatings. Carpets and seats should be thoroughly vacuumed. Leather needs to be cleaned and treated with special leather care products (Meguiar's makes a high-quality Leather Cleaner & Conditioner; Lexol products are also recommended). Vinyl interior coverings require their own cleaner and conditioner.

PROTECTING A CAR IN LONG-TERM STORAGE

The ideal storage conditions are consistent temperature, absence of humidity, and no sunlight or harmful chemicals. Few owners of custom and collector cars have storage that meets these conditions. While a heated or air-conditioned garage or storage building may be a luxury unavailable to most, low humidity and absence of sunlight and chemical pollution is available to anyone through a sealed storage device called the CarJacket. Literally a car-cocoon, the CarJacket consists of a zipper lined sheet of 7.0 mil, nonbreathable, rip-stop polyethylene large enough to wrap around and enclose any size car or light duty truck, including SUVs.

To prepare for storage, the CarJacket is laid out on the floor where the vehicle will be parked. While a wooden or concrete floor is recommended, the CarJacket can be used on dirt if the surface is free of stones or other sharp objects that might puncture the plastic. When storing on gravel, it's recommended that sheets of plywood or OSB be used as a protective platform under the CarJacket.

Cocooning a vehicle is easy. Just unzip the CarJacket, then push or drive the car or truck onto the platform of the jacket. The rest of the jacket can then be wrapped over the car or truck and zipped shut. Before zipping up the CarJacket, a measured amount of des-

The CarJacket's manufacturer John Schoepke unseals his Alpha Romeo to show the car's perfectly preserved condition.

iccant (provided with the CarJacket) needs to placed inside with the car. With the jacket zipped shut, the desiccant will suck the moisture out of its polyethylene cocoon where the car is also protected from sunlight and airborne chemicals.

Unlike a cover which doesn't protect against humidity, vehicles emerge from long-term CarJacket storage with the bare steel on brake disks still shining, electrical connections corrosion free, chrome glistening, and aluminum untarnished. Another advantage over cloth covers, the CarJacket has proven effective in repelling mice, which like to nest in car upholstery and chew on wiring insulation. It's not clear what keeps mice and other rodents from nibbling their way through the plastic; apparently what they can't smell doesn't interest them and not only does the plastic seem unappetizing, it blocks the more attractive smells that are sealed inside.

Likewise, thieves aren't attracted to what they can't see, so storing vehicles in a CarJacket makes them less susceptible to vandalism and theft. The jacket isn't a substitute of proper secu-

rity, but a big gray bag doesn't attract as much attention as shining chrome or bright red paint.

The CarJacket is not a substitute for a garage or other type of covered storage. It's not to be used for covering a car out-of-doors where wind can whip the plastic, scuffing the car's paint or tearing holes that could quickly turn dry storage into wet! But with the CarJacket, any indoor storage becomes as hospitable as a climate-controlled garage. With care, the jacket can be reused year after year (small tears can be mended with duct tape) and the desiccant is recycled by baking in a kitchen oven. CarJackets are purchased directly from the manufacturer: Pine Ridge Enterprise (see Resource Appendix).

UNANSWERED QUESTIONS

The steps to producing an elegant or eye-catching finish and the resources for preserving that finish which have been presented in this book are not intended as all-encompassing or the "final word." If you're using this book as a guide to do-it-yourself, you may have questions on various parts of the refin-

ishing process. Frequent mention is made to instructional demonstrations on video tape, which can be extremely helpful in helping you see artistic techniques such as airbrushing before you do them. The world wide web is a resource of virtually limitless information on practically every topic, including just about every phase of automotive refinishing. You can also seek hands-on training in nearly every step covered in this book. As described in Chapter 8, I-CAR training is available on CD ROM self-study as well as actual classes conducted at high school skill centers and technical colleges. Meguiars offers a car care clinic at its California headquarters.

The best answers to most questions come from people doing the quality refinishing and custom painting themselves. Don't be afraid to ask these experts. In my experience, they're more than glad to explain the process and show you their work. For creative ideas, the best source is what others have done, so visit car shows, camera in hand. After all, what's the purpose of high quality refinishing besides adding pleasure to driving, enjoying, and showing our cars?

In many areas, as of this book's writing, you can still buy lacquer paints and primers — both relatively modern acrylic lacquer and the "authentic" nitrocellulose stuff used on collector cars of the Twenties and Thirties. So why not include this long popular, amateur-friendly paint in the paint processes described herein? Why relegate lacquer finishes to a short chapter in the appendix? Two reasons:

First, you'll remember from earlier discussions that lacquer is a thermoplastic coating, meaning it shrinks and swells. It has great gloss and is easy to repair, but it's not durable. Expensive classic and custom cars painted in lacquer have been purchased at winter auctions in southern or southwestern states like Arizona then shipped north in transports to icebox states like Minnesota, experienced 70-80 degree temperature drops in two to three days, and arrived at their new home with their expensive lacquer finish cracked like an ice cube struck by a hammer.

Second, lacquer is being phased out through environmental regulations. Already, there are areas of the U.S. where lacquer can't be legally sprayed. It's not unreasonable to expect lacquer to disappear as a commercial finish. Already most professionals are side-stepping lacquer in favor of two-part base coat/clear coat finishes.

Thinking lacquer would be in demand when it could no longer be purchased from local refinishing suppliers, a would-be speculator purchased a large stock — only to find very little interest. Yes, lacquer is easy and quite safe to spray, but how often do you want to repaint your car?

If you're determined to paint with lacquer, the choice should be the acrylic variety, not old nitrocellulose. As a finish paint, lacquer reduces 125-150% with thinner. The figure isn't precise as with catalyzed paints. Painters spraying lacquer often hold their mixing stick above the gun cup and watch how the diluted paint flows off the stick. If it seems to flow with the consistency of milk, the mix is ready to spray. Air pressure at the spray gun (for conventional painting) should be 34-45 psi. Gun distance from the work is between 6 and 8 inches. A lacquer finish typically consists of 4 to 7 double coats. To apply a double coat the painter sweeps the gun across the surface left to right, then reverses the pattern and sweeps back across the same area right to left. Flash time between coats one and two is a brief five minutes; for coats three and four the flash time stretches to fifteen minutes.

When lacquer was in its heyday, you'd hear proud show car owners describe a hyper-glossy, mirror smooth finish as so many coats of "hand rubbed" lacquer. The process they were talking about started with several coats that were then allowed to dry and block sanded with 600 grit sandpaper. After cleaning and prepping the surface, several more coats were applied and block sanded. This process might repeat itself until as many as 20 coats had been sprayed. The finish was like a plaster cast of mascara. Don't smile! Oddly, thinner coats produced an almost equal gloss, were less likely to crack, and repaired much more easily.

Amateurs loved lacquer because you almost couldn't goof. The paint dried so quickly that runs were rare. Orange peel or other surface blemishes could be sanded and recoated, or "finessed" out with rubbing compound. If the finish was scratched or scraped, the damage was easy to repair. A friend told of "ruining" the finish on his Model T Ford's running board hours before the car was to be entered in a National show. What to do? He didn't have time to prime and respray the damage. Not a problem: he repainted the "ruined" spot with a brush, wet sanded, and compounded to a perfect match with the surrounding paint. Try that with base coat/clear coat! But remember, paint was cheap and the finish really only had to stand up for that big show.

Today we don't want to have to repaint our cars every 5-6 years, so lacquer is rapidly becoming a relic of the past. If you're set on using it and your supplier can sell you the stock, you won't need a lot of skill and everything else you need to know has already been talked about in this book's earlier chapters.

APPENDIX B: PAINTING TERMS

Accelerator — an additive that speeds the drying or curing time of a paint coating.

Additives — chemicals added to paint for a number of reasons: to speed drying for cold weather painting and to retard drying in hot weather, to harden the finish, prevent wrinkling, improve gloss, and more.

Adhesion promoter — an additive used over a cured finish to improve the bonding of the new coating.

Air dry — allowing the paint to dry in natural conditions without baking.

Atomize — a spray gun diffuses paint into tiny droplets by directing compressed air into the paint stream as it leaves the gun nozzle.

Bare substrate — the raw steel, aluminum, or plastic material without any paint.

Base coat — the color coating in a base coat/clear coat system.

Bleeding — the penetration of the underlying finish by solvents in the paint or primer. If the solvents are incompatible with the base coat, they may bleed through and blister the underlying finish. This condition occurs most commonly when lacquer is sprayed over enamel.

Body Filler — known generically as "bondo," polyester body fillers are water porous and should only be used to smooth minor surface irregularities, not to fill holes or major dent damage.

Block Sanding — using a rubber block to hold the sandpaper helps prevent grooves in the sanding surface.

Buffing/compounding — a process for smoothing the finish using a very mild abrasive; can be done by machine or by hand.

Build — the thickness of the paint measured in mils. A factory finish typically has a thickness of 4-5 mils.

Burn through — buffing or polishing too long or hard in one spot so that the underlying coating shows through.

Carcinogens — cancer-causing agents.

Catalyst — an agent that causes two-part paints to set up or cure.

Chalking — a powdery appearance on old and weathered finishes. Sometimes chalky finishes can be renewed by microsanding and polishing.

Checking — fine line cracks on an older finish caused by aging, often of thick lacquer paint. Checks in an old finish will show through fresh paint unless the blemished undercoat is stripped off.

Clear coat — lacquer, enamel, or urethane paints without pigment are called clear coat finishes. Clear coats are applied over a color coat to increase gloss and depth, and to protect the finish from airborne pollutants.

Color coat — also called the top coat; on a single-stage color finish it is the finish layer. On a base coat/clear coat finish it is the base coat.

Corrosion battery — a spot where moisture and oxygen begins to react with the metal. Once the "battery" is activated, the tiny "seed" of corrosion grows, spreading corrosion and eating into the metal.

Crazing — hairline cracks in the paint. Crazing was a common problem with older lacquer finishes.

Cross block sanding — first sanding the surface in one direction, typically horizontally, then shifting the sanding motion 90 degrees, vertically. This method is used to smooth high and low spots on flat body panels.

Cure — a chemical reaction that occurs as two-part paints dry, leaving the coating impermeable to solvents.

Decomposition — the breakdown of a chemical product.

Double coat — a second coat of paint following immediately after the first.

Dry spraying — paint sprayed with the air pressure set too high, the gun incorrectly adjusted or held too far from the work surface leaves a dry, powdery finish.

Dust coating — a solvent-rich coating for color blending. See also Mist coat.

Enamel — a tough automotive finish traditionally thought of as being slower drying than lacquer and consequently more difficult for beginners to master. Modern acrylic and urethane enamels are much easier to use and have become popular all-purpose finishes for professionals and amateurs alike.

Etch — chemically roughening the surface of a bare metal substrate to improve adhesion of the primer coating. Also to remove rust.

Explosive limits — the amount of vapor from a painting product that will cause an explosive mixture. Lower and upper explosive mixtures are given on the Material Safety and Data Sheets that accompany painting products.

External mix — professional style spray guns mix air and paint outside the spray nozzle. Quick-drying automotive finishes are designed to be sprayed using an external mix air nozzle.

Feathering or "feather-edge" sanding — spot sanding blemishes such as rust spots on the car's finish with rough-grit sandpaper or a grinder leaves sharp edges that need to be sanded smooth before refinishing. The feather-edge process tapers the paint and primer around a repaired area so that the new finish will blend into the old.

Film/film build — the thickness of the paint coating.

Fisheyes — these small circular blemishes are caused by a residue of silicone left on the old finish before painting. Properly preparing the surface with a grease and wax remover product, using a fisheye preventer additive in the paint, and purging water and moisture from the air compressor storage tank and filter are steps that should be taken to avoid this unsightly blemish.

Flash point — the lowest temperature at which a combustible mixture will catch fire. Flash points for painting products are listed on the MSDS.

Flash time — the period needed for solvents to evaporate before a second paint coating can be applied.

Flattening agent — an additive applied to dull the paint.

Flex agent — an additive used when painting over flexible substrates, typically rubber or plastic.

Flop — a metallic's color appearing darker in a side view due to the reflective angle of the metallic flakes.

Flop Adjuster — an additive mixed with the base coat of metallic paints that helps give a uniform appearance to the color, regardless of the angle from which the car is viewed.

Flow — the wet paint film leveling itself on the surface.

Fog coat — a properly reduced final coat sprayed at slightly increased air pressure and greater gun distance from the work surface produces a "mist effect" that is used for shading and blending custom finishes.

Glaze — an extremely fine polishing compound used to heighten gloss.

Guide coats — a contrasting color primer coating is often used to reveal high and low spots that need to be smoothed before the topcoat is applied.

Health hazard — any product that can be harmful to the user's health under the conditions of its intended use.

Hiding — when the primer layer is no longer visible through the topcoat color the painter knows he has reached the minimum thickness for the topcoat.

High Solid — undercoat products, typically primer surfacers, containing more film-building pigment and resin than "regular" primers.

High Volume Low Pressure (HVLP) — a spraying technology designed to reduce overspray.

Hold-out — a property of sealer coatings that prevents top color layers from soaking into the primer base coat.

Internal mix — air and paint are mixed inside the spray gun nozzle. Heavy-bodied, slow-drying paints are sprayed using an internal mix nozzle.

Isocyanate/polyisocyanate— chemical compounds in catalysts that can be toxic.

Lacquer — one of the earliest automotive finishes, nitrocellulose lacquer was first introduced in the Twenties. Because of the harmful effect of lacquer's volatile solvents on the environment and the finish's brittle characteristics, lacquer is rapidly disappearing from use.

Masking — covering surfaces not to be painted.

Metallics — tiny aluminum flakes that give paint a silver glitter.

Micas — various colored flakes embedded in the paint that can cause color shifts.

Midcoat — an iridescence or translucent paint sometimes placed between the base coat and the clear coat. See also Tricoat.

Mils — a measurement of paint thickness where 1 mil is .001 or 1/1000 of an inch. See also Build.

Mist coat — a highly reduced final color spray used to blend a repair into the surrounding finish.

MSDS — Material Safety and Data Sheets required by OSHA to be provided with all chemical products that contain a hazardous substance. Be sure to ask your refinishing supplier for the MSDS sheets on products you purchase.

Multistage finish — finishes with multiple color layers, typically containing a base coat color and a special effects color. See also Tricoat.

Occupational Exposure Limits — the maximum allowable concentration of a toxic substance over a lifetime.

OEM finish — paint products and colors used by the Original Equipment Manufacturer when the car is built at the factory.

Opaque — a finish that is not transparent.

Orange peel — a rough finish texture that resembles the skin of an orange. This condition is the novice painter's trademark since the main causes are improper spray gun adjustment and painting techniques. A slight orange peel is likely to appear in professionally painted finishes as well and is removed in the polishing step.

OSHA — the Occupational Safety and Health Administration, an agency of the U.S. Government that regulates safety in the work place.

Overlap — partly covering an earlier spraying pass.

Overspray — paint mist that carries beyond the intended surface. Proper masking and an adequate ventilation system are requirements to avoid overspray on painted surfaces as well as minimize exposure to toxic painting chemicals.

Ozone — an air pollutant that is corrosive to paint and rubber.

PEL — Permissible Exposure Limit for toxic painting chemicals, specifically isocyanates. The PEL tolerance is shown on the MSDS (Material Safety and Data Sheets) available with all refinishing products.

Pigment — the color ingredient in paint.

Plastic welding — a repair process for thermoplastics where the material is heated and fused with a stick of like-composition plastic.

Polish — smoothing the finish to enhance its gloss.

Pot life — once a catalyzed paint is mixed with hardener, the paint has a very limited workable life, typically no more than a few hours. For this reason, it's good practice to mix only the amount of catalyzed product you intend to use during the current spraying session.

Powder paint — finely ground up plastic that when melted gives a paint-like finish.

Product Information Sheets — literature with painting products that explains mixing ratios and spraying conditions. Sometimes referred to as Technical Data Sheets.

Primer — the base paint coating, which has several functions including creating a bond with the substrate — whether bare metal, plastic, or an existing finish — and filling minor surface flaws.

Reactive reducers — solvent with catalyst used to dilute the paint for spraying and allow the paint to harden. See also Two-part paint.

Reducer — solvent used to dilute non-lacquer paints and primers. Reducers are available with fast, slow, and medium drying rates. It's important to match the reducer to the spraying conditions.

Runs — drips and sags caused by spraying a cold surface or applying too much build while not allowing time for the paint to set. To borrow baseball lingo, a painter's aim is a finish with no runs, no errors.

Sand scratches — marks made in the underlying paint or primer that may show through a final finish. Sealer coatings help prevent sand scratches in the primer from showing in the color finish.

Scallops (also spelled scollops) — a decorative design similar to flames except the streaks are spear shaped.

Sealers — the last primer coating that locks the undercoat against penetration by topcoat solvents and provides a good bonding base for the color finish.

Single-stage color — a color finish without a clear coat.

Solid color — finish paints not containing metallic or mica flakes. These colors are opaque rather than translucent.

Solvents — chemicals that dilute the paint so that it can be sprayed. The solvent ends up in the atmosphere, either by dispersion during spray painting or by evaporation from the paint that lands on the car. Lacquer solvents are considered an environmental hazard because of their high level of Volatile Organic Compounds (VOCs).

Spot repair — refinishing only part of a panel or vehicle to repair damage.

Tack coat — to prevent runs in slower drying paints, the painter will often allow the first coat to dry until it becomes "tacky" and use this coating to hold subsequent paint layers.

Tack cloths — wiping cloths with a sticky coating that picks up dirt, lint, dust, and other surface contamination. Tack cloths are used to prepare a surface for painting.

Tack free — when the paint is no longer sticky but has not thoroughly cured.

Technical Data Sheets — literature with painting products that explains mixing ratios and spraying conditions. Sometimes referred to as Product Information Sheets.

Thermoplastic — material that becomes soft or pliable when heated and returns to rigid form when cooled.

Thermoset — material that hardens when heated.

Thinner — a strong solvent used to dilute lacquer paints, now widely used to clean spray guns and other equipment used in the paint application process.

Topcoat — the color finish, which may consist of one or several paint products.

Tricoat — a complex triple layer color finish usually (though not necessarily) containing a special effect paint such as pearls or a color-shifting chameleon.

Two-part paint — a painting product that mixes with a catalyst to dry or harden. Most two-part paints contain isocyanates and need to be handled with protective clothing and sprayed wearing a proper respirator.

Undercoat — the buildup of primer coatings whose purpose is to provide adhesion, smooth the surface, and provide a stable base for the color coating.

Viscosity — a measure of pouring or flow rate. Thick substances with high viscosity pour slowly. Dilute substances like automotive paints, pour or flow easily.

VOC — Volatile Organic Compound. Chemicals in solvents that disperse easily into the atmosphere.

Wet sanding — dipping specially-backed automotive sandpaper in water during the sanding process extends the life of the sandpaper, helps prevent the sandpaper from clogging, and lubricates paint for a smoother finish.

Wet-on-wet — the sealer coating is allowed to set up, but not thoroughly dry before topcoating.

Zinc chromate — a fast-drying primer that provides corrosion protection by containing "sacrificial zinc" that substitutes for steel in a "corrosion battery."

CHAPTER 3: POWDER COATING

HotCoat® Powder Coating System

Eastwood Company
Box 3014
Malvern, PA 19355-0714
(800) 345-1178;
fax (610) 644-0560
www.eastwoodco.com

CHAPTER 5: TOOLS AND TECHNIQUES FOR HIGH-TECH PAINTING

Conventional and HVLP paint spraying equipment

Ask Dr. Gun
Sharpe Manufacturing
Company
www.sharpe1.com

Spray enclosures

Spray-Tech
100-A East Main Street
Ontario, CA 91761
(909) 391-2981;
fax (909) 391-4281
www.spraytech.com

Spraymex
Spray Booth Mfg.
(800) 490-5777

Col-Met
Spray Booths, Inc.
(888) 452-6684

CHAPTER 6: REMOVING AN EXISTING FINISH

Paint stripper

Klean-Strip
www.kleanstrip.com
Klean-Strip Sprayable —
easy-to-apply liquid spray

Safety precautions

Environmental Protection Agency
www.epa.gov/iap/pubs/
paintstr.html

Shop stripper — semi-clear liquid that removes all types of paint and is harmless to chrome, rubber, aluminum, and factory fiberglass

The Shop
P.O. Box 2790
Creston, CA 93432
www.thegrid.net/theshop

Rust remover

OxiSolv Rust Remover — quickly dissolves iron oxide leaving zinc phosphate coating

Eastwood Company
See previous listing

Rusteco — environmentally friendly organic anti-oxidant

Ecoclean
100 N. Meadows Road
Medfield, MA 02052
(888) 399-2600,
fax (508) 359-7311

The Destroyer — all-purpose rust and ferrous stain remover

The Shop
See previous listing

Chemical dipping services

Pro Strip Professional Metal
Refinishing

Professional Metal Refinishing, Inc.
2415 W. State Blvd.
Fort Wayne, IN 46808
(219) 436-2828
www.prostrip.com

Redi Strip Locations

Redi Strip Company
100 W. Central Ave.
Box 72199
Roselle, IL 60172
(630) 529-2442;
fax (630) 529-3625

Abrasive blasting equipment and supplies

Eastwood Company
See previous listing

TiP Tools and Equipment
7075 Rt. 448
P.O. Box 649
Canfield, OH 44406
(800) 321-9260,
fax (330) 533-2876
www.tiptools.com

Soda Blasting equipment

StripCo., Inc.
www.sodablasting.com

Rust converter/stabilizers

ChemSafe — converts rust and metallic oxides into sable and inert compound

ChemSafe Products
www.chemsafenet.com

Corroless rust stabilizer
Eastwood Company
See previous listing

POR -15 (Paint Over Rust)
POR-15, Inc.
P.O. Box 1235
Morristown, NJ 07962-1235
(800) 457-6715,
fax (973) 887-8007
www.por15.com

Rust Ender — emulsifier that transforms rust into black acrylic coating, for use in severe rust areas.

The Shop
See previous listing

CHAPTER 7: RECOATING AN EXISTING FINISH

Spot sandblaster

Eastwood Company
See previous listing

TiP Tools and Equipment
See previous listing

Paintless dent removal

Fixx-a-Dent, Inc.
4959 N. Buford Hwy. Ste. 6
Norcross, GA 30071
(770) 449-4878
fax (770) 448-8131
www.fixx-a-dent.com

Dent removal tools and training

Ding King, Inc.
1280 Bison Avenue
Suite B-9
Newport Beach, CA 92660
(949) 442-7601
fax (949) 442-7611
www.dingking.com

CHAPTER 8: PAINTING OVER PLASTIC PAINTS FOR REPAIRING AUTOMOTIVE INTERIOR AND UPHOLSTERY

Eastwood Company
See previous listing

Fitzgerald's
Restoration Products
(800) 441-3326
www.fitzgeralds
restoration.com

Repairing plastic: training

I-CAR courses
and services
(800) 422-7872 (US)
(800) 565-4227 (Canada)
www.i-car.com

CHAPTER 9: PRIMER COATINGS

Additional painting products suppliers

Altex Coatings Ltd.
www.altexcoatings.co

Matrix System
Manufacturing
(800) 735-0303
www.matrixsystem.com

Restorer's Choice
Box 2291
Youngstown, OH 44511
(800) 471-3061,
fax (330) 792-9001

CHAPTER 12: SELECTING OR MATCHING A FINISH COLOR

Paint code information sources
Catalog of American Car I.D.
Number book series distributed by:

Classic Motorbooks
International
729 Prospect Ave.,
P.O.Box 1
Osceola, WI 54020
(800) 458-0454

CHAPTER 14: CUSTOM PAINTS AND CREATIVE DESIGNS

High build clear coat

Restorer's Choice
See previous listing

Custom painting products and instructional videos

House of Kolor
210 Crosby Street
Picayune, MS 39466
(612) 729-1044
www.houseofkolor.com

Custom painting and artistic designs

Starek Designs
3828 Woodbury Estate,
Apt. C
Traverse City, MI 49686
(231) 929-7007

CHAPTER 16: CUSTOM EFFECTS WITH POWDER COATING

Airbrush supplies and equipment

Badger Air-Brush Co.
9128 W. Belmont Ave.
Franklin Park, IL 60131
(847) 678-3104
fax (847) 671-4352
www.badger-airbrush.com

Eastwood Company
See previous listing

Paasche Airbrush Co.
7440 West Lawrence Ave.
Harwood Heights, IL 60056
(800) 621-1907
fax (708) 867-9191
www.paascheairbrush.com

Airbrush paints

Createx Colors
14 Airport Park Rd.
East Granby, CT 06026
(800) 243-2712
fax (860) 653-0643
www.createxcolors.com

Medea Artists Colors
P.O. Box 14397
Portland, OR 97293
(503) 253-7308
fax (503) 253-0721
www.medea-artool.com

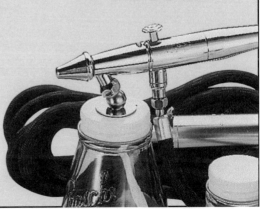

Pinstriping tape and paints

Eastwood Company
See previous listing

Finesse Pinstriping Inc.
P.O. Box 54148
Linden Hill Station
Flushing, NY 11354
(800) 228-1258
fax (718) 961-2980
www.finessepinstriping.com

CHAPTER 17: FINAL STEPS

Fasteners

AMK Products
18600 E 96th St.
Broken Arrow, OK 74012
(918) 455-2651
fax (918) 455-7441

**Restoration Specialties
and Supply, Inc.**
P.O. Box 328
Windber, PA 15963
(814) 467-9832
fax (814) 467-5323

Buffing system

Eale Abrasives, Inc.
Norcross, GA 30093
(770) 279-8111;
fax (770) 279-0727
www.EagleAbrasives.com

**Wizards Products
RJ Star Inc.**
11469 Eighth Street
Northeast
P.O .Box 249
Hanover, MN 55341
(800) 356-7223
fax (612) 467-5125

CHAPTER 18: FINISH PRESERVATION, CARE, AND STORAGE

Car Cover and Storage

California Car Cover Co.
9525 DeSoto Ave.
Chatsworth, CA 91311
(818)-998-2100
Toll free (800)-423-5525
fax (818)-998-2442
www.calcarcover.com

CarJacket

Pine Ridge Enterprises
13165 Center Road
Bath, MI 48808
(800) 5-CARBAG

Car Care Products

Dri-Wash 'n Guard
(800) 820-6893
www.enviro-tech.com

**Gliptone
Manufacturing, Inc.**
1340-7 Lincoln Ave.
Holbrook, NY 11741
(516) 737-1130
fax (516) 737-0453

Meguiar's Inc.
Irvine, CA 92714
(800) 854-8073
Fax (714) 752-5784
www.meguiars.com

Mother's
5456 Industrial Drive
Huntington Beach, CA 92649
(800) 221-8257
Fax (714) 893-1827

Original California Car Duster

California Car Cover Co.
www.calcarcover.com

One Grand Products
3007 Bunsen Dr.
Ventura, CA 93003

Wizards Products
See previous listing

Paint Chip Repair

Pro Motorcar Products
22025 US 19 N.
Clearwater, FL 33765
(800) 323-1090
www.promotorcar.com

NOTES

NOTES

Do-It-Yourself Guide to Custom Painting